THE MYSTERIOUS CASE OF THE
VICTORIAN FEMALE DETECTIVE

THE MYSTERIOUS CASE OF THE VICTORIAN FEMALE DETECTIVE

SARA LODGE

YALE UNIVERSITY PRESS
NEW HAVEN AND LONDON

For information about this and other Yale University Press publications, please contact:
U.S. Office: sales.press@yale.edu   yalebooks.com
Europe Office: sales@yaleup.co.uk   yalebooks.co.uk

Set in Adobe Caslon Pro by IDSUK (DataConnection) Ltd
Printed in Great Britain by Clays Ltd, Elcograf S.p.A

Library of Congress Control Number: 2024942617

ISBN 978-0-300-27788-3

A catalogue record for this book is available from the British Library.

10 9 8 7 6 5 4 3 2 1

For Rosie,
and for every woman whose work has been misrepresented,
overlooked or undervalued

CONTENTS

ILLUSTRATIONS

MAP

ACKNOWLEDGEMENTS

It is a pleasure to thank the many people who have helped me in researching and writing this book, which has spanned a decade punctuated by a pandemic and the death of both my parents. Linda Newey, genealogical female detective extraordinaire, has been a wonderful fellow digger of knotty roots, an ally and a friend. Together, we solved several mysteries that would have foiled less obstinate sleuths, especially the true identity of Clara Jolly Death.

All mistakes are, of course, my own.

I gratefully acknowledge a Covid Research-Reboot Grant from the Royal Society of Edinburgh, which allowed me to recoup research leave lost in 2020–21, and the Daisy Ronco Visiting Fellowship at Gladstone's Library, which gave me time to finish.

For their generosity in sharing images and expertise, I would like to thank James Arsenault, Eddie Bundy of the British Newspaper Archive, David Cook, Richard Graham and especially Nicola Pirkis and the Pirkis family. For assistance with queries, advice and encouragement, I am hugely grateful to fellow scholars and writers including Troy Bassett, Nick Booth, Vic Clarke, Mila Daskalova, Jim Davis,

ACKNOWLEDGEMENTS

Helena Goodwyn, Andrew Hillier, Charlotte Jiang, Guy Lesser, Ian Malcolm, Noreen Masud, Jerome McGann, Gill Plain, Catherine Pope, Matt Rubery and Jenny Uglow. Penny Fielding invited me to present some of this material as a lecture to the University of Edinburgh research group in 2021, which helped its development, as did the Research Society for Victorian Periodicals 2023 conference in Caen. Supervising the PhD of the brilliant Maitrayee Roychoudhury with super-colleague Clare Gill has led to many stimulating conversations about female detection. I am also grateful to librarians Paget Anthony of the Rare Books Room at the British Library, Hilda McNae of the University of St Andrews Library and the staff of Chiswick Library, the John Gray Centre in Haddington and Register House, Edinburgh.

My editor, Julian Loose, his assistant, Frazer Martin, the two anonymous readers who gave such generous and helpful reports and the whole team at Yale University Press have never been anything less than 100 per cent behind me, waving a wand over this project. Even Cinderella's fairy godmother could not dream up a more flattering outfit or a better coach.

My friends and family are wonderful. I am so lucky to have a supportive group of people willing to be moaned to and raved at on the topics of my current writing: special thanks to Sacha and Marina Bennett, Henrik Bindslev, Gavin Boyter, Claire Cunningham, Guy Cuthbertson, Indy Datta, Jonathan Elliott, Miranda France, Rachel Garlick, Angus and Emily Haldane, Rob Hamlyn, Kim Gilchrist, David Lemon, Ben Madley, Susan Manly, Steve McNicoll, Ilse Mögensen, Gerald and Fiona Montagu, Tom and Erin Moore, Helen Morris, Frances Nethercott, Kate Ó Súilleabháin, Mario Relich, Maeve Rutten, Jyoti Sigouin, Annabel Stansfeld and Angus Stewart.

Finally, to my long-suffering in-laws John and Judy Ducker – you are the string that holds the parcel together. Thank you. And to my dearest partner Guy (beta reader, image handler, panic defuser) and daughter Rosie: you could not be loved and appreciated more. I have no clue without you.

PROLOGUE
The Vanishing Lady

This story begins, as so many tales of crime do, in a library. In 2012, I was sitting in the British Library in London. The Rare Books Room is a quiet haven at the heart of the noisy, polluted interchange where King's Cross Station and the fiery Victorian gothic of the St Pancras Hotel converge in a flurry of taxis and suitcases. To enter, you pass a pensive portrait of Charles Lamb, show your card and gain admission. Elderly gentlemen in suit and tie, graduate students in tie-dye: each reader sits, perfectly spaced out from one another, lit by a single desk lamp, in long rows. They are studying first editions of Romantic poetry, sheet music by Satie and Modernist magazines with a print run of only one issue. Considerate typing on laptops fills the room with a sound like gentle rain.

On the desk before me were two racy, rackety titles, both published in 1864. Cheap thrills when they came out, they are now prohibitively expensive. The reason is that these rare books, which pretend to be first-hand accounts, are the first British works of fiction to feature professional female detectives.[1]

The question I was pondering was why? Why did these two books both appear in 1864? What was there in the air of this particular year that led to not one, but *two* books featuring daring, mature women who make their living as sleuths. Stranger still, why did these books appear to be a flash in the pan? Female detectives, it seemed – from the criticism I was reading – appeared in fiction in 1864 like the first swallows of summer and then went extinct, before emerging again over two decades later in the early 1890s. It was a quandary. The case of the vanishing lady.

First, I picked up *The Female Detective* by 'Andrew Forrester' (a pseudonym for James Redding Ware). More than twenty years before Arthur Conan Doyle's Sherlock Holmes first appeared in *A Study in Scarlet* (1887), 'Miss Gladden', who is 'verging on forty' and is called 'G' by the force, solves cases by a variety of deductive methods. She deploys forensic evidence, sending fluff on the clothes of a homicide victim away for analysis and examining the wadding in a gun to discover the reading matter with which the bullet has been padded: a vital clue. She reflects that the English police system 'requires more intellect infused into it', that 'experience shows that the chances of discovery of a crime are in exact inverse proportion to the time which has elapsed since the murder' and that while men seize facts, they are unable to 'work out what lies below the surface'. She announces that she is 'a police-officer' and claims both that women detectives 'can educate our five senses to a higher pitch than . . . our male competitors' and that they 'can get into houses outside which the ordinary men-detectives could barely stand without being suspected'.

'Miss Gladden' is, in other words, a sleuth on a mission. From interview technique to the finer points of keys, she makes a political point of showing that a woman can supply what is lacking and improve what is deficient in the English policing system. Her exploits take her from investigating a headless body in the Thames, the victim of a hit by a European secret society, to considering a child murder: a thinly disguised version of a true crime at Road, in Wiltshire, that had convulsed the nation in 1860.

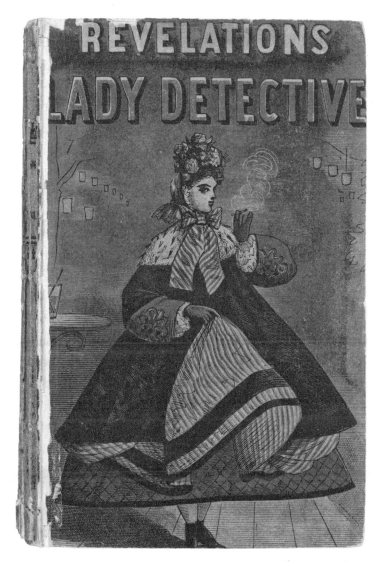

1. *William Stephens Hayward,* Revelations of a Lady Detective *(1864).*

The other volume, *Revelations of a Lady Detective* by William Stephens Hayward, was odder still. Its cover featured a woman who was flirting with the viewer, lifting her skirt to show a neatly turned ankle, while smoking a cigarette. The impression was suggestive. Would there be pornographic revelations within? In fact, this female detective keeps her clothes on. But there are cases between the covers that deal in transvestism, underground sects and erotic violence. Not to mention a circus performer who makes a living by biting the heads off rats.

Mrs Paschal, Hayward's female detective, slips off her crinoline to descend a secret staircase and pursue a countess who by night, dressed as a man, is robbing gold bullion from the vaults of the bank beneath her Belgravia mansion. Mrs Paschal rescues an heiress from an abusive sect of nuns who whip the girl when she refuses to leave them her fortune. She even gets caught in a Mafia shoot-out in a crumbling mill on the Isle of Dogs. The action heroines of modern cop dramas have nothing on her.

Why *had* two female detective casebooks appeared in 1864? Modern commentators did not, it seemed to me, have a sufficient explanation for this freak occurrence. These two books, it was claimed, had not led to successors. It was curious. Why had the character of the professional Victorian female detective suddenly materialised, then *vanished*? There were, after all, no real female detectives at this time. Literary critics said so. Historians of the period said so. The police said so.

As I sat in the library, staring into space, I thought of the magician's trick: the Vanishing Lady. It was a Victorian stage illusion: one of the signature *coups de théâtre* of magician Joseph Buatier de Kolta in the 1870s. In the trick, a woman sits in a chair before the audience. A cloth is thrown over her. Then she disappears.

Pouf!

People gasp. The audience stares in wonder at the empty chair. The trick was performed by means of a concealed trap door and a wire frame that held the cloth in mid-air while the woman did all the work of sliding silently below, out of sight.

I stared at the chair that contained the Victorian female detective. It appeared to be empty.

Yet, in the magician's trick, there is always a body breathing; it is just that you have not seen it move. As I gazed into the hushed space of the library, dimly seeing the heads of readers who were not talking but were still very much there, their fingers chattering over the keys, an impudent thought came to me: *I don't believe you.*

There. I had said it, if only to myself. I don't believe in rain without clouds. I don't believe the magician's floor is solid. I don't believe that there were no Victorian women detectives in 1864.

And, with a shuddering creak, a door opened. That led to a staircase. That led to a vault. Inside which was the material of this book.

INTRODUCTION

Jemima Davis Captures a Coiner

A man walked into the shop. It was November 1883 and the high street in Chipping Barnet was beginning to look festive in anticipation of Christmas. There were likely oranges piled in pyramids, chestnuts in boxes packed with straw alongside red and green apples and mottled pears, brought by horse and cart to the great markets at Covent Garden from the orchards of Kent.

The woman behind the counter looked the man up and down. Jemima Davis was the shopkeeper's wife. At thirty-seven, she had four children (Martha, Adelaide, Hector and Maud) and had been married to George, fishmonger and greengrocer, for almost a decade. She knew her apples, and this customer looked like a bad one. He paid a florin for a couple of bloaters (smoked herring) and, after handing him his change, she inspected the two-shilling piece closely. Jemima had seen forged coins before. Often the queen's head was badly imitated; sometimes the lettering was wrong, or they felt suspiciously light in the hand. There were hundreds of snides – false coins – in

1

circulation, defrauding honest shopkeepers like herself. She was sure this was one of them.

Jemima glanced up from the till. The man had melted. She rushed after him into the street; he was nowhere to be seen. At this point, most shop owners would have folded their arms and written off the transaction as one of those many irritations with which existence is rife. But Jemima Davis was not that kind of woman. She ran along the High Street, peering in at each shop window. There he was! The man was taking tea in a coffee shop. Jemima trailed him to a sweet shop. When she asked behind the counter if she could see the half-crown he had tendered, she saw immediately that this coin, too, was bad. The same was true of the chemist he visited next. Certain now that the man was not just an unlucky punter who had been given one bad coin while shopping, but was himself a counterfeiter, Jemima ran to fetch a policeman.

Constable Bristow, whether out of inexperience or nerves, headed off in the wrong direction to arrest the suspect: he went back to the chemist. Jemima's aim was surer. She caught up with the man in the baker's, further along Chipping Barnet High Street, where he had just used false coin to buy some buns. Jemima confronted him and pushed him back into the shop, from which he was trying to beat a hasty retreat. She grabbed his bag. There was a struggle. When the man tried to escape, she seized firm hold of him. And, despite the fact that he 'threw her through the shop window', she succeeded in holding him fast and long enough that PC Bristow caught up and the suspect was apprehended.

Thomas Wise (forty), a blacksmith who had been working in Liverpool, was found to have twenty-three counterfeit half-crowns and four counterfeit florins on his person, wrapped in a kid glove. He claimed that he had found the hoard by accident in a gypsy encampment, but this story failed to impress the magistrate, who sentenced him to twelve months with hard labour. Jemima Davis's capture of the 'smasher', or forger, was commemorated in several newspapers.[1]

For the modern reader who visualises the Victorian period chiefly through novels written by and for middle-class men and women, Jemima's actions are significant because they remind us that working-class women's bodies and behaviour did not adhere to the constraints we often imagine governed female physicality in the period. We are more accustomed to scenes in which Victorian women faint, paint and look out of windows than scenes in which women run after criminals, wrestle with them and are thrown through windows.

But to understand real female detectives in the nineteenth century, we must recognise that detecting crime and apprehending criminals is – outside of the novel – not typically something that happens through mulling over complex evidence in a candlelit room while smoking a pipe or playing the violin. It is, rather, achieved through present-tense encounter, fast and decisive action, and draws on knowledge of people and places usually better known to those who live a working-class life in those same streets than to outsiders for whom crime is an intellectual puzzle to be solved in private. If we are looking for real Victorian female detectives, we will frequently find them in working-class life.

Who Counts as a Detective?

'Detective' is an adjective, before it is a noun. It entered popular use in 1843, a year after the first 'detective police' were appointed in Britain, as specialists pursuing complex criminal investigations within the police force. The verb 'to detect', however, meaning 'to expose (a person) by divulging his or her secrets or making known his or her guilt or crime' has existed since the fifteenth century.[2] Women, therefore, were able to detect for a good 400 years before the sudden creation of a professional sub-group notionally limited this activity within the police force to a small, designated enclave of men.

In fact, unsurprisingly, women did not stop detecting in 1843. Rather, the new focus that the 'detective police' and 'private enquiry agency' placed in the 1840s and 1850s upon the activity of detecting others' secrets and/or guilt shone a spotlight on the way in which such secrets often involved marital infidelity, cruelty and forms of mental and physical domestic violence that emphasised the legal power difference between men and women. In short, the 'female detective' arises simultaneously and necessarily *alongside* the rise of the male detective because they are symptoms of the same social trend: a public desire to arrest criminals, with a view to creating a safer society, and a private desire to know more – whether about errant spouses, suspect employees, family secrets or potential partners – with a view to securing greater power and security in the individual home and business.

The professional detective was, from the first, involved in the Victorian battle of the sexes: a quest for knowledge and power that pitted men and women against one another as they struggled to discover incriminating information that would support a divorce or separation. As George Sala argued, the private detective

> is radically the outcome and body-servant or the handmaid of the Court for Divorce and Matrimonial Causes. In the last column of one great daily newspaper, I read no fewer than sixteen advertisements of private detective offices and agencies. One offers the services of male and female employés for 'secret watchings' – ascertaining where people go, the company they keep, whether 'the club' is responsible for late hours, and shopping alone occupies 'so much time'.[3]

Before the nineteenth century, gaining a divorce required a Private Act of Parliament: it was an option open only to a privileged few. More than any other development in Victorian life, it was the Matrimonial Causes Act (popularly known as the 'Divorce Act') of 1857, which provided a clear, if not easy, path for men and women to leave unsatisfactory marriages, that led to burgeoning numbers of private detectives of both sexes from the 1850s onwards. A woman, posing as a chambermaid, a fellow lodger or a casual confidante, could in many cases gain evidence of adultery more easily than a man without attracting suspicion. She might even, if the enquiry agency was unscrupulous (and some were), act as a honey trap to lure the unsuspecting husband or wife into an 'assignation' that, witnessed by the agency in question, could seal the deal of a divorce.

Women, notoriously, had to provide higher standards of proof to obtain a divorce than men; they had to gather evidence of adultery aggravated by either cruelty, incest, bigamy, rape, sodomy, bestiality or desertion. Victorian politicians were shocked by the number of women who, undeterred, filed for divorce: they had expected the petitioners to be almost exclusively male.[4] The absolute numbers of Victorians who obtained divorces and separations were small in relation to the number of marriages. But the effect of coverage of cases in the divorce court on social perception of marriage as a site of potential violence and injustice was seismic. The female detective was, thus, from the start involved in a sensational discourse about marriage, women's rights and the threat to women's property and person from male 'coverture' – which erased a woman's legal identity after marriage, dissolving her name, goods and earnings within her husband's title. The fallout from this situation was that while female detectives in reality frequently worked for men, helping them obtain divorces, the fictional female detective became, in many Victorian novels and plays, the poster woman for investigation into male abuse of power.

Professional female detectives worked for private enquiry agencies across Britain and America from the 1850s onwards. By the 1890s, several women would be running their own agencies – a fact so well known that it became the topic of a musical, in which an all-female detective agency sings and dances, advising the audience:

A bevy of lady-detectives are we,
Clever and cute as detectives can be,

No one can equal our skill and finesse,
If you're in trouble, just note our address.
We do all our work without bother or fuss,
No other firm holds a candle to us;
All of the virtues adorning our sex
Centre in us, the renowned Lady Tecs.[5]

From the 1840s, women were also working on a regular basis for the police. Police histories routinely omit the presence of female 'detective searchers' in police stations around the country. These women searched suspects for stolen objects and weapons, examining their bodies for bruises and other evidence of trauma, interviewing suspects and giving evidence in court. Women were also deployed in sting operations and as detectives in the field to gather evidence in cases where a male police officer would have attracted suspicion. The link between 'detective searchers' and the broader development of detection as a career for women has never been made before: it is an essential way in which women became professional detectives. At least one of these Victorian women would have a career spanning four decades.

Some women – like Jemima Davis in her fruit shop or lodging-house keeper Charlotte Pitt, who solved one of the biggest diamond robberies of the 1870s – acted spontaneously to pursue criminals and bring them to justice. They were, like women working for private agencies or female searchers in police employment, reported in the press as 'female detectives', and their accomplishments added to the weight of evidence that suggested women could succeed in this role. All these figures are essential to the developing picture of 'the female detective', as it emerged in Victorian newspapers, journals, novels and plays, and to the debate that was conducted in the press about the qualities that a real or an imagined female detective might possess.

I am thus choosing to refuse the sexist and class-driven hierarchy that suggests a detective only 'counts' once they are salaried officers

6

in the police, or conversely that a detective ought to be a gifted hobbyist with time and money at their disposal to pursue leads in cases to which they have no personal connection. My book boldly accepts the Victorians' own use of the term 'female detective', which was broad.

A conception of 'the detective' as a role necessarily occupied by a professional who devotes their mind to 'solving' cases from beginning to end privileges a view of what detection entails that attributes value chiefly or only to a person who leads and develops the narrative overview of events. This is detection viewed as analogous to authorship. But, just as houses are not built by architects but by masons, roofers, glaziers and joiners, the work of detection is in practice usually a collaborative project that involves multiple roles, some of them physical, social, bureaucratic; work may be temporary or involve long-term relationships. We need, in my view, in thinking about women investigators in the period, to be more open to seeing their participation in this work as 'detection', even when they are not sole directors of the affair. Social class is central to previous prejudice in favour of detective 'managers' rather than coal-face 'labourers'.

When one accepts the definition of detective work current during the nineteenth century, it becomes clear that significant numbers of women were involved and that their activities were a topic of intense interest, speculation and debate. Their existence challenged received ideas about what women should be able to know, where they should be able to go, and their relationship with the enforcement of laws, many of which enshrined women's relative powerlessness compared with men. When discovering a perpetrator, then, the detective was not merely solving a mystery: often she was pointing to the underlying social ills that women faced. This made her a magnet both for sensation novelists, such as Catherine Crowe and Mary Elizabeth Braddon, and for later feminist writers, such as Elizabeth Burgoyne Corbett and Florence Marryat, who used the figure of the female detective in their fiction to point to systemic injustices in social life that affected women, and to imagine the possibility of women using the power of detection to expose and end evils perpetrated against them. 'The Female Detective' was a familiar headline, book and play title long before Sherlock Holmes first cast his lanky shadow over detective fiction in 1887.

The main focus of this book is on Britain; a larger scope would have required a larger volume. British commentators frequently contrast British moral distaste for women 'spying' with the prevailing view in France and Russia, where, they argued, women had long been tolerated in this role. The debate over women and detection was therefore especially acute in Britain in the nineteenth century and was often taken to reflect national values. However, my final chapter journeys to America and examines the case of 'Kate Warne', a real female detective whose myth, posthumously parlayed by her employer Allan Pinkerton, was influential throughout the world, both in encouraging early feminists to demand female participation in the police force and in creating an imaginary ideal of the female detective as a brave, selfless figure, capable of saving a president from assassination. Studying the brisk transatlantic trade in representations of the female detective, I argue that depiction of women fighting alongside (sometimes disguised as) men in the American Civil War was a significant influence on pulp fiction and popular drama where the female sleuth passes fluidity between 'male' and 'female' identities, suggesting the gender role-play involved in everyday life.

Hiding in Plain Sight: The Lady Detective Vanishes

Why didn't we know about real Victorian female detectives before? The reason is partly because the searchable digitised newspapers, court records and genealogical data we now have were not available to earlier researchers. However, it also reflects a desire to protect women from the moral imputations of what was, until the last decade of the nineteenth century, regarded as an unwholesome, even shameful, profession. There was also a degree of misogyny in the accounts of detection dominated by male figures from the police, who often went on to lead private agencies. Women could, moreover, be useful in further casework if their names and faces were unknown.

Where do we look for evidence of female detectives in Victorian Britain? The answer is, overwhelmingly, in the hundreds of national, regional and local newspapers that opened up, particularly after mid-century, the world of crime to the general reader. When one consults court records for these cases and cross-references them with census data and other sources, it becomes clear that, while there may be variations from newspaper to newspaper, the reportage is generally accurate. Women were playing an increasingly active and visible role in confronting crime in Victorian Britain, as well as in engaging in the complex non-criminal investigation that private detectives also undertook, such as tracing the whereabouts of missing persons.

Newspapers, vitally, were at the heart of a circulatory system, where factual reports of female detection shared an organ with advertisements offering the services of female private investigators. In the same newspapers were fictional stories – often long-running serials – featuring male and female detectives and advertisements and reviews for plays where 'The Female Detective' was a common title. The result was a vivifying stream of ideas in which factual and fictional accounts of female detection constantly encountered and influenced one another.

My book is unusual in bringing real-life and fictional detectives together, but I do so with the express intention of showing how real and fictional conceptions of detection in the period are in persistent dialogue with one another, and to underline the gulf between the Victorians' desire (which modern audiences share) for a female investigator who can right the wrongs of her sex and the truth that real female detectives were often enforcers of a patriarchal legal system, paid by men to gather 'dirt' on straying wives, employees or even political rivals.

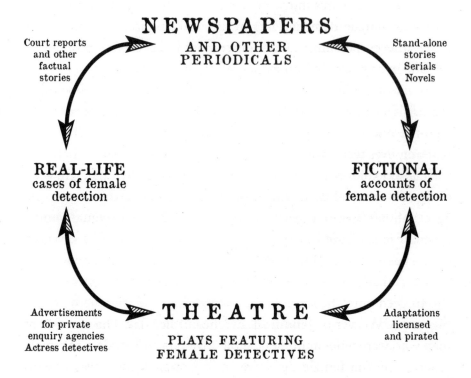

My work draws not only on Haia Shpayer-Makov's trenchant investigations of the Victorian police system, but also on work by Jim Davis, Isabel Stowell-Kaplan, Lucy Sussex, Andrew Maunder, Joseph Kestner, Clare Clarke and many others on women in Victorian sensation drama and detective fiction. It has benefited from the historical research undertaken by Nell Darby in *Sister Sleuths* (2021) on women working for private enquiry agencies, the literary analysis of Florence Marryat by Catherine Pope and Beth Palmer, and the study of female detective journalists by Matt Rubery and Stephen Donovan. My debts are many; I hope that my study gains strength from its interdisciplinarity, which leads it to hop fences, listen at doors and find tunnels (as one of the fictional female detectives in this study does) linking what might otherwise seem discrete Victorian abodes.

INTRODUCTION

This book explores the morally murky yet fascinating world of the Victorian female detective in real life, walking the streets to track sugar-thieves, pursuing adulterous couples to their beds, posing as a servant in aristocratic homes riddled with anxiety about inter-class relations or pulling stolen items from the clothes and bodies of criminals adept at hiding them in the most unexpected places. It asks who these women were, how they became detectives and what their working lives were like.

It also explores the myth of the female detective that grew up alongside this reality. In the East End theatres of London in the 1860s 4,000 working-class people in an evening would crowd together to see Sara Lane – actor-manager and a formidable star in her forties – playing 'The Female Detective'. Her character pulled no punches. Ball-busting, cross-dressing, wise-cracking and gun-toting, she erupted onto the stage as the original female action heroine: the Sigourney Weaver or Jennifer Lawrence of her day. The nemesis of men who were wife-murderers, serial love rats and stealers of female inheritance, the female detective in Victorian theatre was able to shape-shift, playing six different characters in an evening, before finally saving the young female ingenue from a terrible marriage and assisting in the capture of the villain in a thrilling rooftop chase. The mythic female detective, like her modern counterpart, is a figure of desire: somebody who can simultaneously annihilate the linked threats of male domestic violence and public criminality on behalf of women everywhere.

Frequently, real stories of detection from the newspapers found their way into fiction. Sometimes, fictional female detectives would inspire real ones to enter the profession, or colour how they presented their character and vocation. Some real detectives were actresses. These two worlds were connected like rooms in adjacent houses, with voices constantly penetrating through the walls. I want to show you around both of these houses: to introduce you to the Victorian ancestors of the fictional Mare of Easttown and Catherine Cawood

11

in *Happy Valley*, and to real women detectives you have not met: Emily Oxley in Cardiff, Ann Lovsey in Birmingham and, in London, the improbably but factually named Clara Jolly Death.

In a very real sense, we still face the dilemma that Victorians first felt. We still want female detectives to penetrate the labyrinth of male power and fearlessly expose and combat the threat of violence, robbery and corruption. We want them to kick ass. We need them to seek justice for *all* women. In reality, there are still too few female detectives, and those who do exist face a workload less obviously and clearly heroic than that of their fictional counterparts. This tug-of-war between what women wish and what women face is the strong rope that connects us with our Victorian ancestors. The female detective embodies both our intense desire to know the truth and how hard it is to prefer truth to our dreams.

1

SEARCHERS AND WATCHERS
Female Detectives Working with the
Police 1850–1900

One reflection suggested by the introduction of the female police
detective amongst us is, that French manners and ideas are making
rapid progress in this country . . .[1]

Reynolds's Newspaper (1860)

The concept of the 'detective' is Victorian. It was a role invented in
Victorian Britain in an atmosphere of intense public debate
about the proper boundaries of public and private life, the powers of
the state and the right of individuals to lead lives free of intrusive
scrutiny. The Metropolitan Police was formed in 1829: a new force
whose job would professionalise the business of 'thief-taking' and
who, it was hoped, would reassure a nervous population about public
safety. Victorian policing was designed to be chiefly preventive. The
policeman, who would be relatively young and tall (late nineteenth-
century Metropolitan Police were aged between twenty and twenty-
seven and at least 5 feet 9 inches in height), patrolled his beat through
daylight and darkness, a reassuring physical presence in streets still
not widely lit.[2] The new police were visible and could react to public

disorder or complaint, but their manpower and training were completely unequal to investigating the scale and scope of crime committed, particularly in cities.[3] Their very visibility mitigated against undercover operations. Police courts were open to public attendance, so the policemen of any division became well known by sight to local criminals. Most constables were working class; they had only a basic education and some struggled with the levels of literacy involved in report writing.[4]

It was quickly evident that a distinct detective force was needed within the police, to pursue non-routine cases that might include murder, terrorism and organised crime. A detective branch was formed at Scotland Yard in 1842; for a long time, however, it remained tiny.[5] The *Pall Mall Gazette* observed wryly in October 1870, alluding to successful writers of detective novels:

> We learn that that mysterious body whose preterhuman sagacity and marvellous organization – the detective police – actually consisted up to the middle of the year 1869, of 15 persons only, a number hardly sufficient to meet the constant demands made upon the force by Miss Braddon, Mr Wilkie Collins, and others of the same school.[6]

As the *Pall Mall Gazette*'s article acknowledges, the idea fed by fiction of the successful, supernaturally gifted detective far outpaced the reality. Newspapers had played a key role in lobbying for a detective force, but literature also created unrealistic expectations that undermined it. Journalists noted instances of corruption, and of detectives overreaching their remit, as well as failures to solve key cases. In 1868, *Bell's Weekly Messenger* commented: 'As detectors of great crimes, the police have shown themselves . . . inferior to the parochial and magisterial organisation they superseded. Murderers, housebreakers, garotters now seem to escape as a matter of course; if apprehended, their capture is rather due to "information received" than to any special qualities of their captors.'[7] As early as 1863, journalists played on the similarity between 'detective' and 'defective' to suggest that this department of the police was defined by its shortcomings.[8]

Given this yawning gap between expectation and reality, it is unsurprising that the police used all available means to supplement their capacity. Women could be useful in multiple ways. They were less visible. They could go where men could not and had access to certain sites of illegal activity from which men were usually excluded.

Women rarely occupy more than a footnote in histories of Victorian policing.[9] Not until 1914 were there voluntary women police patrols. In 1918, some voluntary patrols were officially incorporated into the paid police force: these were the first women police, who arrived thirty years after Victorian feminist Frances Power Cobbe pressed for the admission of women to the force, claiming that Jack the Ripper would not be caught until there were female police detectives.[10] In fact, women played a much greater role in Victorian policing than is commonly acknowledged, and their invisible labour deserves our attention.

They may not have been part of the constabulary but, across Britain, women were deployed to do detective work, identifying, observing and searching criminals; interviewing, gathering and supplying evidence that secured convictions. Sometimes this involved long-term relationships with law enforcement: Ann Lovsey, whose story will be explored in greater detail below, served Birmingham Police as an employee for at least thirty-six years, between 1865 and 1901. Typically, the women concerned were policemen's wives or other family members, who knew the business of policing and could be trusted to be discreet. These women took risks and developed skills that attracted public notice. Mostly from the working class, these women, like their male police counterparts, often came from rural backgrounds and were 'first-generation' city dwellers. They had to be tough, as violence was a continual possibility in their job, and their work had a strong physical element, putting their bodies on the line.

Female Detective Searchers

From the 1840s, Victorian police stations in London and in many provincial towns employed a female 'searcher'. Her job was to frisk the outer clothes, undergarments, bodies and hair of female suspects for stolen property: coins, jewellery, watches and pawn tickets. Men obviously could not perform this job with propriety.[11] As is common with drug mules today, desperate thieves in the nineteenth century were adept at concealing objects on their person. They might sew a coin into the lining of their dress, the sole of their shoe, or slip it into their stocking as Kate Mularkey did in York in 1892; 'Ruth Morrell, detective female searcher' ferreted it out.[12] One female searcher commented that the fashion for bustles offered many opportunities for concealment: 'when bustles were in fashion many articles were secreted in them, one woman having a dozen pieces of jewellery so packed away.'[13] Some suspects swallowed gold sovereigns, rolled bank notes into their hair, hid a wedding ring under their tongue or forced items into their private parts to escape conviction and the heavy penalties it brought. In 1850, one newspaper described Sarah Elliott, a servant who had concealed two and a half sovereigns, stolen from her employer, in her mouth. The female searcher found them.[14] Stolen goods of all kinds, including clothing, might be 'fenced' at a pawnbrokers, so that the thief carried only paper tickets linking them to their spoils. In 1890, searchers discovered a female French thief with forty-five pawn tickets concealed in her chignon.[15]

Searchers, then, became adept at finding what was hidden, knowing where to look, and studying the behaviour of suspects to judge whether they were hiding something or not. These were detective skills, as Ruth Morrell's title of 'detective female searcher' suggests, and it is unsurprising that this overlooked Victorian profession led women into other aspects of detective work: shadowing suspects and acting as 'watchers', sometimes over long periods, in locations where criminal activity reportedly occurred.

As part of the team of police employees who could be called on at any time of the day or night, female searchers also faced certain risks. Contemporary accounts show that suspects tried to bribe them: in 1845, Mary Randall, female searcher at Southwark police station, was tempted by 'Flash Poll' – alias Mary Morris – who, when unlacing her stays, slipped Randall two half-crowns with the instruction to 'say nothing about it'. They were frequently victims of physical assault. Among numerous accounts of violence against searchers, the *Stroud Journal* in April 1879 reported that Mary Smith, a tramp, while drunk had assaulted Maria Little, female searcher at Stroud police station.[16] In 1886, Theodosia Curtis, the female searcher at Bow Street station, encountered Mary Hearn, a drunk and disorderly woman who was frequently taken up by police: 'When the female searcher arrived the prisoner jumped up, struck her between the eyes, blackening them, and kicked her in the chest ... Theodosia Curtis ... who had two black eyes, said this was the third time the prisoner had assaulted her.'[17]

2. *'Scene in a Police Cell: Assaulting a Female Searcher',* Illustrated Police News *(1896).*

Occasionally, they witnessed extreme violence. In 1854, Susan Marshall, the housekeeper and female searcher at Smithfield police station, experienced gunfire when woollen draper George Umpleby turned in a former employee, James Tucker, on a charge of embezzlement.[18] Tucker drew a pistol and attempted to shoot Umpleby in the head; luckily the shot missed and broke a window. Marshall discovered the suspect, the intended victim and the constable on duty in a heap on the charge-room floor. She gave evidence for Tucker's prosecution. Searchers examined women for bruising and other distressing marks of violence relevant to criminal cases. In 1864, the fifteen-year-old domestic servant Sarah Ann Williams reported her mistress, Isabella Balls, for assault. Sarah claimed that Mrs Balls had gone out one evening, leaving her to nurse the baby. When Mrs Balls returned, she was furious that the kitchen had not been cleaned. Sarah objected that she had been unable to clean because she was minding the baby. The defendant then caught hold of Sarah by the hair, pulling chunks of it out. She dragged the teenager around the kitchen, swearing at her, and kicked her on the thighs and legs, 'causing her great pain'. Mrs Balls denied touching Sarah. When Mrs Crockford, the female searcher at the police station, confirmed the severity of Sarah's injuries, the assembled crowd reacted viscerally:

> There are dreadful bruises at the back of the hip. (Sensation.) There are very large wounds on the front of the leg; they are very bad and appear to have been caused by severe kicks ... I feel confident from the appearance of the bruises, that they had been caused by kicks ... A fall would not have caused such injuries, nor in such places as the injuries are. It will be some time before the bruises are well. (Sensation.)[19]

Mrs Crockford's calm and authoritative account of Sarah Ann's injuries played a vital role in the case, which the teenager won. Female searchers questioned suspects and regularly acted as witnesses, deposing evidence before magistrates and judges. These activities prepared them for an aspect of the detective profession that fiction often ignores: delivering a well-prepared and watertight account of events in court that could secure a conviction.

Elizabeth Joyes, Pioneer Detective

Elizabeth Joyes is one of the first women mentioned by the press as a female detective, in 1855. She was born Elizabeth Woollard in the village of Great Wilbraham, Cambridgeshire, in 1816, the daughter of a thatcher. Coming to London as a young woman with her sister Orphah, Elizabeth was one of many first-generation Londoners who exchanged the seasonal round of rural labour for the new opportunities the city afforded. She fell in love with a neighbour from College Street where she was lodging in Chelsea. His name was James Joyes, and he was a shoemaker who enlisted as a policeman: a cobbler turned peeler, if you will. After their marriage, the couple lived and worked together at St Bride's police station in Fleet Street, where he was a constable and she was 'housekeeper and female searcher'. We know that Elizabeth was 'searcher' at the station from at least 1846, when she was twenty-nine.

James Joyes sadly died of typhus in 1849, after only six years of married life. Elizabeth didn't, however, give up living and working at St Bride's: her police career lasted longer than her marriage. In 1850, aged thirty-five, she was still a searcher at the police station in Fleet Street, in the heart of London. The census for 1851 reveals that then, as now, London was a magnet for workers from all parts of the country: of Elizabeth's male colleagues at St Bride's, who included seventeen constables, two sergeants and an inspector, two came from Scotland, two from Devon, others from Somerset, Gloucester and Kent. On the day of the census there were also a printer and a prostitute (both Irish) at St Brides, awaiting charge in the cells.

Victorian constabularies were communities. Single policemen lived in the station house and married officers were obliged to live close to the police station as they were expected to be available for police work at any time of day or night.[20] They became neighbours as well as colleagues. Policemen began their day with a uniformed drill, to inspire orderliness and discipline. Police stations were, in this sense, more like army barracks than modern police premises. One can easily imagine the importance of Joyes's role as housekeeper in maintaining the domestic harmony of the communal space while, as searcher, she protected the modesty of female inmates and was tasked with examining their bodies, clothes, lives.

Joyes's evidence appears regularly from 1846 to 1855 in the Old Bailey records of cases involving women convicted of theft. Among the women she testified against was Mary Ann Taylor, a young pickpocket who had stolen a purse containing seventeen shillings from a married woman, Sarah Fisher. Fisher noted that Taylor's method was to sit on the horsedrawn omnibus and spread the skirts of her fashionable dress wide, so that they partly covered Fisher's. This gave the pickpocket cover to rifle her neighbour's skirts before alighting with her spoils.

In February 1850, Elizabeth was reported in the *Evening Standard* in her role as searcher. She gave evidence against Jane Turpy (alias Ann Jones), deposing to finding a purse with money in it on the prisoner. The alderman who questioned her noted that 'female pickpockets were the most dangerous kind of thieves, because they were not so much suspected'. In 1854, Joyes testified against Mary Ann Curran, who had duplicates on her person for items pledged to a pawnbroker, including twelve rings and eight coats. Court reports were a staple of Victorian newspapers: short pieces that could be easily sourced by journalists to give readers a snapshot of crime in their area. Joyes's presence was likely familiar to the many journalists around Fleet Street.

In 1855, Joyes appeared in the newspapers again. This time she was responsible for the capture of John Cotton Curtis, 'a middle-aged man of good address and stated to have formerly occupied a highly respectable position in the City'. He was a seasoned thief, whose game was to enter the first-class waiting room at railway stations and take his place among the other well-dressed passengers. He would then wait for a chance – when someone rose to visit the refreshment room or asked him to mind their luggage while they bought a ticket. He picked up the expensive suitcase or bag during their absence, walking out confidently with the stolen articles before the alarm could be raised.

Elizabeth Joyes detected and caught this serial offender on her second attempt. On her first try, on 23 November 1855, she sat for six hours opposite the entrance to the first-class waiting room in the Eastern Counties Railway Station in Shoreditch. Tellingly, she noticed Cotton Curtis by his shabby shoes, which did not fit the profile for a first-class customer. He entered at about 4 p.m. and seated himself on the sofa before the fire (first class waiting rooms were more luxurious then than they are now). Unobtrusively, in his usual manner, he picked up a large portmanteau, which belonged to a vicar, and made off with it. The vicar, who had rather lavish tastes for a man of the cloth, lost his underwear and a fine pair of shoes made by Medwin of Regent Street. Joyes pursued Cotton Curtis but lost him in the crowd. When he returned, however, a week later, she recognised him instantly and secured his arrest. Both the questions at the ensuing trial and the newspaper reports confirmed that Joyes was 'employed as a female detective'.[21] Cotton Curtis himself, with a mixture of irritation and gallantry, observed that she was: 'a special detector, appointed . . . for her acute knowledge of all these things.' It is notable that the idea of a 'female detective' was more surprising to the newspapers who reported her exploits in 1855 than to the judge at the Old Bailey, for whom she would have been a familiar sight. One reporter got muddled and gave her name as 'Elizabeth Fry', the name of the well-known prison reformer, who had been dead since 1845.[22]

Public omnibuses (from 1829) and railways (spreading across Britain from the 1830s) were new engines of mobility in Victorian Britain. They allowed people of different classes and sexes to encounter one another. They made it much easier for people like Elizabeth Joyes, who had grown up in rural Cambridgeshire, to come to London. Circulating bodies, goods and news, they also opened new avenues for crime. Whether it was pickpockets like Mary Ann Taylor, thieving then leaving between bus stops, sexual assaults (or extortion by women accusing men of sexual assault) in railway compartments, luggage theft or large-scale heists from trains, the transport systems that allowed Victorians to get on also allowed criminals to get away. Greater transport mobility permitted offenders, from bigamists to embezzlers, to relocate easily to a new town or country. All these problems created fresh openings for the female detective.

In this case, Joyes's work was overseen directly by the railway company. The transport police were among the first police in Victorian Britain and some railways employed their own detectives to protect tracks and rolling stock, monitor fare dodgers and theft of goods. This was patient work that led to a criminal trial of precisely the same kind produced by the routine detective efforts of her male police colleagues in St Bride's. As Haia Shpayer-Makov observes: 'Most detectives in this period did not handle complicated investigations, nor did they commonly pursue long searches for clues or lengthy readings of crime scenes. Mostly, they gathered information and coped with petty crime.'[23]

In the summer of 1856, Elizabeth remarried to one of her policeman colleagues at St Bride's church, a few paces from the Fleet Street station. Her new husband was widower Walter Tyler, who had been James Joyes's best friend and executor. The closeness of the relationship between police employees here is telling; Elizabeth married twice into the force she served.[24]

Elizabeth Joyes's story illustrates the working community that existed in many Victorian police stations and how women played an integral role in the day-to-day labour of dealing with suspected criminals. Joyes's successor as housekeeper of the Fleet Street station, Elizabeth Harrison, dealt with the appalling case, in 1862, of Ann Cornish Vyse (aged thirty-two) who murdered her two little girls, Annie (seven) and Alice (five). Harrison would sit up with Mrs Vyse all night following the murders, with two constables in an adjoining room.[25] One can only guess at the mental anguish, fear and violence that female detective searchers witnessed.

Victorian policing depended on informal as well as formal relationships. Melville Macnaghten, reflecting on a career as head of the CID, noted that one good management method was to invite officers who were leading an investigation to visit one at home in the evening for a drink and a cigar.[26] In this way, one learned about the progress of cases and encouraged diligence. Under-resourced in their investigative capacity, the police relied a great deal on community knowledge to patch the gaps. Policemen's wives were formally debarred from having jobs outside the home: however, they were mandated to serve by cleaning, ironing and polishing the buttons of their husband's uniform; keeping up a respectable home (if they failed, they were subject to official reprimand from their husband's police force); and sometimes also undertook tasks vital to detective work: watching and following suspects and acting in sting operations designed to secure convictions.[27] The police force, thus, on the one hand rigidly maintained an ideology of 'separate spheres' that situated women in the domestic and men in the public realm, and on the other hand required women's private labour to ensure the smooth running of their public operations.[28]

Sarah Dunaway and the Sugar Thief

Another early example of a policeman's wife acting as a detective is Sarah Dunaway. In London in 1860, Mrs Dunaway, the thirty-eight-year-old wife of police constable Porter Dunaway, was complimented by the magistrate on acting with 'consummate tact and judgement' in catching a thief who had been stealing large amounts of sugar at the West India Dock and the receiver, a grocer and cheesemonger, who had been paying for the sugar, knowing it to be stolen and selling it to customers. Sugar was a valuable commodity in Victorian London. In 1800, annual per capita consumption of sugar in Britain was 18 lbs; by 1901 it was 90 lbs, making Britons the biggest consumers of sugar in Europe. It was an expensive luxury, shipped from the Caribbean and South America as a kind of molasses and industrially refined in London to create the granular sugar now familiar to us as an ingredient in desserts and an accompaniment to tea.[29] Sugar stealing during the transportation process from ship to warehouse to refinery was a common problem.

Edward Payne, the thief in this case, was working as a 'carman' (delivery driver) and was employed to load sugar for Wainwright and Gadsden, sugar refiners in Christian Street, and also for Bowman and Company in Leman Street, a little over 3 miles from the dock. Payne had been, for some time past, siphoning off substantial amounts of sugar from the cargo of ships whose goods he was transporting. He was careful to present his load in good order to Wainwright and Gadsden but used his freedoms around the docks to help himself to 'sugar from another country', which he passed covertly to the grocer in Star Street during his regular deliveries.

The area around Star Street was notorious for its poverty. John Hollingshead in *Ragged London* (1861) paints a vivid portrait:

Star Street is a narrow avenue, leading out of the Commercial Road towards the river, the entrance to which is half blocked up with fruit-stalls, crossing-sweepers, and loiterers. Unlike most of its neighbours, it hangs out every sign of overcrowding for the most careless or hurried passer-by to look at, and it contains, perhaps, within an equal area, more hard-working, would-be-honest strugglers for dear life than any similar street in the same district. Its road is black and muddy, half filled with small pools of inky water, in which stand a number of trucks and barrows belonging to the poorest class of costermongers. The end is nearly blocked up with a public-house, which seems to thrive in the very citadel of want. At some of the low dirty doors wet baskets are standing half full of a common fish called 'dabs'; in some of the wretched parlour windows, under sickly yellow curtains, a few rotten oranges are displayed on an old shutter for sale . . .[30]

A local clergyman found in 1860 that living in Star Street alone there were 702 people (345 adults and 357 children) crammed into 235 small rooms.[31] Unemployment and underemployment of dock labourers, coal heavers, needlewomen and other casual labourers in the nineteenth-century 'gig economy' led to excruciating poverty, as did failure to regulate the dock companies, some of which paid a decent poor-rate to assist the thousands of their employees laid off in a slow market and others of which paid almost nothing. In this neighbourhood, there was not much sweetness and little light.

Sarah Dunaway used her undercover role to observe Payne. She testified that she stood at the corner of Devonshire Street and Commercial Road:

I saw Payne . . . stop his van and horses opposite Devonshire-street. He went into a beershop at the corner of a street, and then came outside and went to his van again, and took from under a tarpaulin which covered several hogsheads of sugar a bag of some bulk – about 1cwt [100 lbs] from the appearance . . . He went down Devonshire Street, which leads to Star-street, and then went to a court at the back of Star-street, and stopped at a private door. The bag was on his shoulder. I have no doubt it contained sugar. It was like the smell of rum, and smelt very strong as he passed me . . . he had to lean close to the wall to enable me to pass. He went into . . . the private back door of a house and shop occupied by Davey in Star-street. I then went into the shop and purchased a few trifling articles. I saw Payne in the back parlour . . . Some one ran upstairs hastily . . . Davey came into the shop, went to the till, which he emptied, put the money in his pocket, and left the shop.[32]

Sarah then left the shop and followed Payne as he exited the house with the folded-up bag that had previously contained the sugar, put it in his van and drove away. On Saturday morning, she watched again. Payne once more stopped his van at the corner of Devonshire Street. Sarah must have given the signal to her husband's colleagues because this time, when Payne arrived at the court in Star Street ready to deliver his stolen goods, two constables were there to arrest him. Payne's house was searched and found to contain a stolen gold watch, among other incriminating items. He was charged and convicted.

Sarah Dunaway would have known the squalor of this locality and the desperate want to which it testified. She was born Sarah Skipper at Shottisham Hall in Suffolk, the daughter of a farm bailiff. Like so many other female detectives, she came to the city from the country, probably in search of work. Her husband, Porter, came from Sussex; his father was a labourer. By 1861 they were living in North Street, in St George's in the East, a mile from where she encountered Payne. She had a boy of ten, Charles, and a baby, William, who would not live to see the next census. Their neighbours in North Street included fellow police constable Hugh Andrews and serjeant Thomas Barnes. The policemen of K division, like others of this period, lived close to one another and to the scenes where crimes occurred that it was their duty to investigate.

Reynolds's Newspaper, clearly impressed by her role in arresting the sugar thieves, described Sarah as a 'very intelligent woman'. Mr Beard, cross-examining, jested, 'A new department of the police – a female detective!', to which the magistrate responded that 'female witnesses, as I have often had occasion to observe in my thirteen years' experience, generally give the best evidence'. A vital part of the role of a detective was not merely to watch, to be in the right place at the right time to seize a suspect and gather the evidence that could convict him, but to be able to present the evidence in a clear, accurate and compelling manner at trial. Her narrative of the theft suggests a logical and procedural mind. *Reynolds's Newspaper* compared Mrs Dunaway favourably with Harriet Martineau, Lucy Stone, Bessie Parkes and 'any other lady author, philanthropist or reformer of the age', opining that she had 'shown herself capable of a man's work' that none of the prominent feminists named could have accomplished.[33] Strikingly, the case becomes, in this reportage, both a piece of evidence in favour of women's equal professional capability and an excuse to jeer at pen-wielding feminists.

From Fact to Fiction and Vice Versa

Joyes's and Dunaway's police work occurred before the publication of James Redding Ware's fictional casebook *The Female Detective* in 1864. In *The Female Detective*, Miss Gladden notes: 'I was engaged at that time (though it may appear to my reader an odd case to call for the operations of a woman detective) upon what has since taken the name of the great sugar-baking case, and therefore I was living in the neighbourhood of Aldgate and Whitechapel.'[34]

It is quite probable that, as a journalist from Southwark, Redding Ware knew of Sarah Dunaway's capture of sugar thieves in London's East End in 1860. Attending police courts, he may also have seen other women who worked with the police – such as female searchers – give testimony. Redding Ware was politically aware; his pioneering fictional casebook *The Female Detective* alludes to a real parliamentary inquiry of 1864 that considered whether policemen were guilty of selling information about individuals' credit to private enquiry offices.[35] The cases he depicts place the female detective in a position where she can reveal the limits of local constabularies; the need for swift, detailed forensic examination of evidence and sympathetic approaches to interviewing witnesses (a skill, his protagonist asserts, women excel at). Although his 'police-officer' protagonist, Miss Gladden, is an invented character, she does not emerge from a historical vacuum. Rather, she imagines possibilities for female professional liaison with the police that reflected current events. Fact influenced fiction.

Fiction also influenced fact. After the success of *The Female Detective* and *Revelations of a Lady Detective* in 1864 and various female detective plays in 1865, a greater number of real-life cases were reported in newspapers under the headline 'A Female Detective'. It is likely both that women were encouraged towards detection by the cachet associated with the role and that activities that had been occurring for some time were reported with a new interest.

For example, Mary Scott, the wife of a policeman in the Newcastle force, was reported in April 1865, under the title 'Another Apprehension by Mrs Scott, the "Female Detective"', to have caught Margaret Edgar, a thief who was stealing bed-tick and flock from an upholsterer's yard in High Friar Lane, where the Scotts lived.[36] The *Newcastle Daily Journal* was well inclined towards Mrs Scott because, a few weeks before, she had caught an 'old thief' who was stealing a bale of paper from the *Journal*'s own offices and given him into custody. She had, perhaps, rescued the very sheets of paper that, when printed, would carry her own story. Evidently Mrs Scott relished her self-chosen role as a female detective: keeping her eye out for those who appeared to be helping themselves to others' property. She appears in at least three cases in the Newcastle papers.

One of the bravest of these ladies was Hannah Lawton, wife of police constable James Lawton. The Lawtons lived in Manchester, where James had previously worked as a file-cutter and Hannah as a cotton weaver. Her father was an 'overlooker' at a mill, so they knew well the realities of manufacturing that shaped the industrial city. Hannah was twenty-eight when she was involved in an undercover sting operation in 1865, apprehending the thieves Joseph Donnelly and James Blackley, with their accomplice Jane Shore, who had broken into the house of a lady in Collyhurst Road, while that lady was at church, and stolen dresses, shawls and jewellery worth over £30. The day was rainy and the thieves were seen shielding their booty with an umbrella as they escaped over the fields with it. Blackley was subsequently observed at the Hop Pole Inn in Blackmann Street, where Hannah was instructed by Sergeant Gill to approach him, posing as a cloth dealer from Bolton, 'desirous of buying wearing apparel'. This she did, successfully securing Blackley's interest in offering her the stolen items of clothing. Hannah was invited to accompany him 'by a circuitous way' to Mrs Shore's house in Back Foundry Lane. She must have been frightened, as she walked with him down the dark lane, that he was leading her into a trap. Among the items she observed in Back Foundry Lane were several housebreakers' jemmies – iron that could easily have been used to strike her. Luckily, Hannah's ruse was successful. She proved cool and effective in her pretended role as fence, offering him £6 10 shillings for the clothes: £1 down and a further £5 when he met her at Victoria railway station.

The promised money was sufficient to secure an assignation and Donnelly was arrested when he appeared at the railway station, while police officers searched the house in Back Foundry Lane, recovering the stolen goods. The *Manchester Guardian* reported this case under the headline 'A Woman Employed as a Detective'. We don't know if Hannah Lawton received any payment for her service to the Manchester police force, but the newspapers – from the *Guardian* to the *Dundee Courier* – were in no doubt that this kind of work was 'employing' women as detectives, an activity both sufficiently novel to merit reporting and intelligible through the lens of the public's increasing familiarity with the idea of the undercover detective. As we shall see, this familiarity was fed equally by theatre and fiction, as was the idea of there being 'female detectives' whose crime-fighting work might involve disguise and impersonation.

Sting Operations, Women and the Law

Without female assistance, it was often difficult to detect and prosecute those who were selling stolen or illicit goods or pocketing their employer's money. Emma Harrison in Worcester, wife of PC Harrison, was deployed in 1869 to observe a teenage draper's assistant who was suspected of stealing from the till: 'There was nothing but marked money in the till. Certain of that marked money was *given to a female detective* for the purpose of purchasing some goods to detect the thief.'[37] The report suggests that it was Emma who marked the money; her husband was then responsible for arresting the boy. The variety of different cities where policemen's wives were involved in assisting the police suggests that this practice was widespread across Britain. Women who participated in sting operations, however, sometimes ran considerable risks. In Glasgow, in May 1887, a female detective was assaulted by the shop owner's brother while buying groceries suspected of being tainted, for analysis under the Adulteration of Food and Drugs Act. The man 'attempted to wrest them from her, knocked her down, hurting her severely'. The *Edinburgh Evening Dispatch*, running the headline 'Assault on a Glasgow Female Detective', had no doubt that his woman had been injured 'in the execution of her duty'.[38] But where did such duties begin and end?

In 1880, female searcher and policeman's wife Martha Diffey (forty-four) posed as the mother of a young woman who wanted an illegal abortion, to secure the conviction of Thomas Titley, a chemist in Charlotte Street, London, who was willing occasionally to supply a 'noxious drug' to women in difficulties. Diffey told Titley that her young, unmarried daughter had been seduced and was desperate to rid herself of an unwanted pregnancy. The ruse was elaborate; one of the policemen, Detective Inspector William Stroud, acted the part of the guilty seducer, who was prepared to pay for the drug. Titley demanded to see Stroud in person. Only after this interview did Titley hand over the mixture of ergot of rye and tincture of perchloride of iron, designed to induce miscarriage. He was convicted and given a sentence of eighteen months' hard labour in the House of Correction at Cold Bath Fields.

Titley had many friends and there was a general public outcry about the sentence and about the police method of 'espionage' – soliciting a crime – that had led to his conviction. The *Dublin Evening Telegraph* reported the case in an article titled: 'The Police Spy System'. People signed a public petition to the home secretary asking for his sentence to be reduced. The home secretary rejected the application.

Martha Diffey ran a substantial risk in performing the elaborate charade that led to Titley's arrest. She and the police officers who worked with her were all indicted and themselves faced a criminal charge. As Titley's defence lawyer put it: 'it was the offence of persons who were acting for the detection and prosecution of crime, but who in this case had procured a crime to be committed from beginning to end.'[39] Diffey, along with her male police associates, had her indictment quashed on a technicality. It was argued in court that she really did have a young daughter who might have been in need of the noxious substance in question: therefore, the request made to Titley was not wholly or provably fictitious. Titley in fact had four children: her eldest daughter Elizabeth (twenty) was a governess and her second daughter Mary Ann (sixteen) was a pupil teacher. Her two sons were under eleven. One wonders how the Titley case, with the public opprobrium it raised, affected her family and her daughters' careers.

As R. M. Morris has pointed out, there was little legal precedent or administrative ruling to guide the operational norms of the police in this period. Criminal law was 'in many ways inchoate so far as their own operations were concerned' and 'the truth is that despite the 1929 Royal Commission much of the relevant law and procedure relating to the investigation and prosecution of crime was not settled until the Police and Criminal Evidence Act 1984'.[40]

Detectives, whether police officers or working for private agencies, would frequently face the accusation that they 'procured' crime if they sought to prove the illegal supply of alcohol, drugs or sex by presenting themselves as potential customers. As we shall see, this difficulty also arose for private detectives in the context of proving adultery in divorce suits. Female colleagues played a morally uncomfortable part in 'sting' operations and in cases like that of Martha Diffey (who was aged forty-four in 1880 but was referred to as an 'old lady' in several papers) were also subject to unwelcome press attention.

Grand Larceny: Smoking out Suspects

The practice of using women to assist the police as detectives appears to have been current in cities throughout Britain. In March 1868, the Wolverhampton papers were convulsed by a sensational case of larceny. Samuel Drew Foulkes, the assistant registrar to the Wolverhampton County Court, had absconded with around £800 in cash, leaving a deficiency of £2,000 (over £187,000 in today's terms) in the accounts. The theft had evidently been carefully premeditated. Foulkes disappeared and was thought to have travelled to Europe; detectives were reported to have searched for him in Jersey, at Boulogne and in Switzerland. The case was remarkable both for the large sum of money involved and for the fact that Foulkes was a trusted official of sixteen years' standing, who had 'the fullest confidence of everyone and entire control of the cash department'. He remained at large for over a year but was traced after his family removed from Wolverhampton to London. Mrs Foulkes rented a respectable house in the suburbs, describing herself as a widow. The police followed her movements and employed 'a female detective of lady-like address' who 'cleverly played her part', posing as a governess and taking apartments in the same house as Mrs Foulkes. She was the fly-on-the-wall who could watch Mrs Foulkes's movements, engage in idle chat, observe any letters she received and be on hand to notify the police via 'secret communication' if the suspect's wife had visitors. In the days before CCTV and hidden microphones, watchers of this kind, who played the long game, waiting in the shadows until criminals broke cover and made contact with their families, were often women. In April 1869, Foulkes appeared at the house, where he was arrested. He was sentenced to five years' penal servitude.

In a similar case in 1885, Nancy Withers, wife of James Withers, the chief constable of Bradford Police, played a crucial role in the apprehension of a member of Bradford Corporation, William Swallow Whitefield, who had defrauded the gasworks company – of which he was a director – of some £6,000 (worth over £600,000 today). Whitefield had been in the habit of claiming sums to pay casual employees for the gas company whose existence and work were purely illusory. He had also been rifling the till in other ways. Withers suspected him and, showing an enterprising mastery of the kind of skills he was usually tasked with suppressing, succeeded in picking his pocket during a corporation meeting, gleaning a letter in his handwriting and, vitally, the address of an intermediary in London (Mr Sample) through whom Whitefield was passing mail.[41]

When Whitefield absconded, then, Withers had a good idea of where his accomplice might be found. But, hearing from a relative of Whitefield's that the criminal was planning to sail for Spain, he knew he must act fast to apprehend him. Withers thus hatched a plan. His wife, Nancy, would arrive at Mr Sample's address, claiming to have a letter for Whitefield that she needed to pass directly into his hands. She would be able to show a document in Whitefield's (forged) handwriting. Chief Constable Withers would be posted in the dining room of a nearby hotel, overlooking the street where his wife was due to act out the scene.

Nancy Withers, a housewife with six children, the youngest of whom was nine in 1885, would not have been trained in detective skills, other than by listening to her husband's accounts of his work.[42] Nonetheless, she succeeded in holding her nerve, meeting 'in character' with Sample on several occasions, maintaining the story she had been given to tell, and eventually convincing Sample that she needed to hand the letter to Whitefield in person. When Whitefield eventually took the bait and appeared, Withers rushed over the street and arrested him. Many of the newspapers only credited Chief Constable Withers with the successful arrest, omitting the essential role played by his wife. The *Bradford Weekly Telegraph*, however, ran the full story. *Judy, or the Serio-Comic Journal* featured in its 5 August issue a charming cartoon by Harry Furniss, imagining the female police officer of the future, inspired by the clever actions of Mrs Withers in capturing the defaulting gasworks official. It was captioned: 'The wife of the Chief Constable of Bradford, having been mainly instrumental in the capture in London of a defaulting gas-manager, we presume that on an early date we may find our muscular sisters joining the police force, and becoming a terror to the gentle burglar.'

In the cartoon, the imaginary female police officer has flowers in her helmet. Her truncheon is stored in a holster that appears also to act as a kind of curtain hook for her voluminous skirt. Despite the floral tribute to her 'femininity' and her very dainty feet, the woman is tall and upright in this cartoon and towers over the crook, who is imaged as a dirty ruffian in a deerstalker (a hat not yet associated with detectives), cowering in fear beneath her moral and physical superiority. The burglar's cosh swings suggestively between his legs, hinting that his masculinity is compromised. Whitefield, a white-collar crook, looked nothing like this villain. Nancy Withers, at forty-seven, was significantly more mature than the lady policeman depicted. But in Furniss's cartoon we can see both the joke that the idea of a female policeman represents in 1885 and a hint that (as the

3. *Cartoon of a female detective,* Judy, or the Serio-Comic Journal *(1885).*

many newspaper stories of women assisting the police attested) this development is not *entirely* a joke. *Judy, or the Serio-Comic Journal* began its summer season with a cartoon of 'Judy' (Mrs Punch) as the Speaker of the House of Commons. Women in the 1880s were penetrating many areas of formerly all-male study and employment and, for some far-sighted contemporary commentators, it was only a matter of time before they did, in fact, enter Parliament and the police force.

From the 1880s, campaigners for women's rights, such as Florence Balgarnie, pressed for police stations to be safer spaces for women accused of crime, with separation between male and female cells and a woman present to attend to prisoners who were breastfeeding or advanced in pregnancy, drunk, ill, wet through or suffering from the effects of poisoning. Women might be assaulted or even raped while being held at a police station, and not all male police could be trusted only to arrest women with just cause. The Sanitary Committee recommended separate spaces within police stations for male and female prisoners and the matter was debated in 1889, but both police and public administrators dragged their feet for years: expanding stations and hiring female staff cost more money than they cared to spend.

Sir Herbert Croft launched an enquiry in 1892 to consider the regular employment of female 'warders' or 'matrons' at all police stations; he asked about existing arrangements. The table of results returned to him was striking.[43] It revealed that across Britain women were already doing the work – routinely, on a case-by-case basis – but their remuneration varied hugely and was, in some cases, non-existent. In Birmingham, pay for a searcher would have been four pence for each prisoner searched and two shillings and sixpence per day or night when in charge of a prisoner. Female staff in police stations, who were expected to be available, year-round and night and day, to watch, search and often take evidence from female prisoners who might be violent, suicidal or dangerously intoxicated were receiving £12 a year and free quarters (Wolverhampton), or £5 per annum (Liverpool), or 7 shillings and sixpence per week (Newcastle), or in Bradford just free quarters, and in Blackpool and Clitheroe nothing at all.[44]

Because they were typically wives or widows of police officers, or women 'of similar standing', female workers in police stations were not sworn in, 'formally appointed' or entitled to pensions. The police would begin, from the 1890s, to regularise the employment of women, but their main aim would continue to be to minimise expenditure on their workforce by keeping female work casualised, however long term. By rebranding work formerly done by 'searchers' as that of a 'matron', the police would also emphasise female employees' caring, maternal role, whereas detection of stolen goods and identifying and interviewing suspects had always been a key element of searchers' work within the station, and often outside it.

Ann Lovsey: 'Well-Known as a Female Detective'

In Birmingham, Ann Lovsey or Lovesay (born Elizabeth Ann Mayo) became 'well-known as a female detective', as newspapers gleefully reported in the 1870s and 1880s. Like Elizabeth Joyes, Ann was formally employed as a 'searcher' at the police station in Moor Street. She lived hard by the police station, at 10 Moor Street, Station Yard, so was readily available at any hour when she was needed. Like the other detectives discussed in this chapter, Ann was a working-class woman, the daughter of a labourer. In 1856, aged twenty-two, she married James Lovsey, an ostler and railway porter. They had four sons, one of whom married a policeman's daughter: this couple also lived in Moor Street, at 11 Lockup Yard. Moor Street was not only a police station where suspects were brought and charged; it was a network of residences where the policing community of Birmingham lived for decades, in and out of each other's homes, or drinking at the Justice Inn on the same street, which was sometimes guilty of breaking the law by selling them pints of beer on a Sunday.

Ann's exceptionally long-term employment by the Birmingham police – over thirty-six years as a searcher and a female detective – flatly contradicts the notion that women had only a casual relationship with police forces in Victorian Britain.[45] Her experience and knowledge of the community in which she worked were crucial to the jobs she undertook.

We first learn of Ann's exploits as a detective in October 1865, when she was reported in the *Birmingham Daily Post* to have exposed a husband-and-wife team of fraudulent fortune-tellers.[46]

In 1872, she identified three bus conductors guilty of embezzling their employers' money. The bus and tramway companies of Birmingham were frustrated that conductors were pocketing the fares and under-reporting the number of passengers who had travelled on each service. This, however, was difficult to prove. Eagle-eyed Mrs Lovsey was tasked with riding the buses, pretending to be an ordinary passenger but calculating the numbers of adults and children who boarded each bus and how much money should have been received at the end of each journey. As a result of her persistent observations and calculations, three young men were prosecuted: Frederick Rotchell (sixteen), George Benson (eighteen) and Joseph Yarnold (twenty).

These were petty thefts by young, semi-literate men who were doubtless sorely tempted to augment their slender wages. Yet the bus companies estimated that 'the amount they were defrauded of by conductors was enormous'. For a single journey, Mrs Lovsey noted that the discrepancy between the returns given by one embezzling bus conductor and the actual money received was 4 shillings 11 and a half pence. If this was repeated many times a day, throughout Birmingham, the annual losses could run to thousands of pounds. Ann Lovsey likewise rode Birmingham's trams. Female detectives were reported as early as 1868 to be riding the buses in Chester to check that the driver wasn't dipping into the receipts, so Lovsey was not an outlier in this occupation.[47]

She was also employed to detect female fortune-tellers, who practised their trade chiefly on young women, especially domestic servants who might be lured to part with money or wares stolen from their employers' larders – bacon, flour, sugar and tea – in exchange for the thrill of looking into a crystal ball or having their hands or cards read. The Vagrancy Act of 1824 ruled that: 'Every person pretending or professing to tell fortunes, or using any subtle craft, means, or device, by palmistry or otherwise, to deceive and impose on any of his Majesty's subjects . . . shall be deemed a rogue and a vagabond.'

Persistent offenders could face up to three months in prison, though a month of hard labour was the most common sentence.

In practice, this law was chiefly used to prosecute the poor. Many middle-class and upper-class Victorians enjoyed the idea of looking into the future, speaking to the spirits or reading tarot cards. The Countess of Blessington famously owned a crystal ball. Readers of *Jane Eyre* will recall that Rochester appears in the guise of a gypsy fortune-teller to read the hands of his house guests. Where working-class women, however, were charging fourpence a time to read the future of young females of their own class, the practice was deemed a public nuisance. A male policeman would have stood out painfully at these gatherings.

In 1875, the *Leeds Times* reported that Lovsey, together with a younger woman called Hyde, had visited Ann Archer's house and found ten women waiting to go upstairs to have their fortunes told. Lovsey told Archer that she didn't want to hear about any 'love affairs' but was interested in whether she would come into possession of some property. A glass globe was produced 'about the size of an egg' and, as Ann deposed to the magistrate: 'She looked into the globe, and said that she could see in it the two gentlemen who would receive my property. I did not look into the globe myself, but I suppose that I should have seen nothing in it if I had.' This response produced laughter in the courtroom. Lovsey had a dry sense of humour.

Sarah Rebecca Smith, a widow of sixty-nine who charged sixpence for a reading, told Lovsey that she would 'go on a long journey', a prediction that Smith doubtless wished were true when Lovsey caused her arrest in 1876.[48] In 1877, Mary Ann Matthews, another female fortune-teller in Birmingham, reassured her client (a female detective in disguise) who confessed to hating her husband that, 'It don't matter how big he is, I can make him glide away.'[49] Matthews further foretold that there was another young man who 'was very fond of her, and would have her in time'. One glimpses here the consolations that fortune-telling provided to working-class women.

The fortune-teller might not be a magical hit-woman, able to dispose of unwanted husbands who were expensive and difficult to divorce. But she was a confidante with whom, for a small fee, one could dream.

Fortune-telling circles were broken by female detectives in the Victorian period not only in Birmingham but in many other cities.[50] Like those of backstreet abortionists, these were cases that only a woman could crack because they involved women meeting in a private setting.[51] As early as 1848, Mrs Henshaw, a female searcher at a Leicester police station, was deployed to attend and expose a fortune-telling salon.[52] As late as 1894, three female detectives assisted in prosecuting a Birmingham fortune-teller who claimed to 'put spells upon people'.[53] One cannot help but think of witch hunts and the age-old mistrust of women who traffic with the occult. Newspaper readers in Birmingham (and Edinburgh and Dundee, where articles in the local press described Lovsey as 'a well-known female detective') were free to speculate not only on how many female sleuths there might be secretly working among them, but also on who was duping people more benignly: the woman pretending to be an oracle or the woman pretending to be her client.

Being a female searcher and detective involved dealing with moral ambiguity and human distress. Lovsey would, for example, certainly have had to deal with the horror in the summer of 1873 when Ann Luke, a hawker well known to the police, presented herself at Moor Street station having drowned her five-year-old son in the canal. Luke was homeless and claimed she had committed the offence to obtain a cell and 'rest my weary head'.[54]

Ann Lovsey, during her four decades working in Moor Street, frequently gave evidence in court. In 1896, she testified in the case of the 'adventuress' Mary Ann Furneaux, who had posed in society as Lord Arthur Pelham Clinton, gaining friends and obtaining credit on the strength of her assumed title and fortune. Furneaux, the *Nottingham Guardian* reported, dressed 'in male attire': she 'affected the fashionable young man about town with Newmarket coat, gaiters, lavender kid gloves, and walking stick'.[55] The *Guardian* failed to explain that

Lord Arthur Clinton was a gay celebrity; dead by 1896, but best known for his association with Fanny Park and Stella Boulton, the most famous British transvestites of the age.[56] If Furneaux was scamming men for money (and she was), she was also part of a complex web of desire that involved circles of Victorians passing socially as persons with gender and class identities different from those they had been assigned at birth.

Lovsey told the court that Furneaux was 'a woman' and that she had searched her ten years before, when she was last brought in. Lovsey, whom the *Birmingham Daily Post* emphasised was 'a most respectable woman', also appeared before the Watch Committee of mayor and aldermen to give a 'detailed account' of the methods she used to search women, reassuring the gentlemen that the process was no more intrusive than necessary and 'in no case was all of the under clothing removed from the person'. Lovsey must have seen it all during her career: from body lice and the chancres caused by syphilis to tattoos, piercings and the marks of domestic violence. Transvestite and transgender suspects were part of the Victorian detective's caseload.

One of Lovsey's sons, William, sometimes assisted her. In August 1877, aged thirteen, William gave evidence against Edward Haynes, a fishmonger's assistant who was suspected by his employer of going to the fish market, buying fish at one price, telling his employer that he had paid a higher price and pocketing the difference. William and a young woman, Mary Ann Glandon, were tasked with following Haynes to the fish market. They gathered enough evidence to prosecute him. The boy, 'who appeared remarkably sharp and precocious, produced several slips of paper in Court on which he had noted the prisoner's purchases'.[57] Doubtless Ann had helped to instruct William and Mary Ann in shadowing figures surreptitiously. William Lovsey would go on to be a well-known alderman in Birmingham, with a remarkable political career.

Diddling fishmongers, fake fortune-tellers and bent bus conductors are not the stuff of conventional crime drama, unless the crystal ball or frozen flounder happens to become a murder weapon. However, petty theft was the routine business of Victorian casework. Ann Lovsey was a pioneer female beat detective, honing and passing on the art of minute, local observation: the ground zero of community policing.

Margaret Saunders, or 'Clubnose'

In March 1877, the newspapers reported the death of a woman who, they claimed, had worked with the police of Scotland Yard as a female detective. Her name was Margaret Saunders, but she was known (the papers announced) as 'Clubnose' due to the dreadful disfigurement of her face that she had suffered during a career combatting crime. Margaret Saunders is the most difficult to trace of the women detectives who may have served with police in Britain in the nineteenth century, as her case hovers uncertainly between myth and reality. Yet its detail and persistence suggest that it may have some foundation in fact.

Though she is not named, Margaret Saunders is first identified in an article of March 1876, 'A Female Detective', which informs readers that

> we have all read romances of foreign ladies moving in the best circles of society, and yet acting as political spies engaged in the defence of some autocratic Government, but it is not generally known that a certain number of females are employed by Scotland Yard authorities to track thieves of the lowest and most dangerous type. It is difficult to imagine anything more unwomanly than the specimen of the low-class female detective I have recently met.[58]

The journalist notes that this woman is 'known in the poor neighbourhood where she resides as a nurse' and will enter a fever hospital or nurse a new-born baby while studying and adapting herself to the 'coarseness and foul language' of her 'low-bred clientele' and thus penetrating their inner circles. She is 'small in stature, but possessing considerable muscular force and indomitable energy'. She is:

> equally dead to all sense of feminine delicacy, of nervousness or fear. She will assume the garb of a boy as readily as the dress of her own sex, and in either costume is ever ready to settle a dispute by an appeal to the 'art of self-defence', which she has often practised with disastrous effect on her adversaries, whether male or female.

This account reports on various near-fatal attacks that the female detective has suffered while engaged in her occupation. In one assault, she has penetrated a thieves' lodging house, but doesn't know the correct argot when asked to speak, and has only just time to put her hand through a pane of glass and sound a rattle to summon waiting police officers when she is struck on the head with an iron bar, a blow that results in an operation to remove 'fourteen small pieces of bone' from her skull. In another case, the unmasking of a large gang of coiners, the female detective is hit by molten lead thrown by the ringleader, resulting in burns and the loss of much of her hair, which she cheerfully remarks will make it easier for her to pass as a boy. She is protected from fatal injury only by the poke bonnet, covered in silk flowers, that she was wearing – whose expensive purchase is cited as evidence that she is not wholly immune to the 'weakness usually ascribed to her sex'. She had, according to the *Irishman*, obtained entrance to the coiners' den by feigning illness and asking a local child for a cup of water: a chilling ruse, as it practises on innocence and compassion.

In this account, the 'female detective' is presented as both admirable in her dogged pursuit of criminals and fearsome in her violent and coarse physical behaviour. She may harbour a womanly weakness for bonnets; but she is also a 'denatured female' who can pose as a nurse yet exhibit no remorse at sending to the gallows the people whose children she brings into the world. She embodies, in other words, in her ugly strength and ruthless ingenuity, a general ambivalence about whether there should be female detectives at all.

In March 1877, it was reported that the female detective known as 'Clubnose' had died the previous week: a woman clearly identical to 'A Female Detective' identified by the newspapers the year before. The story of her death was broken by the 'Man About Town' in the *Sporting Gazette* for 10 March and was quickly picked up by papers across Britain and as far afield as India. A detailed article by William Wilmott Dixon subsequently appeared in *Chambers Journal* for October 1879; he claimed to have encountered Saunders in a London hospital. He reflects:

> She had I think the most hideous and repulsive face I ever saw on man or woman. It was not that the features were naturally ugly, for it was simply impossible to tell in what resemblance Nature had originally moulded them; but they had been so completely battered out of shape, that one would have fancied she must have been subjected to much the same treatment as the figure-head on which Daniel Quilp used to vent his impotent fury.[59]

Like the 1876 article in the *Irishman* that compared the 'female detective' to Sarah Gamp, this one also resorts to Dickens to find a model equal to Saunders's grotesquery. It gives her a voice that at times sounds Irish or Scottish; she uses the word 'gallus' to refer to the 'bad job' in which she sustained the head injuries that caused her death. She is also given a motive; it is claimed that she became a detective to clear her own name after she was accused of involvement in an assault and robbery on a gentleman for whom she had acted as a cleaner. The detective with a personal motive for finding the guilty party is a trope that belongs in fiction, as the *Pictorial World* noted in June 1877, describing Clubnose: 'a woman recently died in London, whose career furnishes incident enough for half a dozen sensation novels'.[60]

All three articles are consistent in mentioning certain details of Saunders's appearance (small, facially disfigured) and career, and each adds new material to the story in a manner that suggests there may have been a real originating incident. There certainly *was* a Margaret Saunders who died aged forty-three in Islington in December 1876, whose death might have been reported in March 1877. Yet the details of her life do not precisely match those attributed to Clubnose. It seems possible that there really was a working-class female detective working undercover with the London police, who helped to capture coiners and who inspired the story.[61] However, the articles that circulated about Clubnose also have the flavour of myth. Already, in the 1870s, the female detective was a character who navigated the debatable and suggestive land between reportage and invention.

Baby Farming and Child Abuse

Most Victorian women who worked with the police were related in some way to male police officers and/or had a job (housekeeper, searcher), which meant they were to be found routinely in the ambit of the police station when their services were needed. This was not, however, true of all women who worked with the police. Fanny Hodson, a middle-class writer and citizen detective, chose to get involved in investigating and prosecuting baby farmers out of a strong sense of moral revulsion at child abuse.

'Baby farming' was a catch-all term for a raft of practices that preoccupied concerned philanthropists in the 1860s and 1870s. Working-class women advertised in the newspapers, offering to take care of infants whose parents wished to put them out to nurse. Sometimes, it was alleged, they personated a childless couple who were seeking to adopt; sometimes they offered to take in women expecting illegitimate births and then to 'take care' of the resulting baby. The allegation was that such women were really contract killers. The babies would not thrive. Undernourished, neglected, plied perhaps with alcohol or sedatives to prevent them from crying, unwanted or vulnerable infants, given in charge by mothers who could not easily support them, would quietly die in a manner that aroused no suspicion. Some of the furore may have been moral panic disproportionate to the real scale of the issue, but several 'baby farmers' were prosecuted, including Margaret Waters and Sarah Ellis of Brixton. Waters, who was discovered with a house full of sick and malnourished infants and suspected of the murders of some nineteen babies, was hanged in 1870.

Hodson combined activities we would now associate with detective journalism and campaigning social work with police liaison over several years: she was the body 'on the ground' who got inside suspected premises, interviewed baby farmers without raising their suspicions, gathered evidence and communicated it to the officers on the case. This led to successful prosecutions. Of Victorian journalists and detectives it was true that 'so overlapping were their tasks that at times they exchanged roles'.[62]

Hodson's method was to respond to suspicious advertisements in the papers, then follow up with house calls, in character. By pretending to be a woman desperate about an unwanted pregnancy, she uncovered the methods, business rates and ideology of those women – abetted by male doctors – who disposed of unwanted babies, whether by abortion, putting them 'out to nurse', or having them 'adopted', which might in effect mean that they were doomed to die in the house of an unscrupulous colleague.

Hodson's investigation, published in *The Times* under the initials A.B., is shocking and suspenseful: entering the premises of midwife and suspected baby farmer Mrs Castle, Hodson worries that her hostess may have drugged the sherry she is offered; she considers the difficulty of escaping the house and has a male companion promise to wait outside for her in a couple of hours and bring police reinforcements if she fails to emerge. She spies evidence of a recent birth, and wonders if she will need to whisk a vulnerable newborn away to safety. Her reportage, with its dialogue and descriptions of the furnishings and music in Mrs Castle's drawing room, at times reads like a novel, complete with detail of the dress and mannerisms that Hodson theatrically assumed to call on various suspects.

Fanny's previously unknown background as the daughter of a minister and wife of an army chaplain helps to explain why, aged thirty-seven, she felt morally driven to engage in the risky undercover project of surveilling Maria Castle, a midwife living in Camberwell Road who had sent at least one child to die at Margaret Waters's hands. Hodson was also well travelled and venturesome: she was married in South Africa and had given birth in Italy and India.[63] Home alone at The Hermitage, Rotherfield, with her husband in India and only her seven-year-old daughter Stella to care for, she relished a challenge. Fanny's familiar manner of writing to the policemen on the case (which disconcerted one officer) suggests that she also enjoyed the camaraderie of shared investigation and was keen to continue: 'If you ever have anything on hand in which I can be of use, pray let me know. A woman's tact is valuable, sometimes.'[64] Finally, Hodson's own painful experience of child loss (her son Doveton had died at twelve days old) doubtless affected her desire to expose the 'ogres' who disposed of tiny children for a fee.

Although she began as a self-motivated amateur aided by a network of friends and servants, Hodson worked with professional policemen, including Sergeant Richard Relf and Captain Baynes, and attended the trial of Waters and Ellis at the Old Bailey. In her letters to the police, Hodson jokingly compares Captain Baynes and his police colleague to 'Box and Cox', lodgers in a farce by John Maddison Morton who rent the same apartment, one working during the day and the other by night. She knew their schedules.

Hodson's literary reading inflects her detective practice. When sending letters to suspected baby farmers, she is keen to make the tone and style convincing for the character she (or one of her assistants) is assuming:

I made my gentlemen aides write as if they were in trouble about some young girl or married woman, and they wrote according to my dictation in various styles, corresponding with their supposed positions and characters, and more or less feelingly – from the man who said he had got into 'an infernal scrape with a woman,' and in a cold-blooded business way asked to know how much it would cost to wash his hands of the whole affair, as he wanted to go abroad, to the timid despairing boy writing with tears in his ink (as it were), who had more love than money, and begged 'for God's sake' to get an answer by return of post.[65]

This is a kind of imaginative authorial practice. When describing her investigation in *The Times*, Hodson compares herself with 'The Amateur Casual': investigative journalist James Greenwood, who published insider accounts of being in a workhouse. Hodson had invented herself as a detective due to reading about the baby-farming scandal. She pursued her investigation through sifting newspapers for advertisements. The culmination of her investigation was her long article in *The Times*, which shared her results and advocated for change. It was, altogether, a literary case as well as a soberingly real one, of flesh and blood.

The Times, introducing the article, maintained both that this kind of detective work was a 'call' that women as well as men might hear, and that – as the formal police detective department was so limited in scope – it was up to everybody to uncover such crime in their midst:

We must request our readers to consider that private volunteer investigations are the only way in which these dreadful mysteries can be detected and exposed ... We have no detective agency except for the prevention of burglary, the protection of tradesmen, and the safety of our purses and pocket handkerchiefs ... It is, then, a public duty, and in the interest of all, that everybody takes the trouble and incurs the risk of such an inquiry as is related in our columns today.[66]

The idea of a citizen detective, who was needed precisely because Britain rightly guarded civil liberties and private life, involved co-opting all newspaper readers, of both sexes, not only as concerned philanthropists but as potential sleuths. The Victorian woman reader was solicited to do as Fanny Hodson had done and bring her literary detective skills to bear on real-world crime.

Working-class Women Combatting Crime

It was not only middle-class women who heeded the 'call' to detection that *The Times* described. Quick-witted, resourceful working-class women could also be impressively active in tracking and apprehending criminals when they became victims or witnesses in the case. They were often described as 'female detectives' in the press and held up as examples of bravery and intelligence.

Isabella and Jean Stewart were the adult daughters of Donald Stewart, a mill-overseer of Park Entry, Dundee. On Saturday 10 February 1866, Donald, who was described by the newspaper as 'an old man' (he was sixty-seven), was on his way home between the hours of ten and eleven at night when he was mugged. Donald was a Highlander born in Laggan, Inverness-shire, and he wore a 'shepherds tartan' plaid, secured in front with a pin. As the *Dundee Courier* lamented:

When within a few yards of his own door in Park Entry, which is a quiet, retired locality, he was suddenly attacked from behind by an unseen assailant, and received a violent blow on the head, which made him reel against the wall. At the same time his assailant attempted to pull his plaid from him; but Stewart managed to retain it until he received a kick in the groin, which brought him to the ground and ... rendered him helpless for the time.[67]

Their father's cries for help brought Isabella (thirty-one) and Jean (twenty-nine) out into the street. Despite the late hour and the violent nature of the mugging, they both ran after the thief, pursuing him down Temple Lane and into the West Port, 'where he was lost sight of among the numerous passengers on the street'. They didn't give up, however. One of the sisters (we don't know if it was Isabella or Jean) found herself in North Tay Street and, as the *Courier* relates:

> with the instinct of a thoroughly trained detective, she reconnoi-tred the premises of O'Farrell, a pawnbroker there, and had the gratification to find the thief there with her father's plaid in his hands . . . which he was about to deposit. She seized hold of him and accused him of the robbery, whereon he commenced a violent resistance, and savagely struck and kicked his female captor in his wild efforts to escape. She retained hold of him, however, until Mr Paterson, a spirit-dealer, hearing her cries for help . . . came to her assistance, and effectively secured and subdued the outra-geous criminal.[68]

The mugger, Lawrence Murray (forty-five), a weaver born in Ireland, had previous convictions as a thief. He lived in Hilltown, a poor neighbourhood of Dundee outside the mediaeval city walls. At the April assizes, he pleaded guilty to robbery but not assault and was given eighteen months' imprisonment. The *Courier* noted that street robbery in Dundee always seemed to happen on a Saturday evening. Little changes: the weekend brings out drinkers and the throng of pleasure-seekers entices the poor and the predatory. What is surprising to a modern audience, however, is that the Stewart sisters, rather than merely helping their father to his bed or calling for medical assist-ance, set off hotfoot in the dark to track down and arrest his assailant.

From the tone of its reportage, the *Dundee Courier* relished this story of have-a-go heroism, which it titled 'Assault and Robbery on the Street – Courageous Conduct of a Female Detective'. Local newspapers were much less certain about other contexts in which women might be used in a detective capacity. In 1876, the *Northern Warder and Bi-Weekly Courier* reported with disgust that 'Ann Hay or Fraser', a female turnkey in the Dundee Police Office, had been sent out with an empty bottle to pose as a customer and purchase whisky from a publican whom they suspected of being an illegal spirit-dealer. To the journalist in the *Northern Warder*, who noted that Ann had not known in advance what she was being asked to do, this practice was a form of entrapment – both of the publican and of the female turnkey – and an abuse of police powers. The writer observed:

> The credit of the Dundee Establishment has suffered before from a somewhat similar course, and although no children have been pressed into the service in this case as 'detectives', as they were before in bringing shebeening offenders to light, still the circumstances are so very extraordinary that they demand investigation. It might be well to know, for one thing, whether there is any official personage responsible for freaks such as this employment of a woman . . . to detect breaches of the Publichouses Acts, or whether they get a clean card, and are told by their head to go out and exercise their wits and get the means of conviction, fairly if they can, but to get the means of a conviction.[69]

Newspapers were the primary forum in which competing stories and ideas about female detection were delivered and debated. The *Dundee Courier*, in common with other papers, ran positive coverage of Hannah Lawton, the policeman's wife who had posed as a clothes dealer to entrap thieves in 1865 and Ann Lovsey and her incrimination of female fortune-tellers in 1872; it also ran advertisements for the 1864 fictional casebook *The Female Detective* and the play *The Female Detective*, which was performed at the People's Theatre in Dundee in 1884. Often, as in the case of Isabella and Jean Stewart, we can see enthusiasm for clever and energetic women – in fact and fiction – who are active in bringing malefactors to justice. Yet there remains distaste for the idea of employing women in the police force, especially where such women might be involved in acts of deception designed to lure suspects to engage in criminal acts in order to secure their conviction.

A Female Detective Force?

Women in the late nineteenth century were occasionally called on to perform a more active role in policing. Rachel Hamilton (née Johnston), known as 'Big Rachel', was sworn in by the Glasgow Police as a special constable during the Partick riots of 1875. Rachel, who was originally from Ireland, reputedly stood 6 feet 4 inches tall and weighed around 17 stone; she worked as a labourer in Tod and McGregor shipyards and as a forewoman navvy at Jordanhill Brickworks. Her physically formidable presence and local knowledge were useful to the police when marches organised by Home Rulers to celebrate what would have been Daniel O'Connell's one hundredth birthday turned into a violent clash between Catholics and Orangemen. Rachel and other constables 'drove the mob across the Kelvin river' and back towards Glasgow.

Women also continued to act on their own initiative to pursue criminals and secure their arrest. In 1890, Alice Ducker, the wife of PC James Ducker, living in Kentish Town, spotted a gang of burglars who, having knocked at the door of a local house and ascertained that the owner was out, proceeded to break open a side gate and enter the property. Mrs Ducker calmly walked down the road, found two constables, and the robbers were apprehended red-handed. This example of what we might now call 'Neighbourhood Watch' caused the *Birmingham Daily Mail* to reflect that this was becoming a regular occurrence – 'only within the last few days several members of the housebreaking fraternity have fallen into the hands of the police through the cuteness of the female mind' – and to suggest that 'if women continue to exhibit such a remarkable aptitude for capturing burglars, a female detective force will certainly have to be organised'.[70]

As we have seen, the question of whether and when women would be formally admitted to the police force as detectives had been discussed since at least 1860, when *Reynolds's Newspaper* pointed out that France already employed female detectives and wondered when Britain would catch up. By the 1880s, the topic was a political hot potato. The Whitechapel murders, which we now know as the 'Jack the Ripper' case, formed the most sensational topic of 1888, generating column after column of press commentary and speculation. It was generally agreed that the investigation was a botched job: the police had failed to protect women from a serial killer, to identify him and bring him to justice. Among the comments the case stimulated was a letter to *The Times* from prominent feminist Frances Power Cobbe, which implicitly addressed Sir Charles Warren himself:

Why should such a thing as a female detective be unheard of in the land? A clever woman of unobtrusive dress and appearance (she need not be 5 ft. 7 in.) would possess over masculine rivals not a few advantages. She would pass unsuspected where a man would be immediately noticed. She could extract gossip from other women much more freely; she would move through the courts without wakening the echoes of the pavements by a sonorous military tread; and lastly, she would be in a position to employ for whatsoever it may be worth that gift of intuitive quickness and 'mother wit' with which her sex is commonly credited. A keen-eyed woman might do as well in her way as those keen-nosed bloodhounds (of whose official engagement I rejoice to hear) may, we hope, do in their peculiar line. Should it so fall out that the demon of Whitechapel prove really to be ... a physiologist delirious with cruelty, and should the hounds be the means of his capture, poetic justice will be complete.[71]

As well as a passionate feminist who lived with her female partner, Power Cobbe was an anti-vivisectionist, who supported the National Canine Defence League. Her idea of Jack the Ripper as a sadistic anatomist who experimented on female and animal bodies encouraged her to imagine his capture by female detectives abetted by bloodhounds as the ultimate form of social retribution. One thinks of the goddess Artemis who, angered by Actaeon's voyeurism of her nymphs, had him torn to pieces by his own hounds.

Power Cobbe also rubbed salt into masculine wounded pride by pointing out that during the Crimean War, when the 'masculine

4. Frontispiece to Life of Frances Power Cobbe *(1894).*

minds' of the generals and War Office failed to solve the problem of hospitals that were overrun, ill supplied and filthy, 'the feminine mind', embodied in Florence Nightingale and her small band of nurses, 'came to the rescue and out of chaos and indescribable misery brought order and relief'. Might not a small band of female detectives similarly solve the crisis of public safety represented by the Whitechapel murderer?

Power Cobbe's letter proposing that there should be female detectives in the police force was widely reprinted and quoted, appearing in papers from the *Dundee Evening Telegraph* to the *Irish Times* and received a storm of responses. A male opponent in the *Manchester Weekly Times* retorted that Power Cobbe's letter 'reads more like a grim joke than anything else ... If there is an occupation for which women are utterly unfitted, it is that of the detective.'[72] The *Yorkshire Post* was also disgusted by the suggestion: 'The argument is complete, conclusive, and utterly repulsive. It conjures up visions of Paris in the third empire ... and generally of a political system of espionage.'[73] The British association of undercover detection with the activities of French female spies in the post-Napoleonic period was strong and allowed conservative critics to ally British national identity with refusal to tolerate undercover 'espionage', especially when conducted by women.

The *Irish Times* concluded that Miss Power Cobbe's proposal

is variously but, upon the whole, not favourably regarded. We are aware that in other countries women have successfully reversed the hint to 'chercher la feminine,' and have shown the keenness of the sleuthhound in running their man to death. The Rue Jerusalem employs female detectives, and so does the director of the 'Third Section' in St Petersburg ... Up to the present Nemesis in her true sex has not been enlisted in the service of justice – save, perhaps, in such base uses as the conviction of publicans violating the licensing laws or decoys for the adulterators of butter and milk. It is hardly likely that Scotland Yard will entertain the notion.[74]

Other papers were cautiously positive about the possibility of female detectives joining the police force. The 'Ladies' Column' of the *Northern Whig*, which devoted itself to reporting recent achievements of women in work, scholarship and the arts, observed that

> Miss Frances Power Cobbe has seized an appropriate moment to suggest that the duties of a detective might sometimes be advantageously performed by women. Across the Channel, as all readers of French fiction are aware, the female detective is a recognised, and sometimes important, personage. The detective profession is not likely to attract many persons who are not specially qualified for it, and if any woman in this country was found to possess the requisite gifts it would be to the advantage of the community that they should be utilised.[75]

Some pointed out that this activity had been going on unofficially for some time. The *Newcastle Daily Chronicle* observed that

> Many of the Private Inquiry Offices make a liberal use of women for the purpose of obtaining information necessary for the cases taken in hand; and in an irregular way Scotland Yard even is not wholly free from indebtedness to astute females in the work of unravelling crimes ... In America, where they are better recognised, and on the Continent, the employment of women in this branch is ... on a far greater scale.

This journalist argued that assistant-matrons in gaols and police officers' families might one day 'experimentally' be trained as part of wide-ranging police reforms to become 'a duly recognised "Force"'.[76] He didn't know or wouldn't acknowledge that female searchers and policemen's wives were doing aspects of this work already.

Some male policemen trying to track down the Whitechapel murderer dressed in 'drag' in their attempt to simulate the East End female sex workers they thought were his targets: an expedient that, rather than success, led to the men being assaulted by bystanders.[77] Such fiascos tended to emphasise the point that actual women were needed. The *Leeds Times* in 1890 reported the conversion of sex workers into female detectives to try to solve the case:

> But by far the most important arrangement IN THE OPINION OF THE SHREWDEST DETECTIVES yet made to entrap the assassinator, should he attempt to add another to his already long list of horrors, is the employment of the class of women he has formerly chosen as his prey. A number of these outcasts, about the same age and character as those who have died by the merciless hand of the mysterious fiend, though not of course officially appointed, have practically been engaged by the authorities to aid in the endeavours being put forth to capture him. They have been converted for the time being into female detectives, for which, provided they can be kept sober, the police consider them well qualified. They are instructed NOT TO REPULSE ANY MAN who solicits them. They are guaranteed that they will be followed, and that there will be help near at hand should their companions attempt to harm them.[78]

If there is any truth in this report, then the police were accompanying sex workers while they arranged assignations, telling the women under their surveillance to take on any man who approached them: surely a violation of their right to choose their clients. Such women may have enjoyed a degree of police protection, but they were playing the part of bait as much as that of 'female detective'. Hallie Rubenhold has argued that the assumption that the 'Ripper' preyed on sex workers skewed the Whitechapel murders investigation.[79] Certainly, media reportage and theatrical productions stimulated by the case could not resist identifying the type of the victims and typifying the female detective as an agent of female vengeance, whose body delivers the Ripper to justice.

In 1889, in a Parisian staging of *Jack L'Eventreur* by Xavier Bertrand, Jack the Ripper disguises himself as a detective and murders one of the female detectives on his trail. In another French melodrama of 1889, *La Policière*, a mother who is a female detective on the trail of a band of assassins discovers that her son is their chief and has just murdered a young girl. In the police station, she hands him a revolver so that he can blow his own brains out. Both these French plays were discussed in the British press.

The Whitechapel murderer's murder of vulnerable women and his mutilation of their bodies made him an apt spectre with which to dramatise the idea of the female detective as the embodiment of Nemesis – in Greek mythology the spirit of retribution for evil acts. Nemesis was often held to be the daughter of Nyx (goddess of night), a child of darkness. She had no father. Linked to the wilderness worship of Artemis, goddess of the hunt and fierce protector of women, Nemesis was a force of nature. Her work, though it restored balance, was to punish: she was a terrifying figure. The male police detective in this period is not usually associated with *revenge*. The fact that vengeance is such an important aspect of the discourse around female detection ('the keenness of the sleuthhound in running their man to death') suggests that the formal establishment of a female detective force within the police in the late nineteenth century raises not only concerns around women's physical and moral safety in the role, but also deep fear of women's anger about crime and how ruthlessly they might pursue men who had wronged their sex.

In 2019–20, in the UK, 82 per cent of all violent crime was committed by men and in 70 per cent of cases with a female victim the perpetrator was an intimate partner or family relative.[80] Victorian statistics are sparser and harder to interpret accurately, but they point to a similar disparity: where women were typically prosecuted for non-violent offences such as prostitution, habitual drunkenness, petty theft and uttering false coin.[81] Overwhelmingly it was and remains men who murder, assault, rape and molest, and most of this

violence occurs in a domestic context. Violence against women, especially domestic violence, began to be more publicly visible in Victorian
Britain, partly through the divorce courts and newspapers, which
related intimate details of the torture some women endured in the
private setting of marriage. The demand for female detectives directly
relates to this increasingly visible violence and the need for women
to expose and end it.

The *Birmingham Daily Post* in 1888 reported on the lady detectives of Chicago: 'Chicago has many female detectives but they are
not known as such. Their identity is successfully concealed.' The
paper printed extracts from an interview with the 'queen of the
female detectives in Chicago … a motherly woman, perhaps fifty
years of age', who argued: 'No one can have any idea … how much
deception and misery there is in the world … Women will suffer
every imaginable indignity and insult rather than let the facts be
known, for exposure means almost invariably the loss of social position – dearer to many women than life itself.'[82]

The 'lady detective', posing as domestic servant, a fortune-teller, a
bank agent, a pedlar of patterns – this article suggests – can penetrate
the concealed woes of domestic life: infidelity, gaslighting, domestic
abuse. Her own deceptions are a justifiable means of getting at the
concealed truth of 'deception and misery' in marriage.

For other commentators, however, a female detective was an
affront to women's purity and the separation of the domestic sphere
from that of public life: '[Miss Power Cobbe] seems to forget the
class of people with whom the detective too often has to work. Would
she send her female policeman into the dens of burglars, street
thieves, and cutthroats? Would she have her visit low beershops and
unravel the secrets of crime in disreputable houses?'[83] Several newspapers reprinted the punning joke: 'A "FEMALE DETECTIVE"
– a blush'.[84] The gag implied that a pure woman was unable to conceal
her feelings; in a sense, she policed herself. She would be found out
(detected) because her cheeks would colour in response to social

embarrassment, indignation or admiration. Her modesty was legible in her unconscious body. If a woman's cheeks were a natural litmus test for shame, how could women coolly confront and apprehend the horrors of crime?

Moreover, there were anxieties about female loyalties and women's capacity to maintain professional detachment. The American *Daily Enterprise* of July 1884 reported that the New York police, while admitting the skills of female detectives, would not employ them: 'there is just one reason ... why they are not to be trusted – no one can ever tell who has most influence over them ... we can't afford to take the risk of employing them and being betrayed by them.'[85] The hazard of emotional involvement in a case is the theme of Leonard Merrick's novel, *Mr Bazalgette's Agent* (1888), where female detective Miriam Lea falls in love with the man she has pursued as a criminal. Luckily, he turns out not to be the thief she's looking for, but *is* the man she's looking for in romantic terms.

Was police work corrupting? Or might women corrupt it? Were women ill-suited to police work because of their labile, frankly emotional bodies that made them more transparent and more sympathetic – endangering professional detachment? Or were women natural actresses, whose ability to feign emotion and assume multiple social identities made them excellent detectives but proportionately dangerous to employers as well as suspects? The questions raised by the threat or possibility of the female detective are essential questions about gender, performance and power in the Victorian period.

In 1854, a report citing the deployment of a female detective in a divorce case by former policeman Charles Frederick Field noted that the woman in question had been employed as a cook but had spied through the wall using a gimlet hole, to observe the adulterous couple having sex. (The proof of this pudding was in the cheating.) The female detective was licensed to interrogate the solidity of boundaries in multiple ways. She might peer through walls. She might cross-dress, appearing to be a man. She might play the role of a governess, or a maidservant, a nurse, a pedlar, a bank agent or a fellow thief. Her existence and her testimony revealed the boundaries of private, domestic space, of gender, class and marriage to be thinner and more permeable than one might assume. To Victorian readers, this was not only a worrisome thought, but also an exciting one.

The newspapers profited from the frisson of positive and negative feeling about female detectives. They eagerly printed stories of real women who were working with the police, such as Elizabeth Joyes and Ann Lovsey, alongside quasi-mythical figures such as 'Clubnose', serialised fiction featuring female detectives and advertisements for theatrical productions in which female detectives were the main draw. It is to the novel and the theatre we now turn, to the female detective craze of the 1860s and the Sensation Plot that exposes marriage as a legalised form of murder and the female detective as its scourge.

2

HOME TRUTHS
Divorce, Domestic Violence and the Fictional Female Detective

Cases succeed each other with hardly any intermission, in which men are proved to have killed their wives by brutal maltreatment: every such death being the termination of a series of sufferings, extending through years ... For every such extreme case, we may be assured there are hundreds which stop just short of the infliction of death, or in which death is inflicted, but not ascribed to its true cause.[1]

'The Nature and Amount of Crime',
Lloyd's Weekly Newspaper (1850)

Most accounts of the nineteenth-century detective story begin with Edgar Allan Poe, whose 1841 'The Murders in the Rue Morgue' was so influential in creating the image of the detective as an eccentric, solitary male savant. Stations on this well-travelled historical line include Charles Dickens's police detective Inspector Bucket in *Bleak House* (1853), Wilkie Collins's Sergeant Cuff in *The Moonstone* (1868), arriving at the comfortable London terminus of Arthur Conan Doyle's *The Adventures of Sherlock Holmes* (1892).[2]

There is, however, an alternative route through the territory. This long-neglected literary line – whose stations scholars have revisited in recent years – features female writers and female detectives as an integral part of its Victorian network.[3] Following this line takes us on a dark, but compelling, journey that shows domestic violence and injustice perpetrated against women to be the jagged rock out of which the female detective tradition is built.

Victorian male detectives are often professionally detached from the events they investigate. Female detectives, by contrast, are more likely to be embedded, entangled in the web of violence that inseparably combines domestic and external threats. If we look only at the lineage of 'professional' detection in literature, then we ignore Victorians' own identification of the origin of the 'detective school' within sensation fiction that specialises in investigating violent acts in a domestic setting, where those acts may not even be legally defined as criminal and the perpetrator (as is often true in real cases) is intimately known to the victim. Poised between strength and vulnerability, the female detective is a controversial agent interrogating the newly visible status of the home as a crime scene, and marriage as a high-stakes gamble in a casino where men control the House.

Although connected with the old town of the gothic novel, the Victorian female detective express departs from Catherine Crowe, whose *The Adventures of Susan Hopley; or, Circumstantial Evidence* (1840) is the most influential detective story you have probably never read. William Thackeray, author of *Vanity Fair*, who knew Crowe, opined that Susan Hopley was 'the first and excellent sensation novel'.[4] It is a ground-breaking book for many reasons. One is that it establishes its pioneer female detective as a servant – a working-class woman – who is intent on finding out the truth behind her master's murder because her brother, Andrew Hopley, disappeared on the night of the crime and has been convicted in his absence. Susan knows at heart that her brother is innocent. She fears that he is dead. She is right on both counts. Her quest, however, to discover who framed her brother will expose the rotten heart of several different households. In each of them, she will discover terrible secrets and rescue women who have been cheated by men who subject them to various kinds of domestic abuse. Women and servants are aligned in this book because of their relative physical and economic dependency: neither is easily able to leave the household in which they live; both rely for reputation and subsistence on 'masters' who may lie to and about them, and even dispose of them altogether without attracting the world's suspicion.

Susan Hopley (1840): Cleaning Up Crime

Crucially, the dark truth at the centre of this female detective plot is the power struggle and violence within domestic life. Like other, later sensation novels, Crowe's *Susan Hopley* stages a cross-class drama that reveals the front drawing room as just as likely to be a crime scene as a back alley. The subtitle 'Circumstantial Evidence' points to the way in which a court may, and often does, draw the wrong conclusion if male magistrates or jurors look only at what they consider the most likely culprit and scenario, based on appearances. It takes a servant to show us behind the scenes and, like Bluebeard's wife, reveal crime in the closets of the patriarchy. All the major villains in this novel are men, mostly of apparently high social standing: they prove guilty of multiple counts of homicide, domestic assault, people trafficking, theft, fraud, impersonation, perjury and false imprisonment.

Susan Hopley does not have the whimsical curiosity or professional detachment of Poe's Dupin (a Chevalier of the Légion d'honneur), Inspector Bucket or Sergeant Cuff – and that is part of the point of her *Adventures*. She doesn't have the luxury of distance. She, too, is at risk from the criminal world in which she moves. Her family life, her name and reputation, and prospects of being able to earn a living and keep a roof over her head are all compromised by the crime of which her brother stands accused. She has no financial leg to stand on that is not in the territory where violence is ongoing. Crowe's complex multi-strand plot, which points towards strategies now familiar in TV drama, evokes a web of male violence shading into every corner of dangerous illegality that stretches from England to France. As the *New Monthly Magazine* in 1852 described the suspenseful quality of the book, *The Adventures of Susan Hopley* are full of

> incident, scheming and cross-scheming, ravelling and unravelling, plot and counter-plot ... A huge favourite was Susan with provincial matrons, who daily scan the lights and shadows of human nature in its avatars at the police-courts and assizes. Her adventures were as good as a twelve-columned murder case.[5]

It is important that the *New Monthly Magazine* situates the imagined reader of Susan Hopley as a woman who also follows true-crime drama in the newspapers, via reports of police courts and assizes. The fictional female detective in the 1840s and 1850s is being aligned with real-life incidents and the female reader's desire to participate in the battle of wits involved in the complex power struggle such court cases expose.

Newspaper coverage of domestic violence showed that this was not merely a problem that affected the lower classes and drew attention to the mental cruelty that often accompanied physical harm in the home.[6] After the 1828 Offences Against the Person Act, the first piece of nineteenth-century legislation to address wife beating, public consciousness of the possible sufferings of women in marriage rose in proportion to the number of periodical articles that conveyed shocking details of real-life torment that was difficult for women and their children to escape. From 1858, details of divorces (inevitably sordid and titillating) became a staple of the burgeoning mass market in cheap newspapers. There were even newspapers wholly devoted to divorce stories. *The Divorce Court and Breach of Promise Record* published its first number on 2 April 1864, priced at 2d, telling readers that it considered its own publicity vital to the justice meted out to straying men:

> The Divorce Court is a comparatively new institution in this country, and therefore ought to be thoroughly and publicly ventilated ... We know very well that in hundreds of cases the punishment of publicity is greater, in the estimation of the wrong-doer, than the mere decree of a court which he has already set at naught; and it is this publicity that is denied to the Divorce Court proceedings more than to any other assembly.[7]

The first number of *The Divorce Court* ran a story on '"The Little Parson" at a House of Ill-fame' about a Wesleyan minister of Bradford who had a regular account at a local brothel. It also detailed the horrors of *Lander v Lander*, in which the wife of a Shropshire surgeon proved that he had

> on one occasion ... attempted to administer prussic acid to her, on another he kicked her out of bed, causing a miscarriage, several

5. The Divorce Court and Breach of Promise Record *(1864)*.

times he threatened to shoot her, once he held an open razor over her, and, finally, he eloped with a married woman named Spedding, whom he had attended during her confinement [childbirth].[8]

This catalogue of connubial crime would not be out of place in a melodrama. It was the new accessibility of divorce that would provide employment for increasing numbers of real male and female private detectives, who might be working to gather evidence for the suspicious wife, or for the dissatisfied husband – competing actors in an increasingly visible, high-stakes domestic battle.

Readers of what one leading lawyer called 'the revolting revelations of the Divorce Courts' became highly aware of the double standard that meant men could divorce their wives on the grounds of adultery alone, whereas women had to provide evidence of adultery aggravated by cruelty or other offences. The legal situation of married women's property also became newly visible through newspaper stories. In 1866, the *London Evening Standard* reported a case of a man who left his wife a day after marriage, refusing to live with her and taking all her money with him: an action morally repugnant but perfectly legal, as technically her goods and earnings were now his.[9] Additionally, cases of domestic violence, desertion and bigamy appeared regularly in columns reporting on the police courts, which were open to the press and the public.

The rise of the female detective on the Victorian page and stage is intimately related to a new public consciousness of domestic violence and crime against women (but also perpetrated by women), through newspaper reportage that made public shocking details of private life. These stories fomented an increasingly live sociopolitical debate about women's legal power in marriage and their vulnerability to abuse of their person, property and inheritance across social classes. The purpose of the fictional female detective is typically not merely to solve a mystery and obtain justice for the victim (though she does perform this task). Her wider remit is to investigate

6. *Domestic violence portrayed in* The World's Doings *(1870).*

the unseen sufferings of her sex, to resist and, on occasion, to revenge them. She thus performs a representative function: warning of violence behind the veil of 'protection' that society seems to offer women and signalling women's determination to penetrate and foil the schemes designed to entrap, exclude or erase them.

Catherine Crowe, the author of *Susan Hopley*, married aged thirty-two, forming a deeply unhappy union with an army officer, Major John Crowe, which she escaped permanently with her young son Willie in 1833. 'I fled for my life,' she reported to a friend: wording that strongly suggests she left her husband fearing violence, even death, if she remained.[10]

Crowe, as a middle-class woman from a family of hoteliers and restaurateurs, was relatively lucky: friends helped her to set up house on her own as a single parent in Edinburgh, where she began to earn a living by writing: her fiction, drama and journalism are aimed squarely at the mass market. Women informally separated from adulterous, abusive or simply incompatible husbands, however, had little legal recourse or standing in this period. It is unsurprising, then, that in *The Adventures of Susan Hopley*, Crowe developed a detective plot that makes an implicit case for divorce, and for the necessity of women's fairer representation in the legal system, where they can suffer torments at the hands of men who wish only to possess their bodies or their fortunes, and who may prove cruel and violent.

This happens not just once in *Susan Hopley* but repeatedly: the chief villain, Walter Gaveston, murders Mr Wentworth (having destroyed his will) solely to marry Wentworth's daughter and inherit her father's wine business without opposition or delay. He proceeds to oppress and abuse his new wife. Gaveston also tries to murder Julia, his former lover, whom he has deceived, impregnated and abandoned, by pushing her into the river. Susan's next employer, Mrs Aytoun, has a coercively controlling husband. When Mrs Aytoun falls under (false) suspicion of stealing fabric, she is so terrified of her absent husband's reaction that she becomes vulnerable to the attentions of another predatory man, who tries (in vain) to seduce her. It is up to Susan to establish her mistress's innocence; she proves that the fabric theft was in fact a fit-up by a male draper's assistant, who has been accusing women while looting the till. Lastly, Susan goes to work for the Cripps family, whose wealthy daughter is lured into marriage by a fortune-hunter posing as a count with a castle in Transylvania. Having acquired his bride's money, the 'count' abandons her.[11] He may not be a vampire, but he certainly sucks the family for everything they are worth. Marriage in this book isolates women, robs them and exposes them to every kind of insult, hardship and danger.

Susan Hopley, as a shrewd detective, is keen to visit the site of Wentworth's murder and her brother Andrew's disappearance. Despite efforts to keep her away, she inspects the ground under her brother's window for footprints and searches his hotel room for clues, quizzing the chambermaid. By this forensic method, she finds a coin, which she recognises as one with a special inscription, which she had observed her master, Mr Wentworth, refuse to part with for sentimental reasons. The chambermaid also gives her a pair of shirt studs, found in her brother's room, but with Gaveston's initials and another mystery set of initials. She keeps these incriminating clues carefully: 'Susan, who was resolved to neglect nothing that could throw the faintest light on the mystery she was so anxious to penetrate, consented to keep the half-crown ... she folded it in paper, and deposited it in the same little box as the shirt studs.'[12]

The female gaze and viewpoint are of paramount importance in Susan's investigations. Although she has only basic literacy, she is a sharp reader, who recognises faces, voices and handwriting, and follows clues such as the fabric of a doll's dress that resembles the fabric said to have been stolen by Mrs Aytoun: 'Susan's attention had been attracted by observing that the doll's frock was of the exact pattern and colour of the piece of silk which had been brought to Craven Street from Mr Green's; and of which sundry yards were asserted to be missing.'[13]

Susan makes connections between information she sees in the newspaper and 'cases' she is pursuing, devoting leisure hours to tracking down a suspect and observing him unseen. She will visit prisons, pawnbrokers and lawyers, pursuing villains and eventually unearthing the body of her murdered brother Andrew – whom she publicly exonerates of the murder of which he had been accused.

As Lucy Sussex points out, there are in fact three female detectives in this novel: all of them are themselves victims of crime as well as, at various times, suspects.[14] Susan saves multiple women who are falsely accused; she also demonstrates that men who injure one woman frequently go on to injure many more, across social classes and in contexts that persistently link offences in the 'private' realm with those in the 'public': showing how violence against women strongly predicts and accompanies wider forms of serious crime. She finally saves Harry Leeson, her youthful master, by jumping through a window to intercept the armed assassins who are about to kill him in his bed. The servant detective is a stoical character, but *The Adventures of Susan Hopley* is an angry book. Susan does not marry. Given what she has seen and endured, who can blame her?

Catherine Crowe's thriller of 1840 not only echoes work in various genres – stage melodrama, the gothic novel, Samuel Richardson's *Pamela* and *Clarissa*, in which women are oppressed by men who wish to possess them – it also created a distinctively new character: a working-class woman whose position as a servant allows her to do what Poe's Dupin will do in 1841, to challenge the narrative of 'circumstantial' evidence, and discover beneath it a buried plot. That plot, in *Susan Hopley*, is so pervasive that it suggests rot in the foundational nature of male power. Crowe's novel suggestively aligns female detection and women's daily domestic labour of a kind that is frequently ignored or undervalued; restorative justice is won not from above but from below.

Susan Hopley was a phenomenal and enduring success: it sold out immediately, was pirated and put on the stage and remained a staple of the Victorian theatrical repertoire well into the 1870s.[15] The youthful Dante Gabriel Rossetti drew vignettes of the individual characters.[16] Crowe's eager readers included those who were themselves servants, paving the way for later 'sensation novels', whose thrilling secrets and revelations about low behaviour in high life (critics sniffily complained) were enjoyed in the kitchen as much as they were relished in the bedroom. Domestic service was the largest employer of women in Victorian Britain: servants were constantly in a position of silently watching their employers and picking up their traces. Imagining themselves into the detective role was easy. Meanwhile a young actress, Mary Elizabeth Braddon, acted in the stage version in 1857 in Brighton, an experience she never forgot; Braddon would go on to become a doyenne of the 'detective school' of sensation fiction, creating her own female detective characters.[17]

Anne Rodway (1856): The Seamstress Detective

Crowe's book was deeply influential. One of its readers was her friend, the young Wilkie Collins, whose first detective mystery is *The Diary of Anne Rodway* (1856), which also takes an oppressed working-class woman, rather than a man, as its detective heroine. Anne Rodway, like Susan Hopley, investigates a suspicious death and uncovers the hidden truth about it. Her fellow 'plain needlewoman', lodger and friend Mary Mallinson is found dead in the street. The official verdict at the inquest is accidental death: they conclude that eighteen-year-old Mary has simply collapsed from exhaustion, causing her to fall and hit her head on the pavement. Anne Rodway is unconvinced. Like Susan Hopley, she sets out to do her friend posthumous justice. Like Susan, she uncovers a web of abuse to which women and the poor are subject. Her friend Mary was exploited by the family for whom she was working as a casual seamstress. Working late for poor pay, she was taking laudanum to get to sleep and take the edge off her misery. Mary was threatened by the brutal landlord, to whom she owed three weeks' rent (and who callously seeks repayment after her death). Finally, Anne discovers that her friend was given a fatal blow by a drunk man, who was boarding a cab and struck Mary before disappearing, allowing the girl he'd knocked unconscious to expire on the street.

Anne solves the mystery of Mary's death by tracing the torn cravat, a fragment of which Mary was clutching when she was brought home, fatally injured but not yet dead. It is a 'dingy strip of black silk, with thin lilac lines ... in a sort of trellis-work pattern.' Anne discovers the rest of the cravat in a local shop that sells second-hand goods. Constantly improvising to obtain more information and more evidence, Anne interviews the owner of the cravat: a cabman, who tells her the full story of Mary's final night. Her assailant was the cabman's fare. Drunk and facetious, he had put out a leg to try to trip up Mary as she was 'in his way'. Mary resented this and asked him, 'What do you mean by that, you brute?' His response was to strike her so hard that he caused brain injury and death. Both men then left the scene of the crime.

It is notable that it is *fabric* that leads Anne to solve the homicide. As a female detective and a seamstress, she is – like Susan Hopley recognising the silk in a doll's dress – more likely than a man to recognise the material that links perpetrator and victim. A 'clue' originally meant a piece of thread, which one might follow to understand the path through a labyrinth. In this story, the literal thread that Anne follows is that of clothing: a line of investigation that leads her to the man who struck Mary down, and also to the family who kept Mary late sewing their garments and who gave her no sustenance when she fainted on the job from exhaustion. Miss Gladden, in James Redding Ware's *The Female Detective*, poses as a seamstress to gain access to a house where a crime has occurred. Her neighbours think it likely that she is a 'milliner or dressmaker', because of the irregular hours she works. There are many similarities between women's work in sewing and in detection, which so often draws attention to the shared material fabric of human life and the hidden threads that connect one person with another.

Domestic violence is the other key thread that runs through Collins's narrative. Mary comes from a household where her alcoholic father often hit her; his behaviour has been catastrophic for the family unit: 'My mother ran away from home, and died in a hospital. My father was always drunk, and always beating me.'[18] As it turns out, the man who kills Mary, Noah Truscott, is her father's alcoholic friend, 'who taught him to drink and game'. Thus Mary is the victim of a cycle of domestic violence that has uncannily repeated itself to cause her death – the return of the repressed spectre of patriarchal abuse, which connects the dark public street (a familiar scene of criminal fears) to the parental home (where women are supposedly safe).

It is important that Mary is quasi-suicidal when Anne encounters her. Wilkie Collins may well have been influenced by the case of

Mary Ann Rodway, of Cheltenham, who committed suicide in July 1855 by taking arsenic.[19] He would certainly have known of the cases of poor needlewomen in the 1840s, such as Maria Biddell, who were driven to suicide by desperation, having pawned the fabric they had been given with which to make shirts at a penny a time.

As Chloe Ward notes, in 1843, the Children's Employment Commission led a government investigation into the millinery and dressmaking trade, concluding that 'there is no class of persons in this country, living by their labour, whose happiness, health, and lives, are so unscrupulously sacrificed as those of the young dressmakers'.[20] Recruited at around fourteen years old, seamstresses often worked twenty-two-hour workdays, and during the busy season, when dresses were most in demand, it was not uncommon for them to work for three days straight without sleep. The scandal of sweated labour in the garment industry inspired protest poetry in the 1840s such as Thomas Hood's 'Song of the Shirt' (1843), which Anne Rodway quotes, plays and paintings by middle-class writers and artists determined to draw attention to the way in which unregulated capitalism was 'wearing out' young women's lives.[21] It is no accident that Anne's diary begins in March 1840, linking it to this particularly dark period in social history.

Wilkie Collins's *Diary of Anne Rodway*, however, brings a new element to this well-worn theme: the female detective. She is a sleuth, who wants to do justice to her dead friend, but her diary also has a campaigning thread – like the 'inspector' in J. B. Priestley's twentieth-century drama *An Inspector Calls*, Anne Rodway, through her investigation, calls attention to the multiple characters and aspects of society who killed Mary Mallinson – or at least made her death inevitable. Like Susan Hopley, this female detective is a public investigator as much as a private one; she needs to expiate a preventable death, but to do so is to excoriate the collective conscience for its despicable treatment of women and find more than one guilty party. The result is a moving story that alludes frequently to Anne's 'trembling' hand as she writes, her grief and her despair. Charles Dickens

7. *John T. Peele,* The Song of the Shirt *(1849).*

congratulated Collins, telling him that *Anne Rodway*, serialised in his magazine *Household Words*, had made him cry.

Anne, as a sleuth seeking social justice *for women like herself*, belongs to a different tradition from that of the male detectives so often cited as the key figures in the history of detective fiction. Taking their temperature from Poe, many works of detective fiction featuring male detectives are emotionally cool. Sherlock Holmes will solve cases with the offhand panache of a blindfold marksman who always hits the target with preternatural accuracy even if it is behind him. By contrast, the female detective in the sensation novel is likely to be emotionally involved and directly threatened by the criminal events and actors that she is investigating. She is the inside investigator, who exposes crime as an inside job. To say that she is not, therefore, a detective, is to make the false assumption that it is bearing the job title rather than doing the work that matters: the very assumption the early Victorian female detective deliberately undermines as a character whose proper business according to her family or her employers is *not* to ask questions, but who obstinately makes it her role – in the process revealing how germane crime is to female experience, and that nobody will save women if they do not act for themselves.

Wilkie Collins created another female detective character in 1857, in *The Dead Secret*, where Rosamond Treverton uncovers the mystery of her own illegitimate birth, which threatens to deprive her of the inheritance she received from the woman – a wealthy actress – she had assumed to be her mother. Collins, who trained as a barrister, is fascinated by the tenuous hold that women have on property, their dependence on paternity and marriage for any form of recognised legal identity. He preferred to live outside the bounds of marriage himself, forming long-term liaisons with two working-class women who bore him company (and, in one case, children) until his death. Most of Collins's contemporaries regarded sex outside marriage as a vice. Collins's novels explore marriage as a potential vice of another kind: a clamp with jaws that can fatally damage those trapped in it.

Collins's early novels featuring female detectives were warm-up acts for the book that made him famous, *The Woman in White* (1860), which features a strong female investigator, Marian Halcombe, alongside a troubled male one. Halcombe was the knockout success of the novel, her popularity (which far outshone that of the notional male and female protagonists) inspiring infatuated Victorian readers to wish to propose to her, or to become her.

Breaking the Legal Stranglehold of Marriage

The Woman in White, much more than *The Moonstone*, is the key text for understanding the evolution in the 1860s of the detective novel as a sensational domestic drama, with violence and gender conflict at its core. Marian, famously, is an anomaly. Her queerly attractive body has the unexpected synthesis of a dream; it fuses conventionally 'masculine' and 'feminine' attributes:

> The lady's complexion was almost swarthy, and the dark down on her upper lip was almost a moustache. She had a large, firm, masculine mouth and jaw; prominent, piercing, resolute brown eyes; and thick, coal-black hair, growing unusually low down on her forehead. Her expression – bright, frank, and intelligent – appeared, while she was silent, to be altogether wanting in those feminine attractions of gentleness and pliability, without which the beauty of the handsomest woman is incomplete.[22]

In having Walter Hartright, his nervous hero, describe Marian in these terms, Collins queries what 'feminine attractions' really are and creates a strong template for future Victorian detective heroines, many of whom will challenge gender norms. Marian Halcombe is her half-sister Laura Fairlie's foil, as well as her staunchest defender. She does not excel at the 'feminine accomplishments' of drawing and singing; she excels at the 'masculine' games of chess, backgammon, écarté and billiards. She is, by her own account, not a domestic 'angel' but tends in the opposite direction. Laura has the qualities of a water-colour study: faint in every sense, fair, malleable, childish. Her virginal whiteness is that of the bride or ghost. It is easy for her to lose her identity in marriage because she is so indistinct to begin with. Marian is, by contrast, sculptural. She is substantial, and she will not be rubbed out without a struggle.

Marian's intellectual strength and assertiveness, her darkness and her determination make her the character best suited to resisting the diabolical plot that gradually envelops Laura in a fog of domestic oppression so thick that she is lost to view. Laura is committed by her uncle to marry Sir Percival Glyde, a marriage arranged before she attains her legal majority at twenty-one. Glyde, like Gaveston in *The Adventures of Susan Hopley*, wants only to possess Laura's fortune. He forces her to sign over her property rights to him. He bruises her arms; locks her in her room; dismisses her maid. Finally, in the culmination of an extraordinary plot, he substitutes Laura – swapping her with a mentally unstable lower-class woman, Anne Catherick, who resembles her because they are in fact related (Anne is her father's illegitimate child). Anne (deemed to be Laura) dies while Laura (now considered to be Anne) is committed to a madhouse. Laura Fairlie thus for legal purposes ceases to exist: her very identity a dead letter in her husband's hands.

The most shocking thing about this plot of Jacobean malice and complexity is that Glyde's machinations are quite unnecessary to attain his end. As Lisa Surridge points out, Glyde's status as Laura's husband, without a marriage settlement limiting his power over her estates, gives him absolute control of her property in any case.[23] He controls her as a working-class husband controlled his wife: largely without let or hindrance from the law. In this sense, Laura and Anne, despite their very different initial class advantages, *are* wholly exchangeable. Collins dramatises the logic of the law of coverture that erased married women's independent identity, demonstrating the gothic in the everyday.

It is understandable, then, that critics could not decide whether the novel was a tissue of improbabilities or, as Margaret Oliphant argued, composed only of what was 'legitimate, natural and possible'.[24] Collins had taken inspiration from a real French case in the late eighteenth century, where the widowed Marquise de Douhault was dispossessed of her estates and her identity by a nefarious brother, who drugged, kidnapped and institutionalised her in order to seize her assets.[25] But the book also played out a panorama of domestic violence very similar to that which unfolded daily in the newspapers where, as Surridge notes, readers of *The Times* at the time of the novel's publication could feast their appalled eyes on cases including that of the son of an Irish peer who had threatened his wife with a meat chopper ... an artist who had beaten his naked wife with a furze brush ... one publican who had struck his wife with a riding whip and a bronze candlestick ... and another who had flogged his wife with a clothesline ... and finally, in close parallel to the 'sensational' plot of *The Woman in White*, a barrister who had induced his wife to execute a deed transferring her inheritance to him ... and a merchant who had threatened to drive his wife to a madhouse or to her grave within six months.[26]

Providing the reader with 'witness statements' from men and women, as if presenting evidence in court, the novel (like *Susan Hopley*) suggested domestic violence, tyranny and fear, as the skeleton beneath the floorboards of the private home that underlay more public and international manifestations of crime.

Marian, carefully gathering and recording in her diary evidence of Glyde's domestic violence for a potential court case, is the heroic counterpart to the evil Count Fosco, an Italian political spy who, as Glyde's house-guest and accomplice, is infiltrating the British establishment. Marian and Fosco's cat-and-mouse game pits amateur female detective ingenuity against hostile professional male surveillance; there is a sense in which it is Marian's threatened rape as much as Laura's threatened murder that drives the reader's page-turning anxiety. Women's watchfulness is presented as the necessary corrective to male voyeurism. Indeed, Marian Halcombe became the poster figure for the female detective as a brave character who is 'the good sister' to the oppressed 'feminine' – whether a full sibling, a half-sister or a self-appointed 'sister of my love' (as Anne Rodway describes herself). Marian's 'masculine' qualities serve her well in a battle that exposes women's relative legal powerlessness, and brings into question the ideology of 'separate spheres' that is supposed to offer women protection but here enables women's disappearance. The female detective in later Victorian fiction and drama will often be able to pass as a man.

Women in the 'Detective School'

Wilkie Collins was known as a writer of the 'detective school' many years before he invented Sergeant Cuff, the professional detective of *The Moonstone* (1868). So was Mary Elizabeth Braddon, actress and author of 'sensation novels', edge-of-seat thrillers that had both women and men investigate secrets in the family home, including bigamy, illegitimacy and murder.[27] Reviewing *Eleanor's Victory* in 1862, the *Morning Post* opined that Braddon 'may be named next to Mr Wilkie Collins in the ranks of the detective school of literature'.[28] The *St James Chronicle* in 1862 also named Braddon as a member of the 'detective school of fiction'.[29] In 1864, the *Sheffield Daily Telegraph* could already observe that

> Of all forms of sensation novel-writing, none is so common as what may be called the romance of the detective ... whether a Pre-Raffaellite delight in the representation of familiar objects, is the true source of the popularity of this kind of plot, it would be rash to decide; but of the fact itself there is no doubt.[30]

These critics understood detective 'romances' to be a subset of the broader genre of sensation fiction. As such, women were central, not latecomers nor marginal, to their history. Sensation fiction typically featured strong women as agents, whether as heroines or villains, or (excitingly) something in between. These thrillers involved the reader in suspense that sought to produce physical reactions – constrained movement, rapid breathing, fixed concentration – akin to a charged personal encounter. The 'Pre-Raphaelite' qualities of the sensation novel point to the way in which the forensic attention to detail appropriate to detective fiction can also be a heightened mode of conveying extreme emotional and sexual tension. Intense looking, by and at women, can be a state of erotic arousal.

Victorian readers and reviewers became accustomed to the idea of the detective heroine as a feature of thrillers whose plots explicitly questioned what virtuous women were allowed to know and whether knowledge of sin and pursuit of criminal justice was liberating for women, or corrupting, or both. The female reader, in immersing herself in the detective plot, became herself a participant in this debate. If she was driven to finish the book, she must surely sympathise with the female protagonist who persisted in her determination to discover the terrible truth, even when that truth impacted her own sense of identity and domestic relationships.

Mary Elizabeth Braddon, like Wilkie Collins, was one of the many Victorians who lived adjacent to the rose-encircled cottage of marriage and cast shade on its cracked roof and invisible panic room. She cohabited, from 1861, with the publisher John Maxwell, and bore him six children. They could not legally formalise their relationship, however, until Maxwell's first wife Mary Ann died in 1874. Braddon's novels teem with trapped, angry and passionate women who behave in ways not sanctioned by society. They earned her considerable moral disapproval, and a lot of money.

Eleanor's Victory (1862): Baring the Sins of the Fathers

In Braddon's *Eleanor's Victory* (1862), the young heroine Eleanor Vane is devastated by the death of her father – apparently by suicide – after an evening in Paris where he has lost heavily at cards. Like Anne Rodway investigating Mary Mallinson's 'accidental' death, Eleanor sets out to find out what really happened on the fatal evening and to trace the men responsible for luring her father to gamble and cheating him to the point of financial, then literal, annihilation.

At first it seems that Eleanor is a kind of Hamlet or Electra figure: she is determined to avenge her father's death.[31] But, as her detective researches uncover the wider web of male vice that threatens not only her father in the past but her own inheritance rights in the present, it increasingly feels that Eleanor is, whether she knows it or not, seeking a revenge *on* the fathers, whose powers deprive wives and daughters of financial control and limit women's ability to know how they have been cheated. Mr Vane was (as his name suggests) an amiable but idle and narcissistic spendthrift, who frittered away the fortune of three different wives and, on his final night, lost at cards the £100 earmarked to fund Eleanor's further education in Paris. In seeking the truth about that night, Eleanor discovers that a handsome but weak young artist, Laurence Darrell, to whom she was initially attracted, was part of the plot that gulled her father to his death. Darrell has also conspired to substitute for a will naming Eleanor as the sole heir of a substantial property, a fake will naming himself as heir.

Eleanor's dilemma in the second part of the novel is how to deal with this knowledge of male violations in a way that allows her own marriage of convenience to a lawyer (which, incredibly, she embarked on to be close to the scene of her detective research) to flourish and yet disables Darrell and his henchmen from further crime. She chooses to forgive Darrell, and – vexingly to the modern reader – he is permitted not only to escape jail but also to inherit part of the property he stole. As ever in sensation fiction, the solution to the detective plot reveals the domestic space to be radically unsafe: a site of female and male suspicion and concealment.

Eleanor is driven to detect by grief and anger. The novel derives its excitement from her relentless pursuit of knowledge. Yet it also questions whether her quest is wise. Through Eleanor's friend Simon, a painter of theatrical scenery, the text posits different models of what female detection involves. The first is cautiously positive:

> The science of detection, Miss Monckton, lies in the observation of insignificant things. It is a species of mental geology. A geologist looks into a gravel pit, and tells you the history of the creation; a clever detective ransacks a man's carpet-bag, and convicts that man of murder or a forgery.[32]

In this model, detection is a form of natural science that a woman might legitimately explore. It involves scrutinising minute evidence that reveals the order in which events occurred. One can pursue such study as a good Christian, though in 1862, just after the publication of Darwin's *On the Origin of Species* (1859), geology might also suggest to the quizzical eye a universe that is neither divinely ordained nor morally ordered.

In the second model, by contrast, detection is posited as an activity that necessarily degrades and denatures women. Simon predicts that Eleanor's investigation will

> blight your girlhood, warp your nature, unsex your mind, and transform you from a candid and confiding woman into an amateur detective, a path that will involve humiliating falsehoods, ... pitiful deceptions ... stupid basenesses, you must practise if you are to tread that sinuous pathway.[33]

In this paradigm, seeking to know is the end of 'girlhood' and, thus, innocence. It necessitates falsehoods and deceptions, even though its aim may be to uncover them. The snake-like 'sinuous pathway' Simon paints is not only winding but also sinful. Its 'base' re-gendered behaviour leads implicitly – like the 'unsex me here' of Lady Macbeth – to Hell.

Braddon's novel never fully decides between these two positions. It invites us to consider whether Eleanor's 'victory' is that she succeeds in avenging her father's death and her own woes by unmasking those who have criminally conspired against them, or whether Eleanor's real 'victory' is conquering her self-will: returned to the 'candid and confiding' role of wife and mother, she forgives the wrongs that men have done her. This is a common theme of the endings of Braddon's novels: traumatised, furious and rebellious women are tamed, confined or otherwise delivered up to keep the peace. But female anger, once detected, is never wholly dissipated.

Although a mystery may have been solved in *Eleanor's Victory*, a full reckoning with male abuse of power remains repressed. The skeleton of buried female anger remains a Tyrannosaur whose size dwarfs those who dig it up.

Braddon was an actress, and the larger question posed by her fiction concerns performance. Simon, in warning Eleanor against becoming a detective, suggests that detection inevitably 'unsexes' women's minds and corrupts them because it involves deception. We do indeed see Eleanor during her investigation flirting with a shipping clerk to gain sight of a register of departures, and making excuses to haunt the house by night where she suspects the real will (which names her as heiress) to be concealed. Yet it is evident to the reader that Eleanor's life when she is not acting as a detective *is equally theatrical*. She acts as a wife with similarly mixed motives and a similarly compromised identity (she travels under an alias, before and after marriage). Her marriage would be a routine – more or less convincingly performed – whether it formed part of her scheme of vengeance or not. Braddon's novels convey the centrality of acting to women's lives and the extent to which the extraordinary events of the sensational plot reveal a situation that is common to ordinary life: women battling to get their own back. It is unsurprising that sensation novels of the 'detective school' were a smash hit on the Victorian stage.

From *The Woman in White* to *The Female Detective*

It has been customary in accounts of female detection to mark a separation between the 'gothic heroine-sleuth' like Eleanor Vane (whom Lucy Sussex asserts is 'nearing her end' in the 1860s) and the character of the professional female detective who pops up 'coincidentally' in 1864, in James Redding Ware's *The Female Detective* and William Stephen Hayward's *Revelations of a Lady Detective*, those fictional casebooks that puzzled me when I encountered them in the British Library in 2012.[34] This separation is, however, unhelpful in that it obscures the electrical connections between the 'amateur' female detective of sensation fiction and the professional female detective who brings expertise and police liaison to the same crime circuit.

Not long after I began delving into the history of Redding Ware's *The Female Detective*, I had a lightbulb moment. Wilkie Collins's *The Woman in White* was immediately adapted (without the author's permission) for theatrical performance; it was staged at London's Surrey Playhouse just two months after the novel appeared as a volume in print. Who had written the adaptation? It wasn't immediately clear, as the pirate was understandably keen to conceal their identity. But, searching contemporary newspapers, the name fell out: James Redding Ware. The man who first brought the indomitable Marian Halcombe to the stage in October 1860 was the same man who published *The Female Detective* in 1864. Bingo.

The manuscript of his adaptation was in the British Library's collection, preserved – like other plays of the period – because a copy had to be passed to the Lord Chamberlain for approval before it could be performed. Paging through Redding Ware's version of *The Woman in White*, I was suddenly transported to the Surrey Playhouse, a popular theatre south of the Thames that could seat an audience of 3,000, chiefly working-class, playgoers. The Surrey theatre in Blackfriars typically staged melodramas: sensational plays that featured heightened emotional situations. Its audience (many of whom already knew Collins's bestseller) would have identified with the victims in the battle between the tyrannical male aristocrats in *The Woman in White* and the women whose lives and inheritance they were threatening. The class and gender conflict in the book were amplified in a space where the struggles could be played out as physical skirmishes, with the audience hissing the villains and cheering the heroines.

Redding Ware's adaptation of *The Woman in White*, daringly, goes further than Collins's original in staging violence in front of the audience.[35] Where in the novel she is silent, in the theatre Laura Fairlie expresses her misery in her marriage directly to Marian:

LAURA: Marian I may as well tell you at once, I am a neglected wife. He has never seen me since I have come of age but to order me to sign my property over to him
MARIAN: How shameful
LAURA: Oh Marian – My life is weary[36]

Like the deserted 'Mariana' in Tennyson's famous poem, whose refrain is: 'My life is weary / I wish that I were dead', Laura voices her quasi-suicidal depression long before she is abducted and forced into a madhouse. Marian, by contrast, expresses her anger with Glyde with physical vehemence: 'If I were a man, I would beat him down and leave his house, never again to enter it.'

Redding Ware uses the menacing lake at Percival Glyde's estate, Blackwater Park – the backdrop in the theatre – as an ever-present threat of women's literal or metaphorical drowning. Fosco and Glyde discuss the female sex, with Fosco barely concealing the sadism that accompanies his obsessive admiration for Marian:

SIR P: Confound all women. What say you Fosco?
FOSCO: Confound all women. No. Percival. I bless them all. You are too violent. The lake is picturesque is it not.[37]

Fosco, admiring the lake, hints that he has a subtler mode of eliminating women than Glyde's. He will affect to worship them, then make them disappear. Fosco later remarks of Marian: 'I adore her for she is magnificent but she must not stand in my way.' He triumphs briefly over his female victims, but is unprepared for the strength of their resistance:

FOSCO: What fools women are, had she thought, she would have known I dared not fire this pistol . . . I should have been foiled. We are safe . . . [alarm bell heard] She has caught at the alarm bell in passing.

Multiple female characters in Redding Ware's production of *The Woman in White* help to foil Glyde and Fosco's plot, using their intelligence to decipher or to leave clues for Walter Hartright to solve the mystery. Mrs Vesey, nurse and housekeeper, notices that the dress the dead body (Anne) is wearing is not the same as the one Laura had on, and so guesses at Glyde's substitution of one woman for the other. Laura, having witnessed Anne Catherick's poisoning, writes 'Save Me Walter' on the window before she is dragged away; she drops a ring tied to a ribbon outside the madhouse to lead Walter to her. Thus Marian is just one of several women who use detective skills to defend themselves against male treachery. Fosco and Glyde not only abuse women, they underestimate them.

The popularity of Redding Ware's dramatisation of *The Woman in White*, which played to packed houses in London and toured successfully to Edinburgh, Bath, Bristol and New York, shows how emotionally Victorian audiences responded to the staging of domestic abuse, its detection and its defeat. This production paved the way for his female detective, who would likewise reveal the home as the primal crime scene and women's vigilance as the necessary corrective to male violence.

Domestic Violence and the Paternal Plot

James Redding Ware had first-hand experience of domestic violence. He first appeared in the newspaper not as a writer but as a defendant in the magistrate's court. The case was brought against him by his father, a grocer and cheesemonger of Southwark, who claimed that the sixteen-year-old James – whom he had reprimanded and beaten with a cane – had threatened to kill him:

He (the father) corrected the defendant by striking him with a cane, and afterwards went down into his shop, and had not been long there when the defendant also entered the shop, and seizing a long and sharp bacon-knife off the counter, approached him in

87

a menacing attitude, and exclaimed that he would have his life for striking him.[38]

Interestingly, James's mother stood by her teenage son rather than her husband. One wonders whether she, too, was sometimes 'corrected' with a cane by her spouse. The magistrate concluded that James, who had received 'an excellent education' and been given a situation in a 'mercantile house', was a 'spoilt' child and ordered him either to stand bail or go to prison. He went to jail.

This incident is telling. It shows us that Redding Ware, long before he wrote *The Female Detective*, had been inside a police court. It also strongly suggests that personal experience of domestic violence informs his fiction. In *The Female Detective*, the home is a place of entrapment: often to be escaped with difficulty, sometimes with fatal results. Indeed, Redding Ware is often at his most successful where he conveys the claustrophobia of the 'locked room' mystery, not merely as a puzzle to be solved but as a metaphor for domestic tyranny. It is suggestive that on the dramatic cover of *The Female Detective*, two women are standing over a patriarch, who lies dead on the floor.

Redding Ware's first 'female detective' mystery to be published concerns Nelly – a daughter whom her father is determined to marry to a rich old man, Mr Trunk. Nelly has other ideas. Unfathomably to her father, she escapes by night from her locked bedroom, which has a high window and has been secured by heavy furniture placed in front of the door. Condemned to imprisonment – literally by her father in her room, and symbolically in marriage to Trunk – only Nelly's Houdini-like ingenuity can break the prison of parental power. Similarly, in 'Tenant for Life', the real problem that the female detective encounters is not the lady but the law. Miss Gladden discovers that the sister of a woman who died in childbirth secretly adopted a baby to supply a 'legitimate heir' for an estate that would otherwise be inherited by a 'wicked and wasteful' baronet (like Percival Glyde). Gladden is professionally driven to uncover the swap, but is evidently delighted when the baronet dies and the woman succeeds.

8 James Redding Ware ('Andrew Forrester'), The Female Detective *(1864).*

In 'The Unknown Weapon', the most claustrophobic case in *The Female Detective*, Graham Petleigh, a mistreated son, tries to break into his father's house to commit robbery by concealing himself in a box delivered to the property. Graham is killed by his father's house-keeper, who thrusts a picador's barb into the box without knowing that the intruder is in fact the heir. The home is not a safe place in these stories. The female detective is the person who reveals its (dis)contents: the innards of the box delivered to the father's door, which are both victimised and violent. In all three of these tales, no legal case is brought. The female detective's investigations are more concerned with uncovering hidden social truths – the precarity of female inheritance, the neglect of children by their parents and the misery concealed within domestic life.

The Female Detective is fiction, but two of the cases it alludes to are real. One is the Road Hill House murder of three-year-old Francis Saville Kent in 1860, where the murderer was a family member. The other is the Hansom Cab murders of November 1863 – which shocked London just before the book's publication. A man (later identified as Samuel William Hunt, a druggist's assistant) hailed a cab near the Great Eastern Station at Shoreditch to take his wife and two daughters on what seemed a party of pleasure. En route, he asked the cabman to stop at the Green Dragon pub, where he bought beer for his family and gin for the driver. Then he asked to be dropped off, and for the taxi to continue with his family to Westbourne Gardens. On arrival, the cabman discovered he had inadvertently been driving a hearse; all three females were dead, having been poisoned by prussic acid in their beer. There was nothing to identify them except a box of ointment bought in Camberwell. Nonetheless, the combined efforts of the press and the police led, within three days, to Hunt's arrest. The case drew attention to the way in which domestic abuse was now part of the public spectacle of crime, and how the anonymous circulation of traffic that enabled the murderer to disassociate himself from the bodies was connected to the rapid print circulation that led to his discovery.[39] It's no accident that this story attracted Redding Ware's notice. His eyes were always drawn to the contained space within which domestic violence occurred.

His female detective – who ultimately maintains her anonymity – refuses to be an object of male surveillance, instead keeping a sharp eye on the home:

> The reader will comprehend that the woman detective has far greater opportunities than a man of intimate watching, and of keeping her eyes on matters near which a man could not conveniently play the eavesdropper. I am aware ... that to reflect that a female detective may be in one's own family is a disagreeable operation. But, on the other hand, it may be urged that only the man who has secrets to hide need fear a watcher.[40]

It is significant here that the imagined figure who has secrets to hide is a *man*. He may, the text teasingly hints, have a woman detective in his own family without being aware of it. This kind of 'intimate watching' is a direct response to the domestic origin of crime, an origin to which the female sleuth in fiction from 1840 onwards had increasingly pointed. The evolution of this character has everything to do with the bitter battle for control of power in domestic life that was, by the 1860s, more publicly visible than ever before.

Indeed, Redding Ware's *The Female Detective*, far from being an anomalous and isolated text, as critics once commonly imagined,[41] is deeply imbricated in the world of the 1860s, with its critiques of the limitations of the police, its exposure of women's actual work uncovering crime and its live debate about the situation of criminal violence within patriarchal systems of control from which women were currently struggling to free themselves. Rather than a mysterious station in the middle of nowhere, it is closely linked to the network of texts that form the female detective line in the Victorian literary and theatrical landscape: a line that stretches from 1840 to the 1900s, featuring work by Crowe, Collins and Braddon, as well as Mary Fortune, Metta Victor and many others. There is evidence that Redding Ware's female detective character reached and pleased working-class readers. In 1870, *The Female Detective* was confiscated from under the pillow of a woman in a Bath workhouse, suggesting that at least one indigent female reader prized this text so highly that she would not sell or pawn it even when suffering extreme poverty.[42] Readings from *The Female Detective* at Spring Garden Engine Works in Newcastle also indicate that working men enjoyed stories of crime solved by an enterprising woman.[43]

James Redding Ware became in later years a lexicographer of Victorian slang. He cited the expression 'confidence-queen' for a female detective.[44] The term suggests a woman who might mislead ('con') others, and who also possesses a regal self-assurance. In *The Female Detective*, Redding Ware makes the case for women acting boldly in the detective role and for the detective profession in England as a force that is needed to augment and challenge the limited powers of the policeman on the beat. His detective may be fictional, but she emerges from a new era of journalism that revealed the ordinary home as a violent and contested space from which women were beginning to seek formal release and the police force as a body that made use of female labour, albeit covertly. His female detective is a figure of desire and of controversy, but by no means an outlier or a fluke. Relating the details of real and fictional cases in the same pages, her 'memoir' implicitly disputes the existence of any meaningful boundary between the 'sensational' nature of imagined violence and the fact of crime as a part of women's daily, lived experience, as victims, witnesses and investigators.

The prototype of a fictional female detective who works with the police may seem to go out of production for decades after 1864. To some, she has seemed to vanish as quickly as she appeared. But this character does not go underground. Quite the contrary. She goes where the lights are brighter and the music is louder. She goes to the theatre.

3

SENSATION AND THE STAGE
The Victorian Female Detective
in the Limelight

HONEYDEW: And so you're a detective eh, whatever could have induced a lady of independent means to adopt such an extraordinary proffession [sic]?

MRS F: My husband was so much away from home and had so many secrets from me that I thought I would do a little business myself, the nature of which he should be ignorant of.[1]

Until recently, the theatre has been the neglected missing link in the story of female detective plots in Victorian life. We are so used to pairing the words 'detective' and 'novel' that it has taken us a long time to look at the Victorian theatre for female detectives. But in fact the female detective was a popular and familiar character on the stage long before Sherlock Holmes was conceived. Audiences from the 1860s to the 1880s became accustomed to seeing the female detective in 'sensational drama' as a feisty theatrical character. Unlike their real-life counterparts, whose secret weapon was the fact that as women in ordinary dress they were not suspected of being detectives, female detectives on the stage were masters of disguise.

Cross-dressing was a notable part of their routine, delighting audiences with their dapper appearance in trouser roles, often smoking a pipe or a cigarette. Indeed, the signal sent by the female detective in the theatre is that, in the face of male villainy, which tyrannises over women (and innocent men), the gender norms that might usually govern female behaviour are dispensable.

Sassy, punning, wittier than the men she defeats, the stage female detective in the nineteenth century has many of the qualities of a comic actress. She is also an action heroine. Brandishing revolvers, whips and handcuffs, she gets the better of conspirators whose vile schemes include murder, robbery and imprisoning women in madhouses – the better to usurp female identity, property and agency. Although the circumstances are typically elaborate and improbable, the ways in which women are exploited by men in these plays are not. The female detective rescues women threatened by domestic violence, abandonment and seizure of assets: by attempts at erasure actuated by a spouse or suitor that reveal marriage as a potential death trap. The female detective's assurance in dealing with rogue males offers the audience satisfaction that is also retaliation.

These roles were written for mature actresses, the leading ladies of the company, including Sara Lane, the doyenne of the Britannia Theatre in Hoxton, and Amy Steinberg, the energetic star of the Standard Theatre in Shoreditch. Successful women who had reinvented themselves, changing their names and working their way up from minor roles to managerial status, Lane and Steinberg were well known and loved by the crowds at the East End theatres, who looked forward to their weekly appearances in melodrama. Indeed, the first female detective plays are melodramas: driven by action, spectacle and high emotional stakes. They are not primarily puzzles to be solved, like a mystery novel at home, but dramatic confrontations between unjust power and defenders of the victimised, to be relished as a battle of wits and of bodies.

9. Interior View of the Britannia Theatre, Hoxton (1858).

The Female Detective Avenges Her Sister(s)

If you had visited the Britannia theatre, Hoxton, in the autumn of 1864, you would have been in for a sensational experience. This was one of the most impoverished areas of London's East End, but its theatre, which had formerly been a saloon bar later rebuilt by Samuel Lane in 1858 on a grand scale, was a much-loved local institution. The showy decor featured pale salmon paintwork, embellished with white, gold and fawn and occasional vermillion and blue. A constellation of sixteen gas-fired chandeliers hung from the oval ceiling, diffusing a soft light, gentler than the 'volcano' of gas in many West End theatres, yet bright enough to ensure that no detail of the performance was lost to those in the cheap seats. The Britannia catered to an audience that ranged from shopworkers and clerks, the swell 'counter-skippers' of Kingsland and Dalston, to factory workers, 'women in crowds, with children in their arms; pert apprentices with torn trousers and a scarlet necktie; girls from the toymaking shops, coquettishly dressed; sailors, redolent of spirits and tobacco "and" in greater number than the rest, street Arabs [children, living on the street] of every shade and complexion.'[2] As Charles Dickens remarked, visiting in 1860: 'Besides prowlers and idlers, we were mechanics, dock-labourers, costermongers, petty tradesmen, small clerks, milliners, stay-makers, shoe-binders, slop workers, poor workers in a hundred highways and byeways. Many of us – on the whole, the majority – were not at all clean and not at all choice in our lives or conversation.'[3]

Most of London's Victorian West End theatres seat between 1,000 and 2,000 people. The Britannia had a vast capacity of over 4,000. Advertising itself as 'Britannia, the Great Theatre', it suggested a scope equal to that of Great Britain itself: at its re-opening in 1858, Sara Lane had posed as Britannia, with toga and trident. It was a stadium, a fairy palace, an Albert Hall for the East End at which all comers were welcome. The cheapest gallery tickets were threepence. For that money, there was a full evening of entertainment from half past six to eleven that might include a melodrama, a comic burlesque, song, dance and acrobatics. Acts at the Britannia included the muscular gymnast Jules Leotard, the original 'daring young man on the flying trapeze', in his trademark skin-tight costume; Professor Pepper's 'living spectres' (ghostly illusions that defied spectators to trace their mechanical origins), and the 'Lilliputian velocipedists'.[4] Diverse performers included the Black actors Mr and Mrs Langan and Mr H. Watson, the 'Great Eccentric Negro Comedian', who transferred from success at the Broadway Theatre, New York.[5] The Britannia's pantomimes, whose magical transformation scenes sometimes involved the appearance of gardens complete with 'fairy fountains' on stage, were justly famous.

Little boys perched on the gallery railing like sparrows on a telegraph wire, bantering their mates in the back row. In the 'Banqueting Hall' below you could buy pastries, fruit and thick beef or ham sandwiches piled up 'like mahogany planks at a timber wharf'. The spectacle of abundance included 'mountains of quartern loaves, pyramids of cheese, domes of German sausage, and ever-running fountains of ale and porter'.[6] A slice of bread cost a halfpenny; a half pint of porter or ginger beer cost a penny. All waited in anticipation before the enormous green stage curtain, which was affectionately known as 'the cabbage leaf'. By local tradition, youths showed their appreciation with trademark shrill whistles and a shower of orange peel, falling like confetti on the lead actors.

The Britannia specialised in melodrama. Bigamy! Murder!! Exotic locations!!! Innocence led astray!!!! Villainy avenged!!!!! Tonight was no exception. This evening, for the very first time, the audience was going to see *The Female Detective; or, The Mother's Dying Child*. The cabbage leaf went up. It revealed an extravagant landscape painting of a ballroom in the Hotel de Russe, Baden Baden.[7] Couples danced a quadrille. Statues flanked a marble staircase, with archways leading to a garden. Sara Lane stepped down the staircase in a pink silk dress. At forty-two, she was in her prime as an actress and hugely popular (she would be playing principal boy in the pantomime for another thirty years). Tonight she was playing Florence Langton, a baronet's daughter, who becomes 'the Female Detective' and saves her sister Una, who is due to be married in a week to Barry Mallinson: bank robber, aspiring bigamist and – in the course of the on-stage action – wife murderer.

FLORENCE (*without, at back of staircase, R*): Una! Una! (*music – descends staircase*) Not here! Now where can my papa and sister have taken themselves to? (sees STELLA and MADAME RITZDORF)

The strange ladies who are living at the hotel; this is the first time I've seen them out of their rooms, and my natural curiosity prompts me to find out who they are. (aloud) Beg pardon, but the young lady don't seem well.

MADAME RITZDORF: No, she is not.

FLORENCE: So I thought! Excuse my natural curiosity ... I've often seen you from our windows ...[8]

As Isabel Stowell-Kaplan has observed, Florence advertises her 'natural curiosity' from the beginning of the play.[9] She takes an interest in affairs that are not apparently her business: a quality that has traditionally been rebuked in women. But it is Florence's powers of observation, her habit of making inferences, asking difficult questions and being persistent, that lead her to unmask Barry as a villain and spare her sister the misery that would have resulted from marrying him. Women have often been depicted as nosy gossips who simply want to know others' secrets. Florence, as a detective, is morally justified in pursuing the truth.

The drama is tense. Barry – alias Percy Allen – has deserted his wife, Stella, who is pining away. Barry needs to marry Una because he requires her dowry to cover his tracks in a bank robbery he committed earlier. Barry is an unscrupulous asset-stripper, determined to put an 'n' into fiancé and come up with personal finance. He will murder Stella in a lonely scene at a boathouse on a moonlit lake, stabbing and then drowning her. Una witnesses this scene without being certain of what she is seeing. In the final act, Barry, on the run from the police, takes Una hostage in a thrilling rooftop shoot-out, where he holds her in front of him to protect himself from hostile fire. Una gives him the slip and escapes, assisted by Florence, leaving Barry to be shot and killed in the dramatic climax.

Florence, as a garrulous character who slips into four different disguises while on Barry's trail, provides much-needed comic relief: as well as liberating Una from her disastrous engagement, she liberates the audience from the gravity of the plot. In a tour de force of quick-change versatility, she metamorphoses into Grizzle Gutteridge (a 'Somersetshire Wench'), Mrs Gammage (an ancient Nurse), Mr Harry Racket (a fast young Man) and Barney O'Brian (an Irish boy 'from the bogs of Ballyragget'). Such protean dramatic changes required great skill: they were a visible masterclass in acting, where the lead actress showed her many different faces, accents and costumes.

> FLORENCE: I hear you're a widder, mim — so am I; matrimony's a serus thing – I declare I never shall forget how I felt when Gammage said, 'With my goods I thee endow.' He kept a furniture shop, mim, but when he died I found I was mistaken, and I was left executioner to an intestine estate, with everybody a trying to circumvent the poor widow's mite, mim. Oh, dear! (cries)[10]

Of course, Sara Lane playing Florence playing Mrs Gammage, who can't tell an executor from an executioner, is not to be taken entirely seriously. Yet the point she makes about women being cheated in marriage recurs throughout the play. Florence Langton constantly berates the male sex, remarking: 'That's just like those horrid men. I begin to think it's high time they were abolished altogether' and 'this monstrosity on two legs, called a man'; 'what men say and what they do are two very different things.' She sings the song from *Much Ado about Nothing*. 'Sigh no more ladies, sigh no more / Men were deceivers ever' – but, unlike Shakespeare's female leads Beatrice and Hero, Florence and Una remain happily single at the play's end. Women's legal vulnerability in marriage is a persistent theme.

It is also true that Sara Lane as Florence 'becomes' male. In undertaking two 'breeches roles' she is acting in a grand tradition that encompasses Shakespeare's Viola, Rosalind and many others: one of Sara Lane's 'happiest impersonations' was 'Jack, a country lad' in *The Flirt*, which she chose to play for her benefit night in December 1865.[11] Playing a man or boy would, however, become a signature aspect of stage performances of the female detective role. In these plays, women pursuing male criminality often penetrate the criminal circle by joining it in a pretended male character. Florence Langton has key scenes where she is placed at the same physical risk as a man and has to escape without breaking cover. First (when she is playing Harry Racket), Barry, with his accomplices Phoebus and Lodovic, tries to get her drunk and drug her, but she only fakes drinking and drunkenness, then throws the drugged glass of ale in Lodovic's face. Second (as Barney O'Brian), her hands are tied with rope and she has to free herself with her teeth.

In a variety of different ways, then – physically, intellectually and in the boldness of her character – Sara Lane as Florence, in *The Female Detective*, demonstrates that she is more than equal to a man. Her decision to deceive others, to 'act', is sanctioned within the play as a counter-tactic to male deception and this provides much of the play's pleasure. Her repartee is loaded with double meanings that the villain doesn't get, but the audience does.

> BARRY: (seizes her) If I thought you were a spy, I'd take your life!
> FLORENCE: (as Barney) What are ye after wanting wid my life? Haven't ye got one of your own? If it's your servant I'm to be, I hope you keep a good table, for the only thing I've tasted these twenty-four hours is an Irish pheasant.
> BARRY: What's that?
> FLORENCE: A red herring, sir.[12]

Significantly, although Roderick Tracy, the Bow Street runner, is also on Barry's trail, the professional policeman fails to nab the crook. Tracy is too easily duped: Barry claims to be his illegitimate son and thus effects his escape. The female amateur detective proves a more determined and effective opponent.

Several features of *The Female Detective* recur in other female detective plays from 1865 to 1900. First, the female detective is always primarily the scourge of villainous *men*. She frequently saves women from marrying or being abducted by men who have betrayed other members of her sex. In this way, although her opponent is frequently also a murderer, a thief and an impostor, she is particularly visible in saving women from a future of *domestic* violence, desertion and exploitation. The female detective's investigations, indeed, insistently link domestic abuse with wider social crimes against property and persons. Second, the female detective works with the police, but she is superior to them, often showing up their limitations. It is not difficult to see why these plotlines appealed to East End audiences. The police were not popular with the costermongers, a large group of street hawkers who sold everything from fruit, vegetables and flowers to pies, ices and shellfish on stalls and barrows outside the Britannia and who formed part of the theatre's most loyal clientele. Sara Lane, as the cunning 'detective' who gets the better of cheating men – playing them at their own game – was a poster woman for female cleverness and for the dependence of the police on community support. It was boasted that Lane could walk unmolested in East London streets where policemen had to walk in pairs.

Sara Lane was popularly known as 'the Queen of Hoxton'. She had been born Sarah Borrow in 1822 in Eagle Court in the City of London, the daughter of a 'coach proprietor' (a cabbie) who subsequently became treasurer of the Britannia Theatre. Sara had a career as an actress and dancer, 'Sarah Wilton', before becoming Sam Lane's second wife, the co-proprietor, and, on Sam's death in 1871, manager of the Britannia. Sara wrote her own dramas (at least eight are credited to her pen, including *Red Josephine; or, Woman's Vengeance*) and staged plays by women dramatists.[13] Like the Britannia itself, she operated on a grand scale: liberal in her gifts, but strict in her rules. The *Era* in her obituary of 1899 recalled that she was

> An autocrat in matters of organisation and discipline ... a true democrat in spirit. To a great extent she gave back with one hand what she had received with the other. She not only allowed those

*10 & 11. Photograph (c. 1870) and cartoon (*The Entr'acte, *1887)*
of Sara Lane.

who worked for her a 'living wage', but when bad times came upon them she provided for their needs. Of comely presence, her temperament was active and cheerful, whilst her tastes leaned frankly to sport. A ticket of admission to the inner enclosure of Newmarket used to be visible tied to the leg of an Arab figure in her drawing-room.[14]

The Lanes ran the Britannia as a 'stock-company', retaining a core cast of actors throughout the year who played weekly in a variety of entertainments.[15] This provided much more secure employment than hosting travelling companies; it also gave the theatre the feeling of a family, which extended to the audience. Gifts were bestowed on fellow actors by Lane and by playgoers, who came to see well-known favourites, sometimes night after night. A later generation remembered the benefit nights and Britannia Festival where:

The packed house, who knew the inner lives of the players as well as they did themselves, ... threw bouquets: not the usual kind – but articles they thought the recipients in need of – joints of meat, boots, intimate wearing apparel & c. In fact stall holders frequently had to put up their umbrellas in case a parcel fell short.[16]

This was an intimate, affectionate relationship. When Sara Lane died in 1899, her body was – according to her wishes – taken to her private room at the Britannia. The coffin left for its funeral journey from the theatre, pulled in a carriage by black-plumed horses, in a spectacular procession to Kensal Green Cemetery through crowds who lined the streets of Hoxton ten-deep to see her final stage exit. It was, in its own way, as dramatic a send-off as that for Queen Victoria two years later. The Queen of Hoxton would have expected nothing less.

It is important that Sara Lane created the role of the Female Detective in its 1860s incarnation in the East End theatre: it defined the character as a strong, mature woman, funny, business-like, highly competent and physically quick, who ran rings around her male assailants. Sara Lane's real sister Charlotte (who would indeed die young, aged twenty-seven, the following year) played Stella, the Mother's Dying Child whom Barry drowned in the lake. The intimacy and fellow-feeling that the Britannia created in its packed auditorium was a vital part of the success of its repertoire, which showcased melodrama – a genre that explores resistance to tyranny and violence through evoking a community of strong, shared feeling. As Jim Davis has noted: 'Britannia melodramas often reacted to social injustice, highlighting the exploitation of male and female labour (including seamstresses and artificial flower makers), poverty, the degradations of the workhouse, class inequality, the treatment of convicts, and the gulf between rich and poor'.[17] One melodrama staged there in 1864 was called *The Mill Strike and the Mutineers*.

The Female Detective; or, The Mother's Dying Child, then, in depicting male financial and physical exploitation of women, fitted perfectly within existing traditions of melodrama at the Britannia, but brought to them a new emphasis on the female detective character as the agent of change and master of transformation.

Colin Henry Hazlewood had already had success at the Britannia with his stagings of Mary Elizabeth Braddon's sensational bigamy novels *Lady Audley's Secret* and *Aurora Floyd*, in which desperate women respectively push their unsatisfactory first husbands down a well and horsewhip men who mistreat their dog. He knew that strong female characters and domestic violence sold tickets. An actor himself, he was accustomed to the expectations of the Britannia's audience (according to the *Era*, 'action, action, action' was their primary requirement).[18] He produced a new drama every two weeks. The immediacy of these works means that they are highly responsive to the moment in which they were first played.

Hazlewood also understood unhappy marriages. He was separated from his alcoholic wife, who sometimes attempted to reach him. The Britannia's stage manager, Frederick Wilton, recorded in September 1865:

> Hazlewood, Dramatic author, in trouble about an accident occurring to his wife, a drunken woman, from whom he has been a long time separated. It appears that she had come to his house in the City Road and attempted to get from the next garden into the one belonging to his house and that as she crossed the wall he pushed her back. She fell on some spikes and received a serious wound in the thigh. He was brought to Worship Street today & remanded till it be seen whether the woman lives or dies.[19]

In the month when he finished writing *The Female Detective*, Hazlewood was himself in custody for possible manslaughter of a wife he no longer loved. The play's theme was, then, secretly close to the bone. For the name of his venture, he drew on the popular *Female Detective* casebook by 'Andrew Forrester' (James Redding Ware) published in the summer of 1864. For the plot, he drew inspiration from two other wildly successful sensation dramas that had convulsed London in 1860, *The Woman in White* and *The Colleen Bawn*. James Redding Ware's pirated stage version of *The Woman in White* (1860) featured a moonlit lake as a thrilling backdrop to the 'white lady' (the Woman in White) who drifts across the stage, like a ghostly bride, with a warning about marriage that feels both supernatural and domestic: 'If I could only see her. If I could only *warn her*.'[20] Florence Langton's efforts to protect her sister Una from a fatal fiancé bear a family resemblance to Marian Halcombe's efforts to protect Laura Fairlie. Both women turn detective to see off the threat of substitution and erasure that haunts Victorian women in melodrama, paralysed and parasitised by marriage.

Hazlewood borrowed the coup de theatre of an unwanted wife being drowned in a moonlit lake from Irish melodrama, *The Colleen Bawn* by Dion Boucicault, which had been the other smash hit of the season in 1860, causing traffic jams of carriages as hundreds of people pressed to experience the climactic thrill of attempted murder, then dramatic rescue from drowning of the heroine, Eily O'Connor, in the 'water cave' – rather as cinema audiences queued to see *Jaws* in the 1970s or *Titanic* in the 1990s. According to witnesses, this sensation scene 'went on from first to last in the midst of an intense and almost painful silence', where the 'excitement of the spectators was protracted to the utmost pitch of intensity'.[21] The effect of water was created by lighting on layers of gauze, with boys moving under it to make it ripple. Hazlewood had previously tried in vain to pirate Boucicault's play and so it comes as no surprise that he pinched its best scene.

As Nicholas Daly has pointed out, *The Colleen Bawn* (1860) was based on a shocking real case of male-on-female violence from the early nineteenth century.[22] In 1819, John Scanlan, a gentleman from County Limerick, was arrested for the murder of fifteen-year-old Ellen Hanley, the daughter of a local farmer and a noted beauty. The two had eloped, but when Scanlan tired of Ellen he arranged a hit: his boatman took Ellen out in his boat, clubbed her to death with his musket, bound and drowned her in a lake. Scanlan was hanged in

1820 for this appalling crime.[23] The case remained notorious; Gerald Griffin retold it in his popular novel *The Collegians* (1829).

The Colleen Bawn, enacted in theatres like a nightly ritual, rewrote the tragedy of Ellen's death and gave it a happy ending. Eily O'Connor, the lily-white girl ('colleen bawn') is rescued from the water and rises again. In Hazlewood's *The Female Detective*, by contrast, the discarded wife *does* die: Stella, like the real Ellen Hanley, is killed by her faithless husband's hand and drowned in the lake. In other words, the melodrama that introduced the female detective to the Britannia was based loosely on a real case and – setting its action in 1821 – it incorporated the terrible truth of that case of marital violence. Melodrama is full of plot improbabilities and exaggerated dramatic gestures; yet that does not prevent it from being current, of the moment, real.

Isabel Stowell-Caplan has suggested that *The Female Detective* was part of a trend towards 'woman-centred sensation drama', which reflected debate about the number of 'surplus women', who (censuses in 1851 and 1861 revealed) would not find a man to marry and needed to pursue alternative careers.[24] She also links the play to the Contagious Diseases Act of 1864, which forced women suspected of prostitution to subject themselves to police inspection: a demeaning and intrusive practice that placed the onus of preventing sexually transmitted diseases on women rather than men. These are significant backgrounds to the prominence of strong female protagonists in the 1860s. But more important to the emergence of female detective plays, in my view, is the spotlight on unhappy marriage and women's legal powerlessness cast by the 1857 Divorce Act. In this heated atmosphere, the figure of the female detective arrived in the theatre as a character in Sensation Drama, pointing her finger at male violence, the difficulty of protecting female property, and the shocking deceit and coercion too often concealed in domestic life.

Hazlewood's *The Female Detective* was an instant hit. Indeed, Frederick Wilton, the stage manager, reported to his diary on

7 November: 'The greatest number of people at the Britannia this evening – ever known there – *4500* in all.' As the *Clerkenwell News* reported: 'this piece abounds with striking situations, and ends with the usual denouement of retribution . . . it was evident, by the applause bestowed on it by a crowded audience, it was a decided success.'[25] The play toured Britain immediately, moving from the Britannia to Shields in December 1864. By March 1865 it had transferred to the Opera House, Columbus, Ohio, with Kate Denin in the starring role. The American press observed that 'the different phases of [the female detective's] fourfold impersonation' gave Ms Denin's 'versatile talents . . . full scope and play'.[26] Since it offered such a brilliant vehicle for the lead actress, it had, under different titles, a long life on the Victorian stage.[27] The celebrated American actress Carlotta Crabtree played the female detective in 1869 in Boston: an extra character (a Dutchman) was written for her, bringing the number of impersonations to six; photographs record Crabtree's charming appearance, cross-dressed as two male characters.

Although the plot may now seem creaky, *The Female Detective; or, The Mother's Dying Child* offered something new and gripping to Victorian audiences: a female character who outs a homicidal husband, exposing the murder that marriage can literally or figuratively be. By 1873 it was appearing with the subtitle *Women Against the World*: a phrase that neatly encapsulates the deep struggle the play exposes.

The Female Detective as Wily Servant

The success of the first female detective play in 1864 swiftly led to a second. Emily Scott starred in George B. Ellis's *The Female Detective or the Foundling of the Streets*, performed in June 1865 at the Britannia, where the heroine is a maidservant. We first meet her climbing over a gate. Nelly in a comic opera would be a soubrette role: the knowing, sprightly young servant who listens at keyholes and unknots the romantic entanglements of her supposed superiors. In sensation

12–15. Lotta Crabtree in various disguises as the Female Detective and (bottom right) as herself (late nineteenth century).

drama, however, the housemaid becomes a detective on the trail of crime. As we have seen, there was an existing tradition in early Victorian sensation fiction of female servant-class detective heroines. Catherine Crowe's *Susan Hopley; or, Circumstantial Evidence* (1840) was swiftly adapted into a popular melodrama by George Dibdin Pitt and remained a mainstay of provincial theatre until late in the century.

Nelly, the servant-heroine in *The Female Detective or the Foundling of the Streets* has, like other female detectives on the East End stage, a sprightly comic tone and an enterprising spirit, which leaven the dark deeds the plot discloses. Nelly's wealthy employer, Mr Denville, is unwell. In the tradition of melodrama, he has two nephews: Philip (kind, honourable and secretly married to Alice) and Robert (the villain). Robert Denville aims to disinherit Philip, kidnap Alice, force her to be his lover and abandon Alice's child on the street. Robert hires an accomplice to kill his uncle and substitute a fake will naming him as the sole heir to the Denville fortune.

Luckily, Nelly has her suspicions. Nick, the gardener who is Nelly's sweetheart, is delivering a note for Robert, which Nell boldly opens:

NELL: Well, now. If I was one of those Detective people —
NICK (laughing): *You* a Detective?
NELL: Yes, me — a detective – and a very good one I'd make. I know why there's plenty in London – Female Detectives too – and if ever I go back I shall join the force. I can tell you. But I merely say – if I were a Detective. I should take this note so – look into it so – and what's this? [looks in] . . .
NELL reading note: '4 o'clock near shrubbery – old man dying – done tonight – don't fail – your friend Robert Denville' – oh – oh – *from information I received*, I suspect mischief.[28]

Though she is a servant, Nelly – like Susan Hopley and Anne Rodway – is literate. She knows that there are real female detectives operating in London. She has also gained some command of the professional language employed by detectives; 'from information I received' is her self-conscious attempt to mimic this. There were doubtless working women in the Britannia's audience who enjoyed and shared Nelly's confidence that they would make very good detectives.

Nelly not only stays up as 'nurse' to watch by old Mr Denville's bedside but also to prevent the plot she has detected, whereby a forged will naming Robert as heir will be substituted for the real one during the night. Jem Roughly climbs through a window:

JEM: Yonder is the old man – all safe – the girl sleeps.

NELL: Don't be too sure of that.

JEM (puts pistol on table): The pistol can stay there (goes to Bed. Slips out blank paper). There my work's done. So now to get my reward.

(NELLY points pistol)

NELL: Another step villain and you get your reward.

JEM seizes. She fires. He is wounded but they struggle – She breaks away – Rings bell. JEM escapes from window.[29]

In this exciting action sequence, Nell and Jem spar verbally and physically: she wrongfoots him by appearing to be asleep, then seizes his weapon and challenges him. He attacks but she manages to wing him with his own pistol and raise the alarm. Nell is (like Susan Hopley) behaving as a good servant should in defending the family that employs her. Yet her own clearly expressed *satisfaction* in acting as a female Detective (capitalised throughout the script) has more to do with her conscious skilfulness in the role and pleasure in the right to knowledge and justice that it confers:

NELLY: No one here. Now that's what I call[ed] cleverly managed, even for a Female Detective ... I can hear them talking. From information I received, I have found out that three great rascals are to have a meeting here presently, and as a woman and a Detective I demand the satisfaction of knowing what it's about. Hush . . . I'll hide here.[30]

One sense of 'satisfaction' is 'fulfilment'; but another is 'reparation', or 'the opportunity to defend one's honour in a duel'. Nelly's self-reported satisfaction as a female detective partakes of all these senses. She invites us to root for her against the male conspiracy that threatens Philip, but especially Alice and their child. She also invites us to compare her prowess with that of a man and to admire her superior ability.[31]

Nelly's love interest, the gardener Nicholas Spray, who is happier with a parsley plot than a murder plot, is more timid than his bride-to-be. He is startled when one of his braces' buttons pings off and, far from coveting an adventurous life, looks forward to nothing more than being 'cosy' with his wife in the evenings. This is a notable feature of male partners to female detectives on the Victorian stage; they are the softer sidekick. It is not merely that Nelly literally 'wears the trousers' when cross-dressing to infiltrate the thieves' gang in Marylebone. She also uses thieves' slang – 'I can stag a peeler [spot a policeman] farther off than anyone', – smokes a short pipe on stage and brandishes a gun.[32] Her sexual insouciance in male attire, performing a conventionally male role, not only presents a challenge that is levelled at the male villains but rhetorically also becomes a form of repartee with the audience. Nelly reassures her husband in a manner that makes her upper hand in the domestic realm very clear:

NELLY: Now you be a good boy. And very soon I'll settle down nice and quiet.
NICK: Do you mean to cut this Detective business?
NELLY: Yes my dear . . . Say goodbye to the Police Force and make you a quiet little wife in private life.
NICK: Do you think you can do it Nelly?

NELLY: Do it – ha ha – why what can't a woman do if she sets her mind to it? I'll bet you – one woman will do as much in an hour as six men will accomplish in a week.[33]

Nelly can 'make' a 'quiet little wife', but playing this role is as much her choice as becoming a detective. She refers to the prime minister as 'Old Nick' (the devil, but also her husband's name) and demonstrates her contempt for male professional effectiveness compared with female work. This play, in common with other Victorian female detective dramas, contains a strong element of comedy. Yet Nelly also arrests criminals who are responsible for fraud, kidnapping, sexual assault, child abuse and attempted murder.

Crucially, like Florence Langton in *The Mother's Dying Child*, Nelly prevents – the day before the wedding – a marriage: here between the villain Robert Denville and the innocent heiress Laura St Clair. The female detective is the scourge of domestic tyrants; her metier is preventing the tragedy of a union that would have transferred an innocent woman's money and power to a brutal man. At the end of the play she puts 'bracelets' (handcuffs) on Robert Denville, an act that would become a routine pleasure in female detective dramas, remarking: 'A Female Detective at your service . . . away with him.'[34] Bracelets, as jewellery, are usually associated with women: a woman putting them on a man is thus not only an act of arrest, but an assertion of power. These handcuffs form a vivid contrast to the 'ball and chain' of an unequal marriage: the female detective limits the brutal man's ability to act. As a form of the 'retribution' that the *Clerkenwell News* identified as the 'usual denouement' of melodrama at the Britannia theatre, this move has a satisfying logic.

Another pleasure of the play is that the trope of the detective 'acting in plain sight' reveals social class as well as 'female' dress and behaviour to be performances that could be swiftly altered. Nelly and Nick pose at a masquerade ball in the final act as upper-class characters, Mrs Catchington and the Honourable Henry James Johnson Napoleon

Francis Charles Catchington, to foil Robert Denville's dastardly schemes and rescue Alice. Nobody recognises the servants in their disguise. Nick observes: 'Since I've been here I've been taken for a Duke three times – a Count five times, and a Lord twenty or thirty.'[35] The comic 'Napoleon' hidden in his assumed name has just a hint of revolution in it.

Ellis's *Female Detective* did not have the theatrical longevity of Hazlewood's *Female Detective*, but after its London run it was performed at Exeter, where local newspapers commented: 'the plot is good and it will take rank among the clever sensational pieces of the day.' The working-class female detective would take a long time to reappear in the novel; the trend in fiction as the nineteenth century wore on was towards middle-class and upper-class detective heroines. Real female detectives in the Victorian period, however, often came from working-class backgrounds and could gain vital information through performing servants' duties. Nelly's detective skills in her master's house were doubtless especially satisfying to working class women at the Britannia accustomed to having to endure injustice at the hands of their supposed 'Lords and masters'.

The Female Detective as Goddess

The female detective on the Victorian stage has much in common with a comic-book superhero. Her detective power is her hidden identity. Only when occasion demands it does she spring into action, delivering blows that send villains to jail. Nowhere is this more apparent than in Colin Henry Hazlewood's second female detective play, *Happiness at Home* (1871), which also starred the redoubtable Sara Lane. Like his first, it opens in Baden Baden – a luxurious setting with chandeliers, music and dancing. The premise is that two naïve young English farmers, Alfred and Edmund Woodreve, have had their heads turned by the unexpected inheritance of a fortune from their uncle. Abandoning their honest toils and rustic sweethearts, Margery and Phoebe, they have gone on a continental spree.

Alfred and Edmund (good old English names) are being fleeced at the gaming tables by various spurious European aristocrats, a 'Count' and a 'Duke' and by two courtesans, Inez and Madame Sylvandiere, who are happy to entertain the two wayward Englishmen if pampered with jewels, watches and other luxuries. At the 'parties' they attend, Alfred and Edmund are asked to sign bills or give temporary loans. The two youths are in so deep that they contemplate selling the lease on their farm to get the thousands of pounds in liquid capital necessary to keep the champagne flowing. The only thing that stands between them and ruin is Diana Jolicour, a mysterious woman who makes it her business to protect the innocent.

Diana is an interesting character in the canon of stage female detectives because she is not a conventional sleuth. She has no family or professional connection to the men she risks her own life to save. She claims to have been an orphan who travelled as a kind of itinerant entertainer, dancing with a bear: an actress-performer, like Sara Lane herself. The 'scamps' of the Woodreves' village chased her; Margery and Phoebe took her in: a favour she will repay. Having inherited money, Diana now lives independent of any father, brother or husband. She gives her winnings at cards to the poor and acts as a detective, seemingly from moral motives alone. Her name is significant: Diana is the goddess of hunting and is associated with female chastity and protecting unmarried women.

The villainous 'Count', 'Baron' and 'Duke', irritated by Diana's attempts to remove their gullible prey, threaten her with violence: 'we have a way of conquering obstacles when we cannot step over them.' They also compare her with a witch:

BARON: That woman's one of the mysteries of Baden Baden. A fashionable lady with a heart – her winnings at cards are all given to the poor, and win she always does, by some method that *I'm* unable to find out . . . She calls me Baron Mousetrap and says she's not to be snapped.

COUNT: Is she here tonight?

BARON: Yes. I saw her in the Gardens just before I met with you. I was watching the two Englishmen and didn't want her to see me, but she did.

COUNT: Of course she did. She sees every thing and every body. I don't believe in witches or I should think she was one.[36]

Diana the divine, do-good detective is sharper than the card sharps. She summons Margery and Phoebe from England with a warning that Margery's fiancé is in trouble. She also prevents the sale of the Woodreves' farm to the unscrupulous usurer Gripeau by faking a lease. Only later will Gripeau realise that he has given the Woodreves hard cash for a forged document.

In the third act, the chastened Edmund and Alfred are back in England, pursued by the loose ladies of Baden Baden and by the 'Baron' and 'Count', who aim to have Alfred arrested for killing the 'Duke' in a duel: they want to extradite him to the Continent, where he faces the guillotine. Again, Diana saves the hapless young men. This time she disguises herself as a *male* private detective and pretends to hire herself out to the villains – who fail to recognise her – promising she will locate Alfred and Edmund. In fact, she directs the police to the Baron and Count and secures their arrest.

The play's title, *Happiness at Home*, has a double meaning. It saves its male ingenues from European wiles, posting them back to England. However, it is also clearly about *domestic* happiness and women's claims on male fidelity. Although the plot involves murder and grand larceny, the primary complaint that the female detective addresses is familiar: men quit the domestic sphere, abandoning their sweethearts. They indulge in licentious pleasures that both deny women conjugal happiness and dissipate money that should support family life. In this sense, despite the plot devices of sensation drama – duels, casinos, kidnapping and police chases – the core values are intelligible and relevant to an East End London audience. Women's detection is made necessary by male defection; Diana is the detective heroine who gets straying, carousing men back to attend to their jobs and families. As the 1902 popular song would put it: 'Bill Bailey won't you please come home?'[37]

The *Era*, reviewing *Happiness at Home*, reported that despite fine June weather, the Britannia was crowded from 'floor to roof', with the scenic tableaux of the set calling forth 'a perfect roar of applause from five thousand throats'.

> Mrs Lane particularly distinguished herself, and the audience seemed especially to enjoy her appearance in the last act as 'the female detective'. Certainly so smart and dapper a thief-catcher never yet issued from Scotland Yard.[38]

Notably, in all the plays featured in this chapter, independent women appear as detectives alongside the formally employed detective police. They are known to the force and granted a certain collaborative authority. Diana, like Nelly in *The Female Detective*, has the pleasure of putting handcuffs on the malefactors. Female detectives in these plays are also granted witty lines that take men down. Diana accuses Alfred and Edmund of looking like 'blighted muffins' after their continental spree. Margery's cowardly and foolish brother Davy, who accompanies her to search for Edmund, confesses 'I'd rather be a lady', that he is 'as innocent as a sucking duck' and remarks, rather camply, 'If a bridesmaid's wanted, I am ready, I am here.'[39] His softness contrasts nicely with Diana's shrewdness, worldliness and bravery. As Diana remarks: 'Oh the weaker sex are not at all weak I promise you.'[40] The persistent upending of conventional gender roles is especially visible in the fight sequences:

> DIANA who is now close at their elbows snatches both pistols from their hands and presents them both at DUKE as he starts back surprised.[41]

The stage heroine of sensation drama can handle a gun. Or even two. In another contemporary melodrama, *Under the Gaslight* (1867), it is a woman who rescues a man from the railway tracks: a cliché of heroism that has been customarily misremembered with the genders inverted. In fact, the East End stage provided opportunities for audiences to see 'dashing women' engaging in a variety of physically demanding feats. Joanna Hofer-Robinson and Beth Palmer observe that

> In sensation plays, women rescue men (*Under the Gaslight*) or take decisive actions to alter the course of events, such as shooting threatening ruffians (*The Red Hand*, 1868) or engaging in a hand-to-hand struggle with a murderer (*The Missing Witness*). They often highlight their own autonomy, as when Ann Chute in *The Colleen Bawn* says: 'I haven't a big brother to see after me – and self-protection is the first rule of nature.'[42]

Guns were not carried (and still are not routinely carried) by the British police force, though there was debate between 1883 and 1886 about whether the police should carry revolvers. But Victorian female detectives on stage handle guns with aplomb and this is part of the thrill of their reversal of customary male power and privilege.

The Female Detective and the Battle of the Exes

Perhaps the most remarkable of all Victorian plays featuring a female detective is *The Lucky Shilling* (1888). Written and produced by John Douglass, with stunning scenic 'effects' painted by his brother Richard, this 'sensational drama' premiered at the Standard Theatre in Shoreditch High Street. Shoreditch had been London's theatre district since before Shakespeare's time. The Standard Theatre, like the Britannia, catered to a crowded, local, predominantly working-class audience: the area was popular with immigrants and had a large Irish and Jewish population. Reopened in 1867, the theatre boasted luxurious fittings, including crimson velvet curtains and four 'noble tiers of boxes', as well as a vast pit and spacious gallery that between them could seat 3,000 people. An immense chandelier, or 'gigantic crystal and sun-light illuminator', hung from the roof, creating, it was said, '3000 jets of light'.[43] There was an orchestra, too. For audience members whose own lodgings were frequently leaky, dirty and bare, it offered a taste of luxury and of wonder. Under Douglass's management, the Standard created plays with panoramic backdrops that had the spectacle and excitement (and many of the VFX) we now associate with cinema. Indeed, one can think of the Douglass brothers as the Coen brothers of their day. Mail-coach robberies, gunfights, live animals and recognisable panoramas of whole London streets complete with 'coffee carts' and human traffic were part of the exceptional thrill of the Standard experience.

Douglass's previous success, *A Dark Secret* – a loose adaptation of Sheridan Le Fanu's *Uncle Silas* – had staged Henley rowing regatta in a water-filled tank with boats and oarsmen; it also featured several gruesome murders and a scene in which one female character horsewhips another. As the *Era* tactfully put it, Douglass's plays 'should not, perhaps, be submitted to the ordinary rules of dramatic criticism', or judged from 'a supercilious, high-art perspective'. Nonetheless, it reported that *The Lucky Shilling* was a 'comparatively probable and really interesting play of its class'.[44]

In *The Lucky Shilling*, shockingly, the female detective is the 'ex' of the villain, Erasmus Percival Flight. She was in love with him when they married; then she discovered he already had a wife, so their union had no legal value. Now they are at war. Their comic skirmishes anticipate the sharp dialogue between needling wives and noodling husbands of divorce comedies in films from Cecil B. DeMille's *Don't Leave Your Husband*, to *The Palm Beach Story* and *His Girl Friday*. Where, in the other Victorian female detective plays we have examined, the detective is a conduit for women's anger about male deception and a saviour of women from male exploitation, in this play she is explicitly taking revenge on her own deadbeat love cheat.

The lawyer, Honeydew, expresses surprise when Mrs Flight introduces herself:

HONEYDEW: And so you're a detective eh, whatever could have induced a lady of independent means to adopt such an extraordinary proffession [sic]?

MRS F: My husband was so much away from home and had so many secrets from me that I thought I would do a little business myself, the nature of which he should be ignorant of

HONEYDEW: A married lady . . . who is your husband?

MRS F: We are not living together now, in fact a sort of separation by mutual consent, he complained of my drinking

HONEYDEW: Indeed!

MRS F: Part of my plan to bring him to his senses

HONEYDEW: Well, your domestic affairs are nothing to do with me, you have been sent here to assist by the criminal investigation department, and by this letter I find you are highly recommended by the chief[45]

The female detective emerges in her clearest light here as a scourge of bad husbands, who prevents them from practising their wiles on new and younger female victims. She has, however, professional expertise and testimonials at the highest level. In 1878, the Metropolitan Police Detective Branch was reformed into the CID. Mrs Flight is working for the new elite force of British detection. It is implicit in all the other plays I have discussed that 'domestic crime is crime': that the cheating, wayward, abusive husband is also the villain, or aligned with the villain, who is guilty of grave felonies against property and person – typically theft and murder. In this play, the connection is explicit. The two male villains have both abandoned their wives. They are also engaged in a large-scale fraud and impersonation that aims to dispossess an innocent young woman, robbing her of her fortune and her freedom.

The person who will stand in the way of this heist and defend the young heiress is Mrs Flight, the mature woman who knows from bitter experience how badly men behave. She is sardonic, quick-witted and brave. Although the younger woman, Hester Wyatt, is the virgin heroine of melodrama, with all the sentimental pathos of that role, the older woman who plays the female detective has the best comic lines. Like other female detectives on the stage, Mrs Flight is a master of disguise, appearing as a housekeeper, an old beggarwoman, a high-born lady and a nun. Her husband and his villainous sidekick fail to recognise her: a very apt revenge on a husband who has been 'looking elsewhere'. She is also an action heroine. The flagellation scene in *A Dark Secret* must have been a success because Douglass reprises it in *The Lucky Shilling*, where the female detective, disguised as a nun, seizes the whip from Mrs Craggs, the cruel matron of the madhouse in which Hester has been illegally detained. Mrs Craggs has been torturing Hester and she has it coming to her:

MRS FLIGHT [disguised as a Sister of Mercy]: If you are going to try your weight and muscle against mine, try . . . I'm going to give you a specimen of Muscular Christianity (swings her round and throws her down)

CRAGGS: Here help! (They close. MRS FLIGHT takes whip and strikes CRAGGS.)[46]

Amy Steinberg was thirty-eight when she stepped onto the Standard stage to play the female detective; like Sara Lane at the Britannia, she was the doyenne of the theatre, the wife of its proprietor and the figure around whose talents his plays usually revolved. Born Alice Rachel Koning, the daughter of a Belgian salesman of Jewish descent, she was no stranger to self-invention. She had been an actress since her teens. Steinberg's Belgian origins made her an able linguist and admirers noted that she was able to act in French as easily as she did in English.[47] She played many action heroines, including Grace Darling, the young woman who became famous for her strength and bravery rowing a lifeboat through stormy seas to

16. *Amy Steinberg,* Illustrated Sporting and Dramatic News *(1880).*

rescue men who would otherwise have perished in a shipwreck. She also played Jane Eyre in the melodramatic adaptation of Brontë's novel, *Poor Relations.* Reviews of Steinberg on stage emphasise her 'well known qualities of energy and defiant originality', alongside the 'vivacity, animation, and point' of her comic acting. The *Era* noted of *The Lucky Shilling* that she threw 'intense energy into the mad-house scene'.[48]

In *A Dark Secret*, Steinberg's character had engaged in an all-female on-stage fistfight, defending her half-sister from the governess who was whipping her. In *The Royal Mail*, Amy appeared driving a real mail coach with horses. One of the on-stage characters exclaimed, 'What will people say – a female driving the mail', to which Amy's character punningly responded, 'Don't they always do it!'[49] Audiences at the Standard, then, were accustomed to action heroines who combatted evil in a direct physical fashion and engaged in potentially dangerous stunts with horses, pistols and even a real balloon.

In *The Lucky Shilling*, two villains are poised to take over the estate of the lately deceased Sir Frederick Gower. One of them, Ronald Flemming, is posing as the heritor Edward Gower. In fact, Flemming is not only an impostor but he has also bumped off the real Edward Gower while abroad, stealing his papers and identity. The other villain in *The Lucky Shilling*, Erasmus Percival Flight, is, as the *Referee* noted in its review, 'the comic villain'. He is a jailbird and con-artist whose catchphrase – which he applies to everything, from handcuffs to bigamy – is 'that's nothing new, you know'.

The heir in the villains' soup is the fact that there is another person to be disposed of before they can take control of the Gower estate. She is Mary Wyatt, Sir Frederick Gower's daughter, who eloped with a sailor and fled to America. If she is discovered within two years and it is established that she was legally married, she is the rightful heir. Providentially, Mary Wyatt has just returned to England with her beautiful daughter Hester and the documents that prove her marriage, but Mary is dying, they have no money, and it is snowing . . . By one of the astonishing coincidences in which melodrama rejoices, the Wyatts bump into Flemming and Flight. Flight gives Hester a coin and – to get rid of her – urges her to buy some brandy for her expiring mother. Mary then perishes in the snow, disregarded by the villains, who steal the certificates proving her marriage, Hester's legitimacy and thus her daughter's entitlement to the Gower estate.

This, however, is where it gets interesting. Hester is arrested for trying to pass bad coin: the false shilling that Percival Flight handed her. The villains thus land Hester in jail, with a criminal record that makes it impossible for her to gain respectable employment. They 'ruin' her, by economic means. This is almost as effective as bumping her off in a conventionally melodramatic manner, by poisoning or drowning her. The point the plot, half-humorously, makes is sharp: men have numerous methods of eliminating women who stand in their way. Murder, marriage, a private madhouse or simply slipping them a duff shilling: all of these can work.

The female detective is the roadblock on the freeway of male power. She will not allow other women to be run down. Mrs Percival Flight, in pursuing and incriminating her former partner, both saves Hester and settles her own score:

HONEYDEW: But your evidence will not be accepted against him.
MRS FLIGHT: I must make a confession. I was married to him, he treated me like a dog. And one day he provided proofs of a former marriage. Whatever love I had for him turned to hate, as his wife I could have died to serve him, now I could see him hanged with pleasure.[50]

The fact that their marriage was not legal disempowers 'Mrs Flight' in certain ways. Percival dismisses her as his 'cast-off mistress'. But this irregularity also confers a great advantage. Before 1898, common law held that wives were not competent to give evidence against their husbands in criminal cases. Mrs Flight faces no such disadvantage. She can tell a court what a rotter her supposed former husband is. The similarity of Flight's attempts to discredit them aligns the female detective and Hester, the ingenue she will save (played by Stella Brotherton, Amy Steinberg's sister-in-law in real life).

Sir Percival Glyde is the villainous husband in Wilkie Collins's *The Woman in White*. Erasmus Percival Flight is a parodic, lower-class

17. *'The Female Detective and Hester'*, Illustrated Sporting and Dramatic News *(1888).*

version of Glyde who commits similarly outrageous crimes: attempting to put Hester in a madhouse to silence her. The relationship between Flight and his wife, however, lends his pantomime villainy a realist edge. They joust verbally. He twits her appearance. She insults his stupidity and his habit of sponging off her:

PERCIVAL: She won't let me alone.

MRS FLIGHT: Let you 'a –Loan' – no – you never pay them. But there I really came to ask your opinion, how shall I have my new bonnet trimmed?

PERCIVAL: Have it plain – If you want it to match your face.

MRS FLIGHT: Shameful. The fact is, we were both deceived in each other. My husband married me knowing I had money.

PERCIVAL: Which I hoped to share

MRS FLIGHT: But it was all settled on myself.

PERCIVAL: Beastly selfish. I thought I was going to have a beautiful mansion to live in.

MRS FLIGHT: I found I'd got a flat with the top storeys always vacant.

Their acid banter situates the battle regarding women's property rights as a life-and-death struggle that is also a domestic spat.

18. 'The Maniac', Illustrated Sporting and Dramatic News (1888).

Douglass saved the most sensational scenes for last in this play. The madhouse where the villains unjustly confine Hester Wyatt was recreated on two floors, so that the audience could see into four different 'rooms' at once. This proto-cinematic, 'split-screen' technique of showing different spheres of action simultaneously and creating suspense as to whether the barriers will be broken between the different 'rooms' in time to save those in danger also provided a dramatic manifestation of the domestic as a potentially carceral space of maximal peril. Looking in, as one sometimes can when passing a multi-storey dwelling in winter, the audience could see different rooms in a building as distinct 'scenes' in which characters experience distinct realities. In one of the rooms, 'the keeper and his myrmidons are plotting'; in another the villains are getting Hester's long-lost sailor father drunk; in a third the female detective is interviewing Mrs Craggs; while in a fourth cell, Hester is being menaced by a madwoman, who is secured by a chain around her waist and makes leaps 'like a baboon' towards the terrified girl. In an echo of *Jane Eyre*, the madwoman, Zillah, is Ronald Flemming's former wife, suggesting the intriguing possibility that she, too, was a woman whom he deceived, who has been driven mad by unjust confinement. The double bigamy plot is a suggestive background to all the other ways in which Flemming and Flight injure women in the play.

Incredibly, when Flight is finally arrested, his former 'wife' pities him and momentarily thinks about taking him back. But his lack of remorse persuades her that he has altogether forfeited her regard. She leaves him to his fate. Then, in a shocking denouement, Mrs Flight is *shot and killed* by his accomplice, Flemming, who fires at her through the window of the police station.

A police chase across the rooftops ensues. In the final scene, Flemming tries to conceal himself on a goods train, but is killed in a shoot-out with police.[51] Douglass had secured railway rolling stock that trundled on tracks across the stage. Douglass's use of real, moving trains on the stage draws attention to the similarity between action sequences in late Victorian theatre and early cinema.

At the end of *The Lucky Shilling*, the two villains are defeated. Hester Wyatt and her beau, Bernard Lyle, are now free to marry and to enjoy her rightful inheritance. But the female detective, who is the real centre of the plot, is dead. Did Victorian audiences gasp, as I did when I read the words: 'he fires. Mrs F is shot'? Certainly, the play draws attention to the persistence of men's ability to determine legitimacy, as much as it shows women's ingenuity in combatting the men who wish to de-legitimise them.[52] *The Lucky Shilling* is highly unusual in making its female detective (technically) a 'fallen' woman, who is also an agent of justice, yet who dies in the attempt to secure it.

The year 1888 was critical in the debate about whether there should be female detective police in Britain. *The Lucky Shilling* was staged in February. In June, a poem, 'The Lady-Detective', appeared in *Funny Folks*, referencing an article in the *Pall Mall Gazette* about the women detectives of Chicago:

Oh, light-fingered gentlemen all –
From practised professional cracksmen
To filchers from barrow and stall –
Deem not that all 'coppers' are lax men!
We know that 'the Yard' is a fraud –
We own that our system's defective:
But beware! – there is prowling abroad
The Argus-eyed Lady-Detective!

What! Hadn't you heard it before?
No wonder – poor fellow – you tremble –
No wonder you sadly deplore
That the sex should thus stoop to dissemble.
No wonder you pour on their head
The torrent of manly invective –

No wonder you shiver with dread
At thought of the *Lady*-Detective!

... But we – we will worship her wiles,
While wheedlingly whispering '*Wire* in;'
And beam when she boldly beguiles
Soft Sikes – the sweet, sedulous siren!
Oh, may her activity prove
Of masculine sloth the corrective,
And Society's voice bless the move
That gave it the Lady-Detective![53]

This poem, while patronising the 'sweet, sedulous siren', who 'boldly beguiles' men, concedes that Scotland Yard needs reform and the policing 'system' is defective. The female detective is the answer to a pressing problem. The first of the Whitechapel murders was reported in August. The newspapers described a 'reign of terror' in London's East End that had caused a 'vigilance committee' to form locally with 'citizens as detectives'.[54] In October 1888, Frances Power Cobbe would demand a female detective force. *The Lucky Shilling*, despite its web of improbabilities, contributed to a live discussion with real-world consequences: its identification of homicidal violence against women as rooted in their domestic lives was as accurate as its plot was fanciful.

The American Female Detective as Action Hero

By the 1890s, women occupied a greater variety of professional roles, real female detectives were highly visible via newspaper advertisements for private enquiry agencies, and female detectives had penetrated the fiction market, particularly in serial newspaper formats. These literary female detectives were masters of forensic skill: studying handwriting, trails of candle wax, drops of blood and scraps of paper. Brave and energetic, they were also studious and often private in their cogitations, deciphering criminal plots from details that would escape eyes less finely tuned to narrative details. For the bookworm, the detective as fellow close-reader was a pleasing mirror.

In the tense, live physical space of the theatre, however, it was still possible for a melodrama featuring the female detective as sharp-shooting action heroine to succeed as Hazlewood and Ellis's plays had in the 1860s. In *The Tiger's Grip*, which played at the Lyceum, Ipswich, in 1898, Hettie Brass – a New York female detective – saves the young heiress heroine, Mary Wood, from a flooding cellar over the Thames where she has been trapped by the villainous burglar, Nat Burke.[55] This play has many elements of an action movie, from bombs and safes to a ticking clock. The tide rises on Mary, who has refused Nat's salacious offer to let her join the gang as his doxy:

NAT: The water will be in soon and when you find it's rising to your face you'll be glad to come to my terms.
MARY: No, never. You wretch! My suffering will soon be over – but were I with you it would be daily – hourly – unspeakable misery![56]

The trash compacter in *Star Wars*, in which Princess Leia and her loyal helpers are about to be crushed, is but a more modern version of the flooding cellar of melodrama, which had previously appeared in *A Dark Secret*. The heroine is threatened with being literally overwhelmed, her body and breath oppressed. The audience shares a sense of constriction, their breath becoming shorter as time runs out. In *The Tiger's Grip*, Phil – Hettie Brass's male assistant – tries to save Mary, who makes a spirited attempt to free herself with a knife that has skittered out of Nat's grasp, across the floor. (Again, these moves will feel familiar from modern cinema.) Both victims fail in their efforts to escape and are tied to chairs by Nat and his sidekick, Bill.

The villains would succeed were it not for the female detective, who arrives in the nick of time. The script reads:

HETTIE: Stand back!
(NAT staggers back amazed.)
NAT: Who are you?
HETTIE: Hettie Brass.
(Snatches off disguise. Lime on HETTIE – who presents two revolvers at NAT & BILL.)
Picture – thus

–Hettie–

Mary on knees	Phil on ground
Nat	Bill

This is the striking tableau at the end of Act II. The limelight ('lime') plays directly on Hettie, who stands at the centre of the stage with her two revolvers trained on the two villains; the ingenue heroine and Hettie's male assistant are both on the ground at her feet. Nothing could declare more vividly the female detective's central and controlling role in the drama and how that role is underpinned by her cool and confident use of weaponry. Hettie's boldness lives up to her surname: Brass. Richard Austen scoffs at her:

AUSTEN: You? A weak woman, contend against an accomplished burglar!
HETTIE: (coolly) Ah, yes: if *I* am weak, this makes me strong! (produces revolver) Now, if you want to save those diamonds I'll help you – and at the same time I shall be able to cop my man.[57]

Wise-cracking and safe-cracking, Hettie is seen throughout the play to be more than a match for the dastardly Nat because she has learned to use the same tools. She carries a 'daisy set' of lock-picks that allow her to open the safe and remove the jewels before the burglar's attempted heist.

Burke tries to torpedo the ship in which Hettie and Mary are travelling but Hettie has boarded a different ship. She poses as a cockney costermonger to track Burke, confusing the police as well as the criminal. As ever, the female detective is seen to be superior in her sleuthing powers to the regular police force, whose assistance is only required at the end of the play to make arrests. Hettie Brass successfully defends Mary from all the men who want to deprive her of her life, liberty and fortune.

The diamonds in this play represent female inheritance – they are the legacy of Richard Austen's dead sister and her husband to the baby daughter (Mary) from whom they were forced to part. Richard Austen, who staked the diamonds to prop up his ailing business, has betrayed his custody of female inheritance in multiple ways. Two different young women stand to lose life-changing sums of money through his fraud. He has also connived at Nat's scheme to get Mary out of the way, if necessary by killing her.

From a modern perspective, Austen deserves to go to jail on several counts; it is striking, therefore, that Mary forgives him at the end of the play, gifting her diamonds to restore his fortunes. Nat Burke, the serial burglar, is imprisoned in his stead as a lower-class representative of male vice. Melodramas featuring the female detective frequently show, through different male characters, the ways in which patriarchal power conspires to harm women yet may have to be accepted to achieve the promised order of the final act. This is equally true of novels featuring amateur female detectives – *The Adventures of Susan Hopley*, *Eleanor's Victory* and *The Law and the Lady* – all of which leave some male malefactors and power structures in play at the end of the story. The female detective's actions scupper the homicidal male plot. Yet the pervasiveness of male efforts to defraud women leave a persistent

THE VICTORIAN FEMALE DETECTIVE

suspicion of dry rot in the 'home, sweet home' of the play's domestic conclusion.

Like Nelly in *The Female Detective* or Mrs Paschal on the cover of *Revelations of a Lady Detective*, Hettie Brass exhibits her freedom to flout social nicety when she 'stands coolly smoking [a] cigarette and blowing the smoke in Nat's face'.[58] Her relationship with her male sidekick Phil is one of professional superior to junior staff. Hettie defines its terms:

HETTIE: my assistant
PHIL: my partner[59]

Though Hettie at the end of the play accedes to Phil's repeated request that she marry him and becomes his 'partner for life', it is very clear that she has the upper hand in their relationship. In one scene, Hettie tells Phil to wait in the outer office. 'Vanish!' she insists when he objects.[60] Just as Nick Spray is inferior to Nelly in George B. Ellis's *The Female Detective* (1865), Phil remains Hettie's accessory rather than the other way around. Like Nelly, Hettie handcuffs the villain; she comments, suggestively: 'Muzzled at last –!' The male antagonist has not only been prevented from attacking, but also from speaking.

These continuities evoke a long theatrical tradition in which women on stage prove their ability to get the better of men using disguise and ingenuity. In the late nineteenth century, however, the assertion of women's equal skill in law enforcement – even when made by a male dramatist – carries a new force and weight. The female detective on the Victorian stage asserts her power in the domestic alongside the professional realm; indeed, her work deliberately conflates these realms, refusing a distinction between the secrets of one sphere and of the other and insisting that where women are threatened domestically with theft, violence and loss of identity, public safety is also compromised.

The Actress Detective in Comedy

MRS SPARROW: Evening work. Yes, I think evening work would particularly suit me. There's so much more to find out about people in the evenings, isn't there?[61]

In the last two decades of the nineteenth century, the female detective also began to feature regularly in stage comedy. This tendency had always been present in sensation dramas, with the female detective delivering comic dialogue and entertaining audiences with her many disguises, including cross-dressing. But sharp social comedy that focused explicitly on sex and gender as areas of role-play and transgressive escapism brought 'detection' into crisp focus. This was the era of runaway hits *Charley's Aunt* (1892), where a male student disguises himself as a wealthy widow and is wooed by male suitors, and *The Importance of Being Earnest* (1895), where friends Jack and Algernon both pose as 'Ernest' to lead double lives. Comedy goosed audiences with the delicious suspicion that everyone was 'playing away' to escape sexual and social constraints.

Bilberry of Tilbury, a 'musical farce' of 1898 by Silvanus Dauncey and George D. Day, which played at Northampton and at the Criterion Theatre in London, is an appealingly flimsy confection, which relies on the corsetry of song and dance numbers to hold up its feathers-and-lace plot. The conceit is that Stella Dashwood, an actress at the Gaiety Theatre, is also the manager of her own female detective agency. Gerty, Amy, Susie and Mabel, her band of female private detectives, have been coached so that they can also appear as The Elysian Girls of the chorus. When not performing high kicks, they are staking out low dives; their access to the world of theatre fits them well for the task of informing neglected wives where their cheating husbands are really spending their time and vice versa. As Stella sings:

If you fancy that your wife
Has grown tired of married life,
And begin to wonder where on earth she's stopping —

Chorus Oh!

I can tell you to a shade
All the visits she has paid,
And if she's really spent her time in shopping.

Chorus Ah!

...If a golden hair you note
On your husband's overcoat,
And it doesn't match with yours, it's so much lighter —

Chorus So much lighter!

I can very quickly nab
If it blew in through the cab,
Or whether it belongs to his type-writer.

Chorus His type-writer!

Then I get a lot of praise
From my use of Rontgen rays
In the case of married couples who're suspicious

Chorus Oh!

If a skeleton one sees,
With another on its knees,
And you know it isn't yours, it makes you vicious.

Chorus Oh![62]

The imagined secret lives in this play are explicitly sexual lives. Hair analysis, X-rays (Rontgen rays): these modern detective techniques are placed at the service of the spouse who suspects their other half of cheating. Stella is compared to Henry Slater, a real detective famous for his employment of ladies, and to Maurice Moser, who had formed a professional partnership with his lover, Antonia, who subsequently founded her own detective business. Audience members could thus relate the play to advertisements for private enquiry agencies visible in the newspaper alongside those for London theatre. The farce as a whole suggests that everyone is travelling under an assumed name: that acting and disguise are socially ubiquitous.

Victorian actresses had fought a long battle to be regarded as respectable professionals.[63] The figure of the 'actress detective' drew attention to the fact that the role of detective deployed all the same skills as that of the actress and might be regarded in a similar professional light. As we will see in the next chapter, several Victorian actresses became detectives, most famously Kate Easton, who, like Antonia Moser, did indeed run her own agency. The 'actress detective' also became a figure in literature: George Robert Sims, a well-known playwright, created the figure of Dorcas Dene, a detective who repurposes skills learned during her theatrical career to appear as a flower seller, a nurse, a parlour maid, a middle-aged German or an American tourist. Dene's protean transformations recall the decades-long tradition – which Sims as an author of melodrama would have known well – of female detectives on the stage.

In *Bilberry of Tilbury*, as in other farces of the *fin de siècle* featuring female detectives such as *Private Enquiry* (1890) and *The Colonel's Wives* (1895), detection becomes a mode of investigating male and female infidelity, disclosing sexual double lives and double standards and the commonplace nature of aliases and alibis in social life. As in melodrama, the female detective in late-Victorian comedy is assertive: she makes the case for her own, respectable yet doubled, professional and private existence. She often 'gets her man' in the last act, both in the sense of apprehending him and marrying him: a broad hint that marriage is no longer predicated on female ignorance and male control.

The Victorian Female Detective from Stage to Screen

This is certainly true of George Broadhurst's comedy *The Wrong Mr Wright* (1897), which features Henrietta Oliver, who, in the tradition of Hettie Brass, is a professional New York detective with a business card and a no-nonsense attitude to men who pursue her, whether with a gun or a bouquet.

In this popular farce, which transitioned from late-Victorian theatre to early-twentieth-century cinema, Seymour Sites is a stingy multi-millionaire, whose business has been robbed of $50,000 by an employee's forgery. Sites is incredulous and indignant when he learns that the detective agency he hired to investigate this crime has put a female detective on the case:

> SITES: As soon as I discovered the forgery I placed the case in the hands of a detective agency, and offered five thousand dollars reward for his conviction. And guess what they did? But you couldn't. They put a *woman* on his track. A *woman* to catch a man clever enough to rob me ... so here I am to capture Bailey, save my five thousand dollars and give those wonderful detectives the royal Ha! Ha![64]

Sites's hubris will, of course, be his downfall when he discovers just how intelligent a female detective can be.

Hearing that the swindler has holed up in a hotel, Sites determines to go there himself; to protect his privacy, he registers under the alias 'Wright'. He brings along his young niece and her maid, who are eager to enjoy some holiday fun by swapping their identities: the maid poses as an heiress and her mistress as a servant. Henrietta Oliver is the female detective who, unknown to Sites, is on the case of the corporate embezzler. Everyone is travelling under false colours. Ms Oliver, who is posing as a milliner, at first thinks Sites is the criminal. Enjoyable confusion reigns until all the couples are freed from suspicion of their would-be partners.

As in other Victorian female detective plays, although property theft is the ostensible concern, more domestic forms of deception swiftly become more central to the plot. The 'holiday' of farce, where people occupy temporary places, suggests the extent to which work-aday identities are also arbitrary suites we occupy and can exchange. The hotel, with its rotating cast of dubious guests, is an apt metaphor for the negotiable frame of selfhood.

Constance Collier, who played Henrietta Oliver, was only twenty-one in 1899, but already a commanding figure on the stage. Very tall for a woman, she had striking and sultry features, with dark eyes, a strong nose and long black hair – at least one reviewer described her beauty as 'Oriental' – that led her to be cast as Cleopatra in early stage appearances. She would become a successful tragedienne as well as a comedienne, enjoying a long career that transitioned from stage to silver screen; she can still be viewed playing opposite Fred Astaire as the formidable Lady Caroline in *A Damsel in Distress* (1937), with the hauteur of a pillar and a voice as fruity as old port. Among the many successful actresses she trained were Vivien Leigh, Katherine Hepburn and Marilyn Monroe.

Although she is a character in farce rather than melodrama, Henrietta Oliver retains many of the features of the female detective in earlier Victorian popular theatre. Described in the script as 'a handsome, dashing woman of about thirty ... dressed in a fashion-able travelling costume', she is unmistakably the lead actress: wittier than the younger female ingenue. Lord Brazenface has bet that he will kiss the first woman who enters the room:

LORD BRAZENFACE: How do you do? So pleased to see you – again. We've met before. I know we have. Where was it? Oh yes, I remember now. It was at the dog show.
HENRIETTA: Perhaps I did see you. I was there. What kennel were you in?[65]

If Brazenface hoped to be bussed, he ends up busted. The Captain (a witness to the dare) remarks, 'You'll never renew the attack after a defeat like that.'

The female detective suspects the mature male lead, Seymour Sites, of being a criminal, identifying him as the thief who stole $50,000 from Sites's business. Technically, Miss Oliver is wrong. Sites is the victim of the scam rather than its perpetrator. But since Sites is a testy, tight-fisted bachelor, there is a sense in which Miss Oliver is correct to identify Sites as alienating his own fortune. As in *The Tiger's Grip* and *Happiness at Home*, it is not the overt villain but the covert villain (the ordinary patriarch) who is fingered as the enduring source of trouble in the domestic realm. He needs to be put in handcuffs (marriage) to become a net distributor of financial largesse rather than an obstacle to others' happiness. By the end of the play, Sites has fallen helplessly in love with Oliver, so the detective arrests him:

HENRIETTA: I have conducted this case so badly I shall resign my position immediately.
SITES: (goes to her) Let me give you another. Take me into custody.
HENRIETTA: You are my prisoner.
SITES: For life.

CURTAIN[66]

Although several late Victorian detective comedies end conventionally, as *The Wrong Mr Wright* does, with marriage, the central theme of Victorian female detective drama is male abuse of power. The female detective snoops on men, unmasks them, bests them and captures them, preventing their future delinquency. The battle of the sexes is a defining feature of these plays.

The essential features of the Victorian female detective on stage developed early: she is a mature woman, who may be in her thirties or forties, with a commanding presence and a sharp wit. If she has a male assistant, he will be weaker. She will be confident in carrying weapons and handcuffs and will shape-shift, allowing the actress playing the part to showcase her skills via transformation into characters of different age, class, nationality and gender. Indeed, the question of what is 'natural' to female behaviour is thrown into relief by the enjoyably venturesome, slangy, wily and tough persona of the detective, who pursues rather than retreats from conventionally male habits (such as smoking) and actions (such as safe-cracking). The female detective on stage will also increasingly be recognised as a professional sleuth; even in 1865 she will be working with the police. The remarkable continuities in these plays between 1864 and 1900 point to the longevity of theatrical traditions and how these develop distinctly from (though in tandem with) those of the detective novel or serial. *The Wrong Mr Wright* would be adapted into a silent film of 1927, with Enid Bennet in the role of Henrietta Oliver. Indeed, female detectives frequently feature in early cinema in, for example, *Papa's First Outing* (1910), James Horne's *The Girl Detective* (1915), *The Detectress* (1919) and *The Penalty* (1920) – which drew on sensational and comic tropes established by popular theatre.

These theatrical antecedents reached huge numbers of ordinary people. The myth of the female detective as a master of disguise, brandishing weapons and detonating puns, swung her way into popular Victorian culture in Britain and America. The female detective on the nineteenth-century stage is not a quizzical middle-class old lady like Agatha Christie's Jane Marple, solving cases like cryptic crosswords by dint of lateral thinking and character recognition. For these swashbuckling stage detectives, the active, malleable body is front and centre of their bid to turn the tables on male opponents. They place themselves boldly between the villain and his mark. Like real female detectives in the nineteenth century, so many of whom were working class, these women can succeed by passing as servants or tradeswomen, attracting no notice from a wealthier class they seem to work for but routinely expose. Fast-talking, fist-swinging, sharp-shooting ladies, they take no nonsense from ruthless villains, whose intellectual and physically daring superior they prove to be. When we celebrate the pragmatic, mature heroines of modern female detective dramas, Jane Tennison in *Prime Suspect*, Mare Sheehan in *Mare of Easttown*, Catherine Cawood in *Happy Valley* or Marge Gunderson in *Fargo*, we are viewing characters who share many of the attributes of drily witty ex Mrs Flight in *The Lucky Shilling*, or commanding Hettie Brass in *The Tiger's Grip*: women experienced in marriage and in carnage, saving the young female victim from the perennially linked public and private threat of male violence.

The truth of women's private detective work in the Victorian era was different from this empowering fantasy. It had elements of theatre: role-play, sudden reveals and farce. But it was often shadier and shabbier. It involved pursuing bad cheques and illicit sex. The gaze of the real female private eye was frequently trained on the goods, the bed and the ugly.

4

SEX AND THE FEMALE DICK
The Secrets of the Private Enquiry Agency

I'm the lady in command
Of this most distinguished band,
Whose experience has never come a cropper,
Chorus Come a cropper!
I can tell you if your hub
Spends his evenings at the Club,
Or another kind of place that's not so proper.
Chorus Not so proper![1]

The couple on the Waverley paddle-steamer were not young, but they were engrossed in one another's company. It was not difficult for Emily Oxley to escape their attention. The man was Tudor Williams (fifty), successful inventor and publicist of the well-known Patent Balsam of Honey, widely touted in newspapers as curing asthma, whooping cough and bronchitis: 'If your children or friends are losing their grip on life and scarcely able to breathe, they should try Tudor's Patent Balsam of Honey,' his advertisements urged.[2] The lady was Lina Louisa Hughes (thirty-nine), a vivacious Welsh hotel manager. She had been married twice: first to George Mortimer, an engine filler, then to David Hughes, brewery director and proprietor of the Boot Hotel in Aberdare, a widower with four children – to whom, he would later testify, she had proved an affectionate stepmother.

The pair stepped off the steamer when it arrived at Weston-super-Mare and made their way to the Royal Pier Hotel. Emily Oxley followed them. They booked a room as Mr and Mrs Griffiths. Emily Oxley booked the next-door room, under her own name. 'Mr Griffiths' requested dinner to be sent up to the couple's room, as they were tired. It was delivered at 7 p.m. Emily listened to the holiday-makers through the wall as they enjoyed their evening in a boisterous manner that suggested they had recovered some energy. At 10 p.m., Emily approached the hotel manager. He formed a small party of staff, who stood behind her when she knocked at the door. Tudor Williams opened it half-undressed, probably expecting to see a hotel servant asking about breakfast. Instead, Emily served him with a business card, identifying herself as a private enquiry agent. Lina Hughes, sitting up in bed in her nightdress, asked who had employed her. When she heard the client was Mr Hughes, she exclaimed: 'My God, we are caught.'

The female detective had completed her mission; she testified in the divorce court on behalf of David Hughes's petition to divorce his wife for adultery. He claimed an astonishing £5,000 in damages, largely for the loss of his wife's 'services': he had been obliged to employ a hotel manager and a childminder in her absence. Evidently, Lina was a popular hostess. The Boot Hotel's weekly takings had fallen off considerably since her departure. The court ordered Tudor Williams to pay Mr Hughes £600 plus costs and granted a decree nisi. The *Illustrated Police News*, a sensational newspaper that favoured eye-catching spreads, featured the story on its title page for August 1896, under the headline: 'Caught! Guilty Pair Tracked By a Female Detective'. It showed a cameo of the detective, peeping through a keyhole, alongside a dramatic tableau of the guilty couple in their underwear. The advertisements

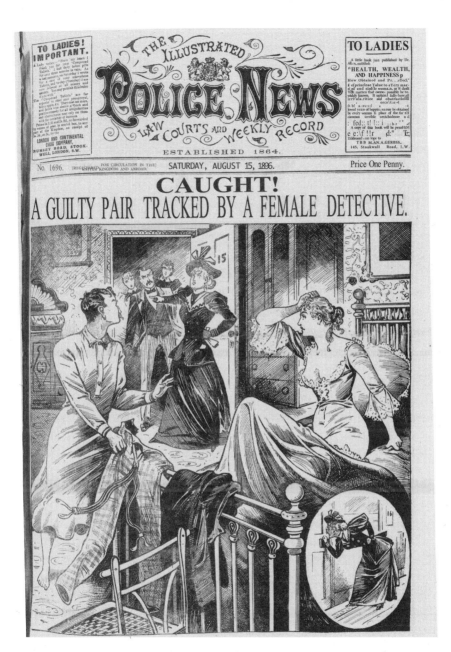

19. *'Caught! Guilty Pair Tracked By a Female Detective'*,
Illustrated Police News *(1896)*.

'To Ladies!', on the front page, signal that the *Illustrated Police News* anticipated female readers, whose gaze would be magnetised by the stare of the adulterous woman and of the female detective, who plays a starring role, fashionably dressed in jacket and hat as she points accusingly at Tudor Williams, like a gun dog directing the hunt towards the quarry. However, the paper omitted Emily Oxley's name, referring to her merely as a 'smartly-dressed, sun-browned little woman, the wife of a retired police constable, now turned inquiry agent'.[3]

If you search for Emily Oxley in the 1891 or 1901 census, you will find her listed merely as 'wife' of William Oxley; her professional employment as a detective is not formally recorded. In fact, Emily Oxley had been working with the police since at least 1891, when, as a 'searcher' at Cardiff police station, she found twelve shillings and sixpence on the person of Margaret Davies, a sex worker who had robbed a sailor client. Her routine work as a private detective involved shadowing suspects in adultery cases. In 1897, she gave evidence in a trial concerning an adulterous couple who had been conducting a liaison while the husband, a marine engineer, was at sea. Emily Oxley watched the house where the suspects conducted their affair, standing on Wyndham Crescent, Cardiff, one Saturday from 10.30 p.m. to 2.30 a.m., noting the light and shadows in the bedroom window and how the suspects remained together in that room. She tailed them to the Atlas pub; she interviewed the neighbours; she watched the man digging the back garden. In another adultery case, she took a room as a lodger in the house where the suspect, Mrs Hellings, lived; Mrs Oxley reported that she sat on the stairs all night, watching to see if Mrs Hellings and her lover left the couch below. She investigated their clothes and shoes. She knew the smell of their bodies. As a lodger, posing as 'Mrs Captain Jones', she shared a bed also used by the suspect's niece. Much of the work of the real female detective in the Victorian period was of this kind: intimate, patient, uncomfortable and fraught with moral ambiguity. The breathless pace of narrative fiction and the glamour of theatre were rare.

There were plenty of female detectives working for private enquiry agencies in Victorian Britain, as we know from the many firms that advertised their services. Frequently, however, where there is a real case involving a female private detective, her name is redacted. A commentator in 1889 noted that women 'seldom figure in an arrest for two reasons: – first, it would tend to destroy their influence; and, second, they would have to go to the police court, which is not pleasant for any woman'.[4] Women are, until the twentieth century, rarely listed as private detectives in the census. Additionally, most private enquiry agencies were founded by former policemen, like William Oxley, who inherited an investigative culture where women were deployed, but rarely acknowledged. Some former policemen turned private eyes wrote self-publicising accounts of their crime-solving successes. Maurice Moser of the Metropolitan Police published *Stories from Scotland Yard* (1890); Jerome Caminada of the Manchester Police published *Twenty-five Years of Detective Life* (1895) while continuing his detective work in private practice. The literary depiction of 'true crime' and the business of private detection thus grew hand in hand: both led by men who emphasised their own ingenuity as solo male protagonists. This confirmed the silence surrounding women's quotidian labour in the detective sphere.

Women only gradually in the course of the nineteenth century stepped out of the darkness that shrouded the 'private enquiry' business with its 'secret watchings', a realm of disclosures that traded on anonymity and confidentiality. If the female detective in Victorian theatre was highly visible, attractive and charismatic, making play of her numerous disguises, her skill in handling words and weapons, the real female private detective was – at least in the early days of the profession – a shadowy figure, whose power lay in obscurity. Positioning herself as a servant, a lodger, a bystander or a companion who happened to be a good listener, her role was typically to observe others and to obtain information about them, while remaining unremarked. The plainer and more insignificant she was, the better she could do her job. One manager of a private enquiry agency noted that he preferred his agents to be: 'small and commonplace looking … quick of hand, foot, eye … a past master in the art of making conversation take certain channels while appearing to talk of other matters'.[5] Deflecting attention, appearing to be a person beneath notice, the female private detective was often, like a mosquito, most effective when she appeared to be doing nothing at all.

This chapter aims to shine a light on the reality of Victorian female private enquiry agents in Britain, the kind of cases they investigated and what we know of women who undertook this work. Twenty named female detectives make an appearance here, though we know much more about some than others. I am particularly interested in the way that private investigations were reported in the press. The ambivalence between excitement, attraction and distaste that accompanied reportage of real female detection reflected lingering uncertainty about whether the profession was 'unwomanly' and might involve coarse knowledge and indecorous acts. While the glamour of theatrical and fictional depictions of female detectives in newspapers increased the public's appetite for real-life stories, it also, I will argue, made readers especially sensitive to the sordid details of cases that failed to resemble the heroics of fiction. I will be examining two cases in detail where the female detective was vilified in the press. However, there was also creative cross-fertilisation between real-life scenarios involving female detectives and fiction. Cases in the papers inspired writers. Some impostors were inspired to pose as female detectives, creating intrigue and confusion. And when middle-class women such as Antonia Moser created public personae for themselves as 'lady detectives' in the later part of the nineteenth century, they drew on self-invention and marketing strategies familiar from theatrical advertisement and fiction, to play a *role* that had become established in the public imagination through a mixture of real-life cases and fictive stories.

The Agency and Private Knowledge

Private enquiry agencies flourished from mid-century; in 1858 they were already reported by one newspaper to be 'thick as blackberries in London and the regions'.[6] They advertised openly in the daily newspapers and, from their advertisements, we can glean a good idea of what their business involved. 'Blackmail', 'libel', 'missing friends' and 'family secrets' were some of the problems they promised to help unravel. They could attempt to solve thefts and deal with threats that clients did not care to make public, to find absconding lovers, family members, employees, or to solve mysteries of parentage and inheritance. They could also make discreet enquiries about prospective romantic partners, business partners and commercial enterprises. Many enquiry agencies were attached to solicitors' offices and others boasted that they had a direct line to banks: if your daughter had become engaged to a charming but bankrupt bounder who already had a wife in Australia, a private enquiry agency was the way to find out before it was too late. Commercial work might involve investigating infringement of patents and trade secrets or watching colleagues who were suspected of fraudulent activity. Some private agencies were also involved in election watching and other political surveillance.

However, as an advertisement in the *Morning Post* unashamedly proclaimed 'DIVORCE, DIVORCE, DIVORCE' was their key line of work.[7] Private detectives could confirm the misgivings of a spouse who suspected their partner of adultery; they could gather evidence of infidelity and present it in court. They also had a strong record of finding men who had abandoned their wives and might have remarried bigamously under a new name; such investigations ended years of uncertainty on the spouse's part about whether she was free to form a new relationship. Before Internet search engines, social media, the credit agency and CCTV, the private enquiry agency offered Victorian men and women the promise of information that was otherwise inaccessible and often had been deliberately withheld from them. It was a source of confidential advice about the kind of worries that strike in the small hours, with some agencies boasting that they were open 'day or night'. Antonia Moser reassured potential clients that her agency was the answer to 'Where to go when in trouble, whether of a legal, social, or private nature'. As a confidante who could find answers and could potentially also hold to account those who were deceiving or distressing the client, the private detective was an agony aunt with a gun. It was a powerful lure.

Many Victorians had reasons to distrust the police: some because they lived precarious lives that would not bear legal scrutiny, others because they disdained to open their doors, exposing family business to members of a social class lower than their own. There were also questions – such as those regarding missing persons – that might or might not be matters for criminal investigation; until the outcome was known, it often seemed best to keep wayward wives and disappearing daughters out of the public eye. The enquiry agency, then, played various possible roles, connecting private, professional and public identities, like a vascular system below the skin of social front.

James Anderson Peddie in his fictional but shrewd *Secrets of a Private Enquiry Office* (1881), claimed that more ladies than men sought detectives' services:

> The wife is generally tied down to her home and children, and only accompanies her husband when it is convenient for him to take her. The husband, on the other hand, is constantly going about, and subject to all kinds of temptations, which, perhaps, he does not always resist. He can leave his home when he likes, and return when it pleases him. There is always some ready excuse at hand.[8]

The confidentiality of the private enquiry agencies and the fact that they offered a way to penetrate the otherwise locked doors of gentlemen's clubs, commercial offices and lodgings in St John's Wood where men kept their mistresses, made them attractive to women. In

20. *James Anderson Peddie,* Secrets of a Private Enquiry Office *(1881).*

February 1881, the detective agency T. K. Walsh advertised in the *Evening Standard* that it had a 'private writing-room for ladies' as well as 'a large staff of experienced detectives, male and female, always ready'.[9] Walsh's advertisement sat suggestively near to the ads for all the London theatres, where 'DIVORCE – SIXTH TIME TONIGHT' was running at the Vaudeville.

Female detectives were a particular boon to the private agency because they could penetrate private and domestic spaces unsuspected, gaining a view of what went on behind closed doors. Female servants were ubiquitous in Victorian society and it was not difficult to place a female detective in the guise of a maid, cook or governess in or near a household where secrets were suspected. Often, however, a female detective's power lay in the simple fact that women were not 'seen' as professionals at all, their inquiries were easily camouflaged in small talk. As Kate Easton, who ran her own successful agency, explained: 'Disguises? Of course, I have many, but one of my best roles is to be myself. As an ordinary caller, as an ordinary guest, the detective very often scores. It is in private, not in public, life that the greatest secrets are revealed.'[10]

Easton gave several examples of the kind of mystery she had been called on to solve. In one case,

a young man of good family had stolen some valuable papers belonging to his mother. I had not the slightest clue to work on, but I finally traced him to a remote country village, thence to London, where I had to face him and lay the facts of the case before him. He returned the papers without prosecution in the end.[11]

One of the great advantages of a private agency was that they could hush up the matters they investigated and ideally produce a resolution of this kind. The London newspapers in May 1897 described a diamond and emerald bracelet, a precious gift stolen at Daly's Theatre from a young woman connected to the Spanish Royal Court. She offered £500 for its safe return through an enquiry agency: an easier proxy than the police for a receiver to contact.[12] Easton regarded herself as especially successful in tracing missing persons. On one occasion a mother contacted her, stating that her only daughter had disappeared and she feared foul play; Easton found and returned the missing girl within twenty-four hours – the daughter and a female friend had gone away with 'two married men, well known in London'. This foolish sexcapade was swiftly stopped.

The real female detective often unearthed stories where the affair was 'an inside job' that might, under other circumstances, have been a case for the newly invented methods of psychotherapy, which also sought answers to private troubles through close examination of family dynamics and sexual life. Real private detectives rarely dealt with murder or bank robberies; but their investigations could still turn ugly, as they exposed hurt and anger in disclosing truths about sex, money, family feuds and domestic violence that lay behind the curtain of social propriety.

Women in the Shadow Market

Women certainly assisted private detective agencies as paid employees in Britain from the 1850s, when the 'boom' in private investigation was triggered by the gelignite of the Divorce Act. As we have seen, as early as 1854, Charles Frederick Field (formerly of Scotland Yard) employed Sarah Grocott to work as a cook and Ann Price to pretend to take an inventory in a Marylebone lodging-house while investigating adultery.[13] As early as 1860, changes in legislation were proposed to tackle the new phenomenon of spouses employing private detectives to procure evidence in divorce cases.[14] But it was in the 1870s that female detectives joined private agencies in large numbers.

The Times for January 1875 printed two advertisements in the 'small ads' section which make it clear that female private detectives were prized in London at this time. The first advertisement, for the

'Confidential Agency' of Leslie and Graham in Holborn, notes that they are assisted by 'men of 20 years' experience, and female detectives'.[15] The second, for confidential agents Arthur Cleveland Montagu and Company in Cornhill, offers 'a large staff of experienced detectives, male and female'. These back-to-back advertisements show that women private detectives had been operating for some time (if they were 'experienced') and that their services added value to the firms that could boast them. It quickly became standard practice for private enquiry agencies to mention that they had female detectives on their staff.[16] In 1881, the *Western Daily Mercury* advertised, in Bristol, a 'Private Inquiry Office for the West of England', stating in capitals:

MALE AND FEMALE DETECTIVES,
Divorce, Libel and all Private Matters carefully investigated.
Elections Watched. Charges Moderate.[17]

Similarly, in Liverpool, an 1888 advertisement in the *Journal of Commerce* announced, alongside offices to let and ships in dock:

PRIVATE ENQUIRIES
MISSING FRIENDS TRACED, Inquiries Made, and Suspected
Persons Watched &c.
Female detectives employed.[18]

The fact that elections were among the possible objects for surveillance and that such advertisements appeared in papers aimed at businessmen suggests how, for Victorian readers, 'private enquiry' could bridge the public and private sphere.

In 1871, the pantomime at the Theatre Royal in Hull opened with a 'private enquiry office in Fairyland, in which are found several police officers, who are described in the play-bill as being anything but efficient, showing that even fairies are as much troubled as poor mortals with stupid policemen'.[19] Presumably the investigators of this bureau included female fairies. The pantomime audience, which included many women and children, must already have been sufficiently familiar with what a private enquiry office was to appreciate the joke.

Enquiry offices were typically situated centrally in cities, in places where a person might walk in casually without drawing undue attention to themselves. In London they clustered around Chancery Lane and the Strand, near the legal firms, the newspaper offices and theatres, all of which could prove relevant to their enquiries. Provincial private enquiry offices often doubled up as other kinds of business, implying that retired police officers could not always make sufficient income from investigating family secrets alone. Some private investigators were also estate agents, accountants or auditors. Henry Haynes (late superintendent of Wiltshire Police) hedged his bets, informing Swindon newspaper readers in June 1870:

> Conducts enquiries in LIBEL, DIVORCE, and other CASES requiring SECRECY, with Despatch, either in London or Country; also on the Continent . . .
>
> N.B. AGENT for NEWTON'S CELEBRATED MANURE, PLASTERERS' HAIR and ASPHALTE ROOFING FELT[20]

When not on the scent of crime, Mr Haynes had celebrated manure to pay his bills. The fact that many private enquiry agencies dealt with other goods and services was likely also an advantage for clients, who had a ready excuse if they did not wish to share the real reason for their visit.

The Women Writter and the Debt Dodger

Private enquiry offices were sometimes part of solicitors' offices that offered services including debt collection.[21] The system of financial credit in Victorian Britain meant that tradesmen typically presented

accounts to middle- and upper-class families for payment at the end
of the month or quarter. If a customer could not cover the invoice, or
disappeared in the meantime, the tradesman was left unpaid. Then,
as now, spouses who were legally separated did not always pay the
maintenance due to their estranged partner. One line of work for
private enquiry agents was tracing defaulters and issuing writs to
individuals who sought to avoid their legal obligations. This formed
a novel area in which female detectives operated.

The *Pall Mall Gazette* in 1889 published a witty article discussing
'Women "Writters" and the Way they Work', inspired by the case of
a 'young lady', Miss Millicent Lucas, employed by Flowerdew & Co.,
confidential enquiry agents and process-servers of Selborne
Chambers, Chancery Lane.[22] The *St James Gazette* for 3 December
1888, which was reporting on a case in the City of London Court
where Millicent Lucas had served the summons, commented that
she 'was found to be very successful as a process-server. We can
readily believe it ... The idea seems capable of infinite extension.
Perhaps even the recalcitrant debtor might be tapped on the shoulder
by a lady tipstaff and locked in his cell by a sweet girl gaoler.'[23] *Funny
Folks*, a comic magazine, imagined the dialogue between Millicent
Lucas and her mark in humorous terms:

MR M. P. CURIOUS (who has hitherto successfully defied his credi-
tors): A – when they told me a charming lady wished to see me I
was – a – charmed. To what do I owe this honour?
LADY BAILIFF (strictly business): Tain't an honner – *it's a writ*.[24]

The woman 'writter', like the woman writer, presented a new way of
holding men to account. Male journalists were alternately troubled
and titillated by the prospect of female honey traps, luring unwary
malefactors to lower their guard. Mr Flowerdew noted that he had
employed three ladies for about a year, whose principal skills were
'nerve, intelligence and presence': 'a well-dressed woman is as a rule

free from suspicion, and consequently has access to so many places and persons which a man would not have. There are repeated instances of that, such as to gentlemen at their clubs & c'.[25] Ingenious methods of serving writs to those who refused to open their door included placing the writ in the milk bottle that they hoisted up to their window in the morning. Mr Flowerdew claimed that his was the first firm to train both sexes in the art of serving a writ.[26]

Additionally, Flowerdew's private enquiry office employed twelve people 'inside' and two dozen 'outside' as detectives, including several women: he emphasised that effective detectives 'are not found but made': it was training that made the private eye successful. It is notable here that the private enquiry office is one branch of a legal firm that offered services such as translation into multiple languages and document copying. Flowerdews were 'Law Accountants and Costs Draftsmen' as well as 'Law Stationers, Printers and Lithographers'. This range of services that an 'agent' might provide suggests how the business of private enquiry often worked hand in glove with the legal profession, despite being itself poorly regulated by the law.

When we picture the private enquiry office as a mysterious enclave up a back stair conducted by a pipe-smoking hobbyist, we are rarely correct. Flowerdew's chambers were in Chancery Lane; Frederick Field's were in the Temple, the hallowed enclave of London's foremost lawyers. Detectives in these environments needed to possess office-based skills. Fictional sleuths rarely engage in accountancy. In 1895, Jewell's private enquiry office in Ipswich advertised for two lady agents and one male one; the ladies did not need to be experienced but all 'must be able to keep books when not otherwise employed'.[27] Mr Flowerdew, who operated on a profit-share basis with his long-term appointees, favoured 'plodding', 'systematic' and plain candidates. This rather prosaic 'Man of Mystery' (as the *Pall Mall Gazette* dubbed him) added that he would be happy to employ a lady of seventy, if a suitable applicant presented herself.

Sex and Shoplifting

Another prosaic but vital area in which female detectives operated was in protecting goods from theft, particularly in large department stores. We tend, now, to discriminate between 'store detectives' and private eyes. In the nineteenth century, however, these were not always separable job descriptions. Florence Alexander, a detective who worked for Aylmer's agency at 319 Strand, was hired in 1890 on a freelance basis by Crisp and Co., a general drapers in Seven Sisters Road, to patrol its Christmas sale. She apprehended a shoplifter, Sarah Watt (aged thirty-four), after following her for an hour. Watt, 'a married woman', had stolen 'a lady's jersey, four lengths of fur trimmings, nine flowers, two birds, and a pair of children's shoes' and secreted them in a canvas bag within her 'dress-improver' or bustle.[28] Annie Betts, who had a long career as a detective, performing various kinds of agency work, was similarly hired to pose as a sale customer by John Barker of Kensington and caught a female machinist, Hannah Kelly (sixty-eight), stealing silk.

It is important to recognise that, while the female detective in the theatre and in literature is almost always a defender and exemplar of her sex, who roots out predominantly male villainy, the real Victorian female detective was frequently employed in cases that targeted and exposed female offenders. Whether she was listening at a bedroom door for evidence of adultery or pursuing a female shoplifter, the private detective was just as likely to be a traitor to the sisterhood as an ally.

In the 1887 divorce suit of Francis William Robins against his wife, Mary Agnes Robins, a female detective, Mrs Bartley, testified that she had shown photographs of Mary Agnes Robins and her putative lover, Charles Cochrane, to waiters at the Star and Garter Hotel in Richmond and at the Clifton Downs Hotel. The waiter identified the couple as having taken a room for three hours together: evidence pointing to Mary Agnes's adultery.[29] She, in turn, claimed that her husband was guilty of cruelty and adultery. He had struck her on the wrist with his belt and with a poker: she had bruises and a black eye.

He frequently spat at her. He was 'also in the habit of mistaking the servants' beds for his own'. He had certainly been conducting an affair with his children's French governess, Camille Bernier.

This case, like many others where the wife was obliged to produce a higher and more comprehensive form of evidence than the husband – because women could not gain a divorce on the grounds of adultery alone but had additionally to prove cruelty or desertion – served to underline the sexual double standard for late Victorian newspaper readers. It did not matter whether the husband had been the first to stray, or to make the marital home emotionally and physically unsafe. If the woman could be proven to have slept with a rival, the male appellant was likely to win. While female detectives in the theatre and in fiction might help women to escape from predatory and abusive men, real female detectives often abetted men within a legal system that discriminated against women.

This was not always true, however. In the divorce suit of *Drummond v Drummond* (1893), the female detective, Mrs Haddy, was employed on Mrs Drummond's side and testified to her husband's adultery with Clara Watts, a sex worker who had accompanied him to a flat in Great Russell Street. Reportage of divorce cases often offered clues to the kinds of evidence that were admitted in court, the standard of proof required of men (for adultery) and women (for cruelty), witness statements, methods of gathering evidence and the kinds of costs that might be sought by aggrieved parties. In short, they offered a hand-book for would-be divorcees. Moralists, including Queen Victoria, worried about the tendency of newspaper reportage of divorce to increase the break-up of families. It is no wonder that some readers progressed from reading the accounts of decrees nisi to perusing the columns of advertisements, often within the same newspaper, in which private enquiry agents featured so prominently, with a view to beginning their own divorce proceedings. In this sense, the female detective, however problematic her role in the divorce suits of individual women, was a harbinger of change for women in general.

On the Origins of Sleuths

The backgrounds of Victorian female detectives varied considerably. Some patterns, however, can be deduced from the available evidence. In the Victorian age, your family's profession was a strong determinant of the work you were likely to do. We shouldn't be surprised, then, that a significant number of female private detectives were related to police officers and/or to male private enquiry agents. They thus had access to professional knowledge and contacts when they were learning the business of shadowing, searching, interviewing and giving evidence in court. This was, as we have seen, true of Emily Oxley. Born in 1850 in Godalming, she was the daughter of Eliza and John Hackman, a brick-maker's labourer, who signed her birth certificate with an X, meaning that he was illiterate. Emily, aged twenty, was a dressmaker. A year later, she married William Oxley, a soldier in barracks at Aldershot. William moved from the army to the Cardiff police force, where he rose to the rank of detective-sergeant but suffered poor health and retired, aged only forty-one, in 1894 on the advice of a police medical officer: the newspapers remarked that Oxley had served for twelve years as a fireman and plain-clothes policemen in the neighbourhood of Bute Street, Cardiff, one of the roughest areas of the city. They implied that police work had broken his health. Emily, then, played an important role in pursuing the private enquiry business that they ran from 1895 onwards: she was working as a detective from 1891 until at least 1903. She occasionally worked with her sister, Mary Ann Green (a domestic servant before her marriage), who also lived in Cardiff: they watched the premises of suspected adulterers together and successfully prosecuted a dentist who was practising without a licence. Emily Oxley had no surviving children of her own. She and her husband adopted two daughters late in life.[30] Perhaps the fact that, during her childbearing years, she did not have as many childcare responsibilities as some Victorian women allowed Mrs Oxley to devote more time to detection that involved travel and overnight watching.

Further examples of female agents who were related in some way to policemen or private enquiry agents were Patience Lawrence, Antonia Moser, 'Clara Layt', Mrs Bartley and Caroline Smith. Caroline Smith's case is of particular interest because in 1880 she petitioned a magistrate to serve an order against her dead-beat police constable husband, William Smith. Caroline Smith was born Caroline Greenwood, the daughter of a bootmaker in Sydenham, Kent. Aged eighteen in 1866, she married William Smith (who, at twenty-two, was already a police constable) in Lewisham, just two months before their first child was born: a shotgun marriage that presaged a rocky relationship. By the time of the 1871 census, the couple were living in Milton Street, Marylebone and had a four-year-old daughter (Caroline), a two-year-old son (William) and a baby (Sydney), who was nine months old. Caroline, at this time, reported her occupation as 'machinist': probably she worked in the garment industry, stitching some of the parts that went to make up the expanding industrial market in mass-produced clothes. By 1881 Caroline was a single mother with five children (the eldest, was now fourteen and Bernard, the youngest, was seven), living on the Holloway Road and listing her occupation as 'Private Enquiry Agent'. As the *Northampton Mercury* reported under the headline 'A Female Detective' in June 1880, two years before the Married Women's Property Act that enshrined women's right to keep their own property and earnings after marriage:

At the Clerkenwell Police Court, London, on Saturday, Mrs Caroline Smith applied to the magistrate for a protection order for her goods and earnings against her husband, who had twice deserted her and her family. She stated that she gained her livelihood by making private enquiries for solicitors. The order was granted.[31]

Mrs Smith's petition grants us a less rarefied view of female detection than fictional accounts of lady sleuths. She is picking up piecework, not so very different from that in the garment business, which can likely be fitted in around the demanding day of a single parent. Her 1881 census return records no servant, parent or sibling assisting in her household. Doubtless her teenage daughter looked after the four younger children. This determined, working-class woman – one of the thousands who had moved from a family background of rural labour to the heart of London – was single-handedly supporting a family of six by trying to find answers to clients' questions. Probably some of them concerned similar domestic desertions and family break-ups to the one she had suffered.

Some female detectives were actresses. Used to one-off 'engagements' where they were required to play a part, actors possessed skills in impersonation and were accustomed to late hours, city streets and mixed company. It is little wonder, then, that they were valuable to private enquiry agencies who desired flexible working and women who could assume any character. This was true of Kate Easton, a London actress and singer who set up her own agency in Holborn. It was also the case with Margaret Cooke, Matilda Mitchell and Dorothy Tempest. Tempest, born in Dublin, combined her acting work with detective work, which included serving writs for solicitors. As Nell Darby notes, Tempest

> was working regularly on the provincial theatre circuit from 1895 to at least 1900, and again from 1905 to 1910, with mention of her as a private detective in the press primarily in 1903 and 1904 ... The pattern of press mentions clearly indicates that when theatrical jobs were not forthcoming, Dorothy worked as a private detective.[32]

These different professional lives, operating on what we might now call a 'zero hours contract basis', could stop up each other's financial gaps. This did not, however, prevent them from touching and inflecting one another, sometimes casting doubt on the moral difference between

21. *Court sketch of Dorothy Tempest*, Penny Illustrated Paper *(1904)*.

licensed and unlicensed deception. In one newspaper article, Dorothy Tempest is advertised as a performer in a pantomime of *Robinson Crusoe* at Eastbourne, playing Coraline in an under-the-water fantasy scene.[33] In another, as 'a lady detective', she appears in Regent Street, in a sting operation taking down a stage magician and his wife, 'Keiro' and 'Madame Keiro', who were practising a different kind of theatrical illusion: palmistry and clairvoyance.[34] As we have seen in Chapter 1, fortune-tellers were commonly arrested using female detectives in Victorian Britain. One wonders if Dorothy Tempest felt any compunction about assisting in the prosecution of fellow performers in the entertainment industry. When L. T. Meade created the fictional female sleuth Diana Marburg, who is both a palmist with clairvoyant powers *and* a professional detective, she trod a fine line between depicting a woman who served the law and one who, technically, was breaking it.

Some female detectives were women whose fathers had died when the family was still young and who had therefore had a strong motive to find flexible, discreet work. Annie Betts, who sometimes assisted Dorothy Tempest, fell into this category. Others were separated single mothers, such as Caroline Smith, or widows, such as Beatrice Craven and Emma Taylor, a farmworker's daughter who married a ship's carpenter and emigrated to America.[35] Importantly, until the last decades of the century, the majority of women involved in detective work were working class. Like barmaids, hotel staff and temping servants (all of which jobs some Victorian female detectives performed alongside or following their detective roles), they worked potentially long hours on a casual basis, in sometimes unsavoury circumstances, for a fee. This contrasts markedly with the image of the female detective in fiction, which tends to present female detectives as middle-class women who are not mothers and who have taken up the profession improvisationally, perhaps initially out of financial pressure but with increasing excitement and sense of power. These fictional female sleuths undertake cases of significant moral importance that offer intellectual challenges and rewards; developing their expertise and personae, they are in much greater control of their cases and their working lives.

In the last two decades of the nineteenth century, when middle-class women began entering the workforce in larger numbers and pressing for entry to hitherto male-dominated professions, the rhetoric around detection as a possible job option for middle-class, even university-educated, women became more positive. In 1888, the *Hampshire Telegraph* reported that £200 per year was the salary offered by one private detective agency to its best operatives.[36] *The Queen*, in the same month, cited a recent report by Captain Monro, Her Majesty's Inspector for Constabulary for Scotland, tentatively recommending official employment of women as police detectives and noted that approaching '£400 per year in some instances' or £80 per month were inducements paid to female detectives by some private agencies.[37] The *Cheltenham Examiner* in 1890 suggested that 'some ladies can earn as much as £500 a year at it' and noted that one proponent of this 'remunerative if not congenial' *craft* was 'a student of Newnham College, where she achieved high distinction'.[38] Although the financial rewards were likely exaggerated, these figures dwarfed the kind of salary available to governesses or female clerks.

Hearth and Home, a women's magazine, which – despite its domestic title – ran a regular column on professional career options for women, anxiously entitled 'What to do with our Daughters', noted in June 1892 that detection might present a valuable employment opportunity, however distasteful:

> This is not an occupation that many ladies would like, but apparently there are some who think differently. We have heard of one, a University graduate, who engages in it simply because it has an irresistible fascination for her. It is impossible to give 'Judex' any useful information with regard to the pay, it varies so much, and depends upon so many different conditions. If employed by 'the case,' the detective might get a guinea a day and all expenses, but if this seems high, it must not be forgotten that 'cases' may be 'few and far between.'[39]

Hearth and Home admonished 'Judex' for failing to supply her name and address: an omission that suggests the enquirer was embarrassed. Between the 'irresistible fascination' of detection – in fiction, in theory – and the sordid reality of work for a private enquiry agent lay a perilous strait that newspapers tried to bridge for middle-class readers. *Tit Bits* in 1890 published a breathless piece in which a lady detective at Moser's agency boasted of her fashionable wardrobe, high pay and European travels, noting that her interest in detection had begun at boarding school, when she and other girls solved cases they had taken from the novels of Gaboriau. The *Sketch* in 1894 reported an 'interview' with an attractive lady detective of twenty-seven, who explained:

> My father was a Scotchman, and that most wretched of men, a poor army officer. At his death there was nothing for me, so far as my relatives could see, but to become governess or a companion. The idea of such dependence was hateful to me, and so were the two or three situations I filled before my mind travelled else-where. I had always been particularly fond of detective stories, like a good many other young people whose own life is uneventful, and while I was in the position of companion to an old lady I unearthed a plot against her ... That gave me an idea of escape from bondage. I applied at a certain detective agency and was soon given a trial.[40]

It is intriguing that, by the 1890s, detective fiction was being posited as the inspiration for women's real-life detective careers. The idea that there were female Cambridge graduates who bravely solved mysteries while enjoying European travel was an appealing fantasy for newspaper readers. In Grant Allen's *Miss Cayley's Adventures* (1899), Lois Cayley is just such a Girton graduate, the fearless daughter of a deceased captain in the 42nd Highlanders, who – like the supposed interviewee in the *Sketch* – falls into detective work through becoming companion to an old lady. It seems likely that Allen had read the *Sketch* and turned it into a full-length portrait. Dora Myrl, the fictional detective protagonist who made her debut in *Pearson's Magazine* in 1899, is also a Cambridge graduate and an orphan who makes her way from lady's companion to professional sleuth.

In truth, however, the lives of female detectives were more likely to be working class, more precarious, more humdrum, more morally ambiguous and less financially secure. There is a fascinating tension between the ideal of the female detective as a highly educated, middle-class trailblazer in charge of choosing and managing her own caseload and the reality of casual or semi-casual agency work. Detection in fiction is a metier or vocation rather than piecework. The detective heroine often has a strong, altruistic family motive for undertaking her quest, whether it is to exculpate a falsely accused lover (Annie Cory, Lois Cayley), convict those who have injured a parent or friend (Anne Rodway, Eleanor Vane) or support a disabled husband (Dorcas Dene). Her emotional zeal and intellectual curiosity can thus be honourably aligned. She accepts a quest, whose end is chiefly to serve truth and justice. The real Victorian female detective pursued information that was often unwelcome, under conditions that were often unpleasant, for rewards that sometimes scarcely justified the risks and effort involved in the pursuit.

In fiction, the 'case' is like a tangled and knotted ball of wool that must be resolved into a thread with a beginning and an end. The 'clue', which originally meant a physical thread that could be followed to the centre of a maze, leads the detective protagonist to dead ends and twists, but eventually unravels to disclose the goal of discovery. This linear model, which tends to assume a discoverable malefactor and a singular crime, deliberately simplifies the web of social behaviour and power dynamics that produce dispossession and violence. In looking at real cases, we are confronted by different models for understanding the detective gaze, why it is deployed and whom it serves.

These difficult, messy and painful cases can tell us more about the domestic realities of Victorian class, race, gender and violence than more successful cases nimbly 'solved' by a dispassionate sleuth. I will look at two cases in detail where the female detective publicly 'failed', in order to consider the emotional cost and moral ambiguity of detection and the ways in which women, on both sides of the court-room, often paid the price in a case where the principal actors were men.

Clara Layt and the Mystery of the Leery Laird

The case of 'Clara Layt', who was tasked in 1897 with attending the home of William Hamilton Broun and his wife in Haddington, Scotland to investigate a suspected 'snake in the grass' in their domestic life, nicely illustrates many of the difficulties – moral and practical – that attended the work of the real Victorian female detective.[41] This unusual case shows how legal firms and private enquiry agencies often worked closely together, yet detectives might still operate on highly problematic and contested legal ground. It is also remarkable because we can deduce an unusually full amount of information both about the client and about the detectives: we possess unique evidence about the case in Clara's handwriting, in her witness statements and in the words of her employers.

Clara was employed by the firm of Steggles and Darling, who ran their agency out of 22 Henrietta Street, Covent Garden, from an elegant building that still stands, a stone's throw from the bustling attractions of the Victorian fruit and flower market. Richard Steggles had been a superintendent in the Metropolitan Police from 1867 to 1893 and so had a wealth of experience in criminal cases when he took the well-established step of founding his own private detective business on his retirement from official duties. Alfred J. J. Darling had also been a chief-inspector in the Metropolitan Police. They knew each other from the Met's musical band in which both were players.[42] They reported that Clara Layt, aged twenty-five in 1897, had been a private enquiry agent for four or five years. She was an experienced detective; during her employment with Steggles and Darling she had already completed 'many detective duties' in 'hotels and private places' and was a trusted employee. Unfortunately, this case was going to go badly wrong; and that is the only reason we know anything about it.

In April 1897, Clara found herself on a train to Haddington in East Lothian, a small but historically significant and prosperous Scottish market town. The brief was this. Clara was to go to Colstoun House and pose as a linen maid: a servant to William Hamilton Broun and his wife Lady Susan, who were leading members of the local gentry. While in post, she was to listen out for poisonous gossip about the couple and to interview, as if by chance encounter, key figures among the domestic servants, local tradespeople and other inhabitants that her employers might indicate.

It was, from the first, difficult to pinpoint what the crime (committed, suspected or anticipated) might be. But the atmosphere at Colstoun was certainly tense. The Hamilton Brouns couldn't get servants to stay in post: there was a high turnover of domestic staff. There were broken eggs in the chicken house; two ponies had been injured and one had subsequently died; rat traps appeared to have been deliberately sprung. Horses had been moved from one field to another overnight. This menacing behaviour, William Hamilton Broun thought, must involve malicious report that someone was spreading. He worried that the local post office was tampering with his letters; that the employment agency he used in Edinburgh had been got at, such that improper persons were being foisted upon him as servants. He feared that the person ultimately responsible for all these problems might be his wife's former husband, the Earl of Connemara, whom she had divorced in 1890. On a visit to London, Broun consulted with his solicitors, Gedge and Kirby; they recommended a private enquiry agency, Steggles and Darling, with whom they had worked in the past.

Clara Layt arrived on 7 April 1897 and worked at Colstoun House until 13 May, except for a four-day absence, when she sought permission to return to London for family reasons. Richard Steggles deposed that this was an unusually long engagement for a private detective: cases were more usually closed within a week or a fort-night. Clara was obliged to perform the arduous duties associated with being a servant. She reported that, while posing as a linen maid, she worked from 8 a.m. to 9 p.m. each day, mending stair carpets, table-linen and bed-linen, while also casually approaching fellow-servants, tradesmen and townspeople, asking them about the Brouns and the household at Colstoun with a view to gathering information about how her employers were perceived and where their detractors might lie. Clara met with Lady Susan Ramsay to receive instruction every morning and with William Hamilton Broun every evening to give an account (which he wrote down) of what she had gleaned. Additionally, Clara sometimes walked the 2½ miles from Colstoun into Haddington to interview people specified by Hamilton Broun, including the local barber and solicitor, and stayed up until 3 a.m. to gauge, at her employer's request, whether anyone was prowling around Colstoun by night (in fact the only person doing so was Hamilton Broun himself). As Clara later testified in court, she had little spare time to report back to Steggles and Darling in London.

Colstoun House dates from the fifteenth century; it has a claim to be the oldest house in Scotland to have been lived in continuously by the same family. A plain but imposing fortified structure, it was surrounded by 2,000 acres of farmland, market gardens and forest. The Brouns were very conscious of their place in Scottish history: their ancestor Sir David Le Brun had been present at the laying of the foundation stone of Holyrood Abbey alongside David I in 1128. Colstoun was famous for its ancient pear tree, said to have been gifted by the magician Hugo de Gifford of Yester, who prophesied that the pear would confer unfailing prosperity on the family who possessed it. Pears, accordingly, decorated many of the rooms at Colstoun. The need to remain prosperous, to fulfil the pear's enchanted legacy, must have exerted a certain pressure on a family worried that their neighbours laughed about them and their servants disliked them. By Clara Layt's account, the house in 1897 was dirty

22. Postcard of Colstoun House, Haddington (1915).

and infested with rats. She boarded for three nights in the room of the lady's maid, Kate McIntosh, but could not sleep for the smell. She had also tried sleeping with Margaret Mitchell, the kitchen maid, but then transferred to a room by herself. The state of disrepair in the house seems to have arisen from the fact that Lady Susan inherited the title without inheriting sufficient money for the property's upkeep. Indeed, problems of marriage, divorce and inheritance lay behind most of the couple's social ills.

William Hamilton Broun (born William Hamilton Briggs), who in 1897 was forty-three, had been a medical officer in the army in India. He had married, in 1894, a woman seventeen years older than him and far above him in rank. Lady Susan Georgiana Ramsay was the eldest daughter and heir of the Marquess of Dalhousie; she was sixty and had divorced her first husband, Lord Connemara. Briggs took Lady Susan's family name rather than the other way round. This unusual step was, in itself, a source of malicious gossip. Lady Susan had inherited Colstoun because of the lack of a male heir in the Broun family tree (which descended from her mother). Colstoun contained Indian treasures, including swords, scimitars and daggers 'of exquisite workmanship and studded with diamonds, rubies, emeralds and other gems' acquired by the Marquess of Dalhousie as spoils when he was commander-in-chief of India and had brought the Koh-i-Noor diamond to Britain.[43] Yet the fabric of the property was in decline and the house had an air of decay; Lady Susan had no children.

Lady Susan's first marriage, to Robert Bourke, Lord Connemara – an earl's son and Anglo-Irish MP – had been an unmitigated disaster. During their divorce proceedings in 1890, she had accused him of cruelty and of multiple counts of adultery over fifteen years, including sleeping with her maid, Hannah Moore. Unusually, and scandalously, Lady Susan had explicitly accused her husband of 'knowingly and wilfully communicating to her a venereal disease'.[44] This history would prove sadly relevant to the toxic situation Clara Layt found herself addressing when she arrived to work as a detective at Colstoun.

Clara's letters to Steggles and Darling are preserved among other evidence in the case, in the National Registry Office of Scotland. They are tiny, pencilled notes: 11.5 by 9 centimetres, with wax seals no bigger than a child's fingernail. In them, Clara makes it clear that the servants and tradesmen knew something of Lady Susan's past history, but that they tended to assume she was the guilty party in her divorce. The first letter reads:

Dear Sirs
I arrived here quite safe last Monday.
There are two new servants only here a week. They tell me this place bear [sic]
A very bad name & that no one stay [sic] because it is so dirty which I find quite true.
They also know that Mr Brown is the second husband of Lady Susan. They say he had to change his name from Briggs to Brown.

I saw Lady Susan this morning and told her what I had heard so far. Yours obediently, C. Layt[45]

Clara's second letter is more expansive, supplying interview notes from conversations with various locals:

Postman said
Lady Susan carried on with soldiers when abroad who were under her husband that was why he got a Divorce. when her first husband was here there was plenty of money, but Lady susan is very poor now. and everyone in haddington gave her a bad name. the servants don't like Mr B – because he is very mean & wear silent boots to watch them that is the reason they leave.

Station in Haddington
Name Cowan
Said Mrs B married below her rank. not any of her friends go to see her. The Queen had recognised her husband but not Lady S.

Kitchenmaid
Told me Lady Susan had been divorced two or three times for carrying on with men. And her children would not live with her. I asked who told her she said it was in the papers.

Head gardener
said he was leaving because Mrs B would not give him <u>coals</u> & he is afraid things would go wrong.
he told me his mother told him what the place was before he came. Also someone in Haddington stoped [sic] him & said Coalstoun had a bad name. could not tell me who. Was a stranger.

These notes show that Clara Layt was literate and wrote a good hand, but that her grammar and spelling were patchy (perhaps

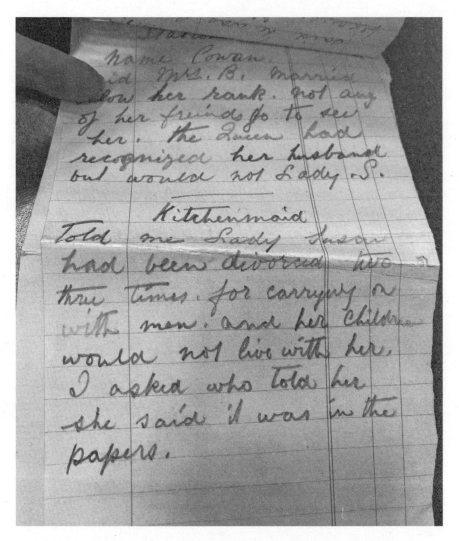

name Cowan.
...d Mrs. B. married
...low her rank. not any
of her friends to to see
her. the Queen had
recognized her husband
but would not Lady ~S.

Kitchenmaid

Told me Lady Susan
had been divorced two ~
three times. for carrying on
with men. and her children
would not live with her.
I asked who told her
she said it was in the
papers.

23. Clara Layt's letter to Steggles and Darling (19 April 1897).

aggravated by tiredness). The gossip she reports is credible, as it
pertains to matters that Clara herself would be unlikely to have
known before her arrival. It is intriguing that even the kitchen maid
claims to have read about her employer in the newspaper and judges
her poorly. There was clearly a range of complaints and anxieties
surrounding the Colstoun family, who were not keeping up their

position in a manner that local employees and tradespeople would respect. The rumours about Lady Susan's sexual indiscretions seem unwarranted. But the grievances concerning dirt and the family's financial straits are consistent. Clara interviewed the local solicitor, who told her he had processed claims for pay from servants who had been dismissed without receiving the salary due to them. Archival papers suggest that the family were also being pursued locally for allowing the water supply to become contaminated.[46] The servants' objections to William Hamilton Broun's 'silent boots' are entirely borne out by the suspicious habit of spying on his staff that his own testimony reveals. One of her employer's messages to Clara stresses that she should '<u>burn</u> after reading' (underlined three times): an instruction she chose professionally to ignore.

At first, Hamilton Broun seemed delighted by the evidence Clara was gathering, describing her as 'the wonder of the age'. After a couple of weeks, however, his pervasive mistrust extended to Steggles and Darling and he began to wonder if Clara was manufacturing the kind of poisonous gossip he feared was circulating. Steggles and Darling, sensing Hamilton Broun's volatility, dispatched two further operatives to pose as servants while investigating: one of them, Leonard Jolly Death (or D'eath), was the son of another leading detective, who conducted his own London agency. It is notable that the third detective, Ernest Hamilton, was dismissed after a few days because he did not play the part of gardener sufficiently well to be credible. Victorian detectives had to know how to act as servants, in a twenty-four-hour play that might extend for weeks.

After a month of investigation, which had produced no definite evidence that there was indeed a 'snake in the grass' who was disturbing the domestic peace on his estate, a dissatisfied William Hamilton Broun refused to pay the £71, 4 shillings and a halfpenny that Steggles and Darling charged for their services. Broun objected that since the detectives had discovered nothing untoward, they had not been successful. Steggles and Darling promptly sued for recovery of their lost fee, on the grounds that the work had been completed whether a culprit had been found or not. Several Scottish newspapers reported on this case, which promised the spectacle of anxious aristocrats and bumbling sleuths.

Clara deposed at her trial before Lord Kincairney that she had done as she was instructed. She had made discreet enquiries and heard some rumours, but the evidence was too vague to point to a specific slanderer. The servants called up as witnesses in the Court of Session, such as Thomas Aitken, under-gardener, claimed that, if they had chatted with Clara Layt, it had been about a moorhen's nest in the grounds rather than scandal. A table maid, Elizabeth MacNeil, denied that she had said that her master was ill-tempered and often 'boozy' after dinner. Who was telling the truth?

Lord Kincairney, passing judgment, was forced to acknowledge that the case presented considerable difficulties in determining what constituted the contracted work and whether it was properly supervised and executed. He decided that Steggles and Darling should be awarded £50 of their fee and half the taxable expenses. But he dismissed Clara Layt's evidence, stating that it was 'coarse to the point of brutality' and adding that he was obliged to decide either that all her interlocutors were lying or that she was. He chose to disbelieve her. When one examines the court transcript, there is nothing at all coarse in Clara's language: her statements merely repeat the interviews conveyed in her letters. Presumably, it was the allusion to 'a very bad disease' and to Lady Susan's sexual behaviour prior to marriage to which Lord Kincairney objected. The newspapers duly recorded that Clara Layt had only partially fulfilled her duty: she had performed some aspects of the job, but her reports were deemed to be fabricated. The male detectives were judged to have fulfilled their duties. The *Musselburgh News*, a local rag, savoured the resemblance between this case and a novel: 'Steggles and Darling may sound very like some of the firms to be met with in Dickens, but it isn't one of those ... Another detective, who was also employed on the job was called Leonard Jolly Death, which looks like more Dickens.'[47] Trading on the real 'female detective' in their headlines, newspapers nonetheless enjoyed the sense in which the whole case seemed like fiction.

Clara Layt, of course, may have concocted or embellished her reports. However, it seems more plausible that the servants and tradesmen, who would likely continue to live and work in or near Colstoun, decided to deny what they had told her in order to manage their future careers. It is striking that both the female detective, Clara Layt, and the female employer, Lady Susan, were the parties chiefly exposed to public criticism and derision in a case where the primary actors (Hamilton Broun and Lord Connemara) were men and the factors that had led to scandal, social isolation and financial embarrassment stemmed from female inequality and the sexual double standard.

In fact, neither client nor detective was being wholly open about their history. 'Clara Layt' was actually Clara Jolly Death, a married woman with two young children living in Fulham, the wife of Leonard Jolly Death, an experienced private enquiry agent. She was presumably hired out as a single woman for reasons of propriety. This concealment of the female detective's true identity was one to which the whole firm of Steggles and Darling was party.

For his part, William Hamilton Broun was not being wholly honest about the misery that had led him, in a fit of what can only be described as paranoia, to bring a guinea-a-day detective into a crumbling household to listen at its draughty keyholes and document its unhappy retainers. It seems highly likely that Lady Susan was suffering from syphilis, which had been communicated to her by Lord Connemara. If his adultery was prolonged and she was willing to make a public statement about venereal disease in the divorce court, it implies that the matter was grave. I am struck by her maid's remark that one 'could see from Lady Susan's face that she was not a virtuous woman'; if her nose was being eaten away, as happened to many tertiary syphilitic patients, this would have been visible and obvious to her servants. The contemporary treatment for syphilis and for Bright's disease (the reported cause of Lady Susan's death) was very similar; in marrying the much-younger Briggs, the doctor who had advised her in India, Lady Susan may have been motivated less by love and more by ensuring that her treatment would be kept quiet. Were Broun also suffering from syphilis, his paranoid delusions and sudden mood swings would be more explicable. If this were the case, his suspicion that Lord Connemara had infiltrated the couple's life in Haddington and poisoned it was figuratively true. Whether Hamilton Broun had syphilis or not, he was not fully master of Colstoun. When Lady Susan died, the property would pass to her male relatives. His high-handed, angry behaviour towards critics (real and imagined) strikes the modern reader as an anxious, defensive response to a situation where he felt others were threatening and undermining him. In a sad twist to the tale, Lady Susan died intestate, aged sixty, during the court case, eight months after Clara Layt's departure from Colstoun. It seems likely that her husband's enquiry and its publicly humiliating aftermath exacerbated her illness. She was never able to testify in court.

The case is important in showing the miseries of the Victorian class system from both sides: Hamilton Broun was both afraid of what Jane Austen called the 'neighbourhood of voluntary spies' constituted by domestic servants and local people and so desperately wanted to know how they viewed him that he hired his own detective to find out. The case also documents the potential oddity, intimacy and physical hardship of real detective work for women in the nineteenth century, who might find themselves sharing a bed, in verminous accommodation that stank, with servants accused of slander. Rather than exposing a clear villain – a murderer, thief, impostor or blackmailer – the detective often brought to light murky, complex and intractable family issues where there were victims but no single malefactor to bring to justice. Rather than being viewed as a heroine, the real female detective might easily find herself accused of being a charlatan or a conspirator in the psychodrama she investigated.

The Dark Side of Detection

The legal parameters surrounding private detection in the Victorian period were complex and, to a large extent, uncharted. As early as 1860, a judge criticised a divorce case where

> the petitioner had unfortunately followed the example which had been lately set of employing persons calling themselves 'detectives', in order to detect or pretend to detect the guilt of his wife ... it appeared that [the detective he consulted] had suggested to the petitioner the gross iniquity of 'putting someone upon' the respondent ... of introducing some one to her for the purpose of debauching her.[48]

Many agencies sailed close to the wind. The firm of Steggles and Darling, which employed Clara Layt in Haddington, was in 1897 involved in 'A Singular Divorce Case'.[49] The petitioner for divorce, Reginald Stanley Lee, a commercial traveller, pleaded that he had suddenly became aware that his wife was living with another man. The defence argued that Lee had been perfectly aware of this irregular arrangement and had benefited from the money and jewellery his wife's new lover provided. In court, a contract was produced that Lee had signed with Steggles and Darling (the firm *hired by his wife*) to pay them £25 in the event of his winning the divorce case. He had been guilty of collusion. His divorce petition was dismissed. Although they were not charged with any offence, Steggles and Darling had been playing both sides of the divorcing couple, suppressing evidence, trying to influence the outcome of a trial and benefit financially from swinging the case in favour of the male appellant.[50]

In 1884, a private enquiry agent was sentenced to seven years' imprisonment for perjury that had resulted in 'seventy or eighty' licensed premises in Poole receiving a summons for illegal supply of alcohol.[51] Female detectives were apt to be disbelieved in court on the grounds that they lied professionally. Even the highly respectable Emily Oxley, whose professional record was impeccable, was jeered at by a magistrate in 1900 for having assumed the pseudonymous identity of 'Mrs Captain Jones' in order to pose as a lodger and gather evidence in the Hellings adultery case: 'Is lying or misdirection justifiable?' he asked.[52] The lawyers debated whether one should ever admit evidence in court provided by detectives paid by one party in a dispute: they were not reliable witnesses. Where did allowable professional fiction end and criminal misdirection begin? Certainly, women – whether as detectives, as clients or as suspects – were liable to be caught in the moral crossfire of a largely unregulated, but burgeoning profession.

An American journalist in 1878 wrote that 'the divorce detective of the present day is generally a woman'. He added that:

> The majority of divorce detectives are as unscrupulous as they are clever. They hesitate at nothing to procure the necessary evidence against or for the party. They will manufacture it rather than miss it, and incite to the very crime which they were paid to detect. Of course they are not faithful to their trust. How can a woman who would undertake such a role as this be faithful to anything or anybody save her own interest? A smart, No.1, female detective who recently figured in a famous divorce case, acted both for the man and his wife. To the husband she reported the peccadilloes of his wife, to the lady she narrated the iniquities of the husband.[53]

We do not know the name of this correspondent or how authoritative his sources: he claimed to have spoken with John S. Young, the head of the detective police in New York. However, several troubling cases from the late nineteenth century corroborate the notion that female detectives were working for private agencies gathering evidence to incriminate respondents in divorce suits, that husband and wife might well be employing rival agents to investigate one another, and that the detectives' methods were sometimes unscrupulous. This was certainly the case with 'Ellen Lyon', a detective in the divorce case of Gertrude Alexandra Barrett, which unfolded in 1892.

Ellen Lyon and the Case of the Injured Bird

Gertrude Bird's story would not be out of place in a sensation novel. She was born in 1872 at Agra in India to Daniel Henry and Sarah Augusta Bird. Her father worked for the government telegraph department and her mother was only fifteen at the time of the marriage. Gertrude was mixed-race: contemporary newspapers described her as being of 'creole' appearance. Orphaned young, she worked as a lady's companion, drifting across the colonial marketplace, like a feather that had lost touch with the wings that kept it airborne. She became engaged, while in India, to John Edward Barrett, a member of the Indian civil service, and married him in London in the summer of 1891. Gertrude was nineteen; her husband was thirty-five. The marriage was almost immediately a failure. After five weeks, Gertrude left her husband, running away to Paris. By her account, she returned and reluctantly tried to live with him. But in February of 1892, Barrett proposed that his sister should come to live with them in India and, when Gertrude demurred, he struck her repeatedly in the face. This act of violence led her to leave him for good. She later said that he had threatened to poison her.

Gertrude didn't have a plan. Women in her situation – not single, yet no longer living as wives, and untrained to earn their own living – were not recognised in Victorian society. She had lived most of her life in India and had no friends in London and little money. She cut a youthful, forlorn, lonely and inexperienced figure in the itinerant world of London lodging houses. While she was in a boarding house in Foxton Road, Earl's Court, she was approached by the lady apparently living in the room opposite hers, who called herself Countess Carina (*carina* means 'nice' in Italian). This lady befriended Gertrude for a couple of days and unsuspecting Gertrude gave the countess the new address to which she was moving: 166 Earl's Court Road.

While at this new address, Gertrude was again approached by a fellow boarder; this lady called herself Mrs Watson. Gertrude later testified:

> she said that her husband was an electrical engineer, and was away a great deal, and she had a lonely life, having no children, and was seeking for a young companion—she told me all her troubles, and I told her mine, and she asked if I would be her companion—I had no means of living then except the prospect of getting alimony, but I afterwards got an order for £44 a year pending the suit—I told her I would think over the matter; I finally accepted it next day.[54]

Mrs Watson was, in reality, Ellen Lyon – a female detective working for the firm of H. J. Clarke. She had been appointed to watch Gertrude Barrett and, if possible, to obtain evidence of the runaway wife's misconduct that would enable her husband to divorce her without fault or alimony. Cleverly and cruelly, 'Mrs Watson' was offering Gertrude the two things she desperately needed: a shoulder to cry on and a respectable source of income to tide her over until her divorce was finalised. No wonder Gertrude accepted. In fact, however, she was being played.

When they went walking in the streets around Victoria Station, Gertrude 'happened' to spot her husband and pointed him out to Mrs Watson. (Doubtless the encounter had been pre-arranged with John Edward Barrett so that he could see that his wife was being watched as he had mandated.) While Gertrude ducked into a stationers' shop to avoid being seen, 'Mrs Watson' volunteered to tail

Gertrude's husband and see where he went. According to Gertrude, Mrs Watson afterwards reported that she had followed Mr Barrett onto the top deck of an omnibus and that she had approached him 'and he enjoyed her conversation very much, and he had gone to Bedford, and she knew him to be what I represented, because he winked and blinked at her all the time'. This suggests that John Edward Barrett picked up women off the street and that Gertrude had complained to her apparent friend about his infidelity. Mrs Watson's story of the bus journey was likely concocted to reassure Gertrude that sympathetic Mrs Watson was on her side and that they were fellow victims and allies in the world of brutish spouses.

In fact, Ellen Lyon was a double agent. She was working to nail Gertrude for adultery – and was prepared to supply any man with whom her unsuspecting confidante might pair off. During her life in India as a paid companion, Gertrude had only been to the theatre once. When Mrs Watson told her that she had tickets for the Empire and the Alhambra, Gertrude was naturally happy to go. She had, after all, been engaged to keep Mrs Watson company, so these parties of pleasure were also notionally work engagements. It was the middle of March; they drank champagne and sat in the five-shilling seats. The Empire put on variety shows: on 17 March, when Gertrude claimed they were in the audience, the bill included Macart's Dogs, Leodiska's cockatoo, Aenea the Flying Dancer, and the Colibris Midgets, 'the attraction of the Paris season', who appeared with miniature carriages and ponies. For a frustrated and anxious twenty-year-old, this kind of diversion doubtless conjured more carefree days.

They ate at Café Monaco. Each time, Mrs Watson would endeavour to push Gertrude gently towards some man whom she claimed was a friend: for a kiss as they alighted from a cab, or a private dinner. Gertrude declined. Mrs Watson urged her to have fun and to allow men to spend money on her, but her companion was uneasy. She was young and naïve, but not wholly daft; she knew that as a woman separated from her husband her reputation was fragile.

By contrast, her financial situation was desperate – she had already pawned some of her jewellery – and she was bored and lonely.

'Mrs Watson' continued to advise, then to press, Gertrude Barrett into assignations. First she encouraged her to go with Henry Clarke, the proprietor of the detective agency himself, who appeared in the guise of 'Stephens of the Stock Exchange'. Then she proposed supper with a man calling himself Charles Wilson and claiming to be the son of an MP. Surely Gertrude knew, when this man, who advertised that he had a yacht and promised her diamonds, asked her to go away with him, that she was being asked for sex? In court, she claimed that she did not. Either way, she got cold feet. She went out with Wilson for dinner; he became very drunk. They retired to rooms at Wellington Street in St John's Wood where, according to her testimony, Wilson slept on a sofa with a blanket over him and she slept in the bed. Probably they did. From the point of view of H. J. Clarke detective agency, the main point was that the landlady, Mrs Muchmore, should have *seen* Gertrude and the man wearing nightclothes, in rooms where they had mutually slept: that would be enough in court to 'prove' adultery. Whether they had slept together in a sexual sense was immaterial.

The unhappy couple left separately the next day (Charles Wilson hid Gertrude's nightclothes to delay her escape and did a runner without paying for the room); then Henry John Clarke appeared at the door, demanding witness statements. The charade had been played out. Poor Gertrude testified that she was 'overpersuaded'; the man was 'a friend of my companion'. She called him 'a vampire', suggestively conflating sexual predation and literal consumption of her blood. Whether she knew she was being pimped or not, it was evident that she was desperate and cornered. Divorce papers were served against her. She subsequently became ill, ended up in hospital, then in the workhouse: a grim and shocking fall for a woman who had been born into middle-class colonial life. When she recovered, Gertrude unsuccessfully sued Ellen Lyon to try to recover three diamond rings she had pawned for which Lyon held the tickets. Lyon claimed that the lawsuit was brought 'out of spite'. John Edward Barrett was granted a divorce in 1892. But in 1895, the legal tables turned.

A judge at the Old Bailey convicted H. J. Clarke and Ellen Lyon of conspiring to procure Gertrude Barrett to commit adultery and, in 1895, Clarke was committed for two years and Lyon for one year of hard labour. Gertrude Barrett, meanwhile, reinvented herself, training as a nurse and becoming one of the many 'New Women' of the 1890s who earned their own living. The newspapers, which had followed the Barrett divorce case for several years, were full of smug depreciation of female detectives and the immoral lengths to which their odious activities might lead. The *Midland Daily Telegraph* opined that 'not a shred of pity will be wasted' on Lyon and Clarke:

> The accused had, in the course of their not very refined occupation, shown an excess of zeal, as indeed there is a temptation to do to persons following their peculiar avocation . . . it is to be trusted that their imprisonment will act as a check on prying self-styled detectives, who have great inducements to better their instructions, and transcend the path-line of strict integrity marked out for ordinary humanity.[55]

Contrary to the *Midland Daily Telegraph*, I do feel a shred of pity for Ellen Lyon, the female detective in this case. It is hard to be sure of her history as she hid under various names, but she may have been the daughter of a coach-builder and grown up poor in Leytonstone, an area of North London close to modern-day Stratford. If this is the right Lyon, her family were involved in coach-painting, railway sign-writing and other artisanal work. She was already a domestic servant aged fourteen.[56]

In 1892, she was twenty-five; her employer, Henry John Clarke, was forty. According to a court witness, Clarke and Lyon had been a cohabiting couple in 1891 in Holborn-Buildings under the alias of Mr and Mrs Watson.[57] Clarke paid Lyon to befriend Gertrude Barrett and to attempt to introduce her to men. It was certainly an unsavoury role, yet the promise of champagne and theatre must have been just as tempting to a working-class woman as they were to her middle-class mark. Personation was itself a form of theatre; in this case, Ellen had been hired to play Mrs Watson rather than Mr Holmes. But could a person of her limited education and experience have been expected to discern the legal difference? Ellen Lyon, aged thirty-four in the 1901 census, was apparently single and childless, living with her mother and engaged as a forewoman in 'lace paper work'. She was supervising the making of doilies.

The plaintiff in the case, John Edward Barrett, escaped prison while the two women implicated both suffered permanent damage from his cruel attempt to frame his wife to obtain a cheap divorce. As was true in the Haddington case given to 'Clara Layt', the Barrett case exposed domestic violence and sexual abuse as the ground zero of crime against women, whose explosive effects rippled out into the community, producing aftershocks of shame, scandal, dependency and potential exploitation. The female detective – even when not explicitly a double agent – was liable to stand on both sides of the wall separating the 'respectable' from the 'unrespectable' Victorian woman. In witnessing and perhaps becoming an accessory to crime, she crossed the boundary she was notionally policing.

This inherent doubleness made her gaze powerful, though she herself was compromised. The activities she witnessed and exposed troubled the differentiation of a secure private space, in which women would be protected, from a public sphere that was predominantly inhabited by men. This was true when she infringed the supposed sanctity of the bedroom, but even more obvious when she was engaged in unearthing political secrets, whether to protect the public from anarchist bombs or to steal an election by smearing a candidate.

Female Detection and Politics

Some Victorian private detective agencies were involved in political activity. The extent of this involvement is difficult to determine, but the number of agencies that advertise 'election watching' among the services they offer suggests that the practice was well understood. Here, again, the moral status of the female detective was ambiguous; she might be asked to spy on candidates, to 'dig dirt' on them or to act as an agent provocateur.

Bribing electors was commonplace in the nineteenth century. Police detectives in Derby in 1852 found that an agent was methodically giving two sovereigns apiece and free beer to men willing to vote for Horsfall, the Tory candidate.[58] Detective agents could watch the activities of political rivals for evidence of foul play; they could also seek (or plant) material advantageous to their candidate. In 1865, the *Tipperary Free Press* objected that Charles Frederick Field, formerly one of the most famous detectives of Scotland Yard, 'amidst the excitement of a general election . . . issues from his secret lair in the Temple an electoral manifesto. "Election Matters attended to for solicitors, Parliamentary Agents and Candidates." What sort of "matters" can they be to be "Attended to" by a detective spy?'[59]

Cooke's, an agency in Charing Cross that boasted it had been established since 1879, advertised in 1894 that it dealt with 'espionage, elections' as well as 'general detective work and all family matters requiring secrecy'.[60] In 1892, a private detective agency reportedly offered the services of male and female detectives to gauge voter intention, sniff out opposition manoeuvres and find out if candidates had compromising pasts.[61] In 1893, a journalist for the *Spectator* cited an interview with the head of a private enquiry agency:

Among other curious statements made by the chief of this office was . . . that at the General Election of 1886 he had some seven hundred men scattered all over the country, 'seeing that the work of organisation was being carried out properly, and watching both friends and opponents of the people who employed them.' 'I have been speaking all along of "men,"' he says, 'but you must not imagine that our staff consists only of men. As a matter of fact, we employ very few, except as managers or superintendents. Most of the members of the staff are women.'[62]

Heated accusations were made in Parliament in July 1884 that women had been employed to spy on Irish MPs and as agents provocateurs encouraging the Fenian contingent towards terrorist acts and even contributing money to the 'dynamite fund'.[63] Further reports from that year in Dublin suggested that at least one female 'London detective or English spy', 'of extremely captivating manners', had travelled to Ireland, staying at two of the principal hotels, and speaking 'very patronisingly of dynamite and very warmly of the cause'.[64] The Irish MP, Timothy Healy raised the matter in Parliament with William Harcourt, the Home Secretary, calling attention to the 'presence of a female emissary from the Home Office in Ireland'. The newspapers named her as 'Mrs Detective Tyler'.[65] Harcourt denied any knowledge of the matter. Healy claimed that a telegram from the Home Office to this female detective or spy was 'in the possession of a friend of mine'.[66] At this time of acute tension between Irish Home Rulers and those who opposed Ireland's political independence from Britain, rumour was rife and feelings ran high. The thought of Britain employing women as part of a covert Unionist operation, seducing Irish politicians into expression of treasonable sentiments with the intention of incriminating them, understandably provoked outrage among Irish MPs.

The *Limerick Chronicle* alleged in 1883 that 'several female detectives have been added to that branch of the service in this city, and that on Tuesday night one of these female officers who was on duty near the Post Office narrowly scanned the appearance and dress of all persons who came to post letters.'[67] Given the timing, it seems likely that – if there was truth in this report – women were being employed particularly to recognise political suspects and those who might be communicating with them. As far back as 1865, James Stephens, Fenian leader of the Irish Republican Brotherhood, had been arrested at a house in the outskirts of Dublin on information provided by a female detective. Stephens, in hiding, used the alias 'Mr Herbert':

> Herbert seldom ventured beyond the grounds of the estate, being ... much of the time actually disguised as a gardener, but his wife and daughter frequently visited the markets and bazaars of the city ... On their return from one of these shopping excursions early in November the unsuspecting pair were attended afar off by a female detective from Scotland Yard, who had identified Mrs Herbert as the wife of James Stephens ... the man wanted above all others by the British crown.[68]

In the 1894 arrest of the anarchist terrorist Jacob Polti, who was convicted of plotting a bomb attack in London, it was also alleged that a female detective had been used to ascertain his whereabouts. The police subsequently denied this. Whatever the truth of these persistent rumours and accusations, the idea of the female detective as an agent whose actions might uncover plots and foil political assassins had become imaginatively embedded in public conscious-ness by the 1890s. George R. Sims's fictional female detective, Dorcas Dene, penetrated an anarchist bomb plot in 1896, while Florence Marryat's remarkable novel, *In the Name of Liberty* (1892), which I shall discuss further in the next chapter, conjures a woman – Jane Farrell – who has been abandoned by her husband and is successfully recruited by the police for counter-terrorist work to foil a Fenian-anarchist bombing campaign in London.

A female detective was also involved in the investigation by journalist William T. Stead, who wrote in 1885 one of the most sensational news articles of the nineteenth century. 'The Maiden Tribute of Modern Babylon' was an exposé which claimed to show that young girls were being sold into prostitution in Britain by working-class parents and that child-trafficking for sex was a problem known and winked at by the police, who routinely received bribes and sexual favours from brothel-owners and sex workers. When questioned in court about the conduct of his investigation, Stead admitted having used a female detective, Mrs Fibey, whom 'he brought from the north', to investigate the 'character of the house in Lady-lake Grove' where he suspected child-trafficking occurred.

Such private enquiries crossed boundaries between campaigning social work, journalism and cases conducted by private detective agencies that led to public prosecution. Even well-intended sting operations could, however, turn ugly, as W. T. Stead's investigation into child-trafficking did: he was charged in court with having abducted the girl whom he had taken from her parents (without of course actually debauching her) to demonstrate the ease with which young women were being trafficked. The real Victorian female detective dealt constantly with moral ambiguity and moral compromise.

Self-Invention and (the) Female Agency

One of the truths exposed by the numerous cases of private detective agencies flouting or skirting the law in the second half of the nineteenth century was that, outside of the police force, anyone could call themselves a detective. It was a largely unregulated profession, for men and for women, with a strong element of self-invention. As the novelist Elizabeth Burgoyne Corbett pointed out in her bestseller, *Secrets of a Private Enquiry Office* (1891), all one needed was an office with a brass plate on the door. In this respect, as in some others, being a detective and being a writer were very similar.

For those who were gulled into parting with their money, goods or secrets by inexperienced or deliberately fraudulent detective agents, the fictive nature of the profession was a problem. In 1892, a young woman called Margaret Preston or Parmley from Newcastle arrived in Edinburgh representing that she was a female detective sent by Scotland Yard.[69] With this story, she obtained respectable lodgings for three days for free. On questioning by a local constable, however, she was revealed to be a fantasist with a notebook. She was sent to prison for thirty days: a rather harsh penalty, perhaps, for a flight of fancy. In 1900, a twenty-four-year-old joiner, Charles Robert Francis, conned a ten-guinea bicycle out of a shop in Bangor, by representing himself as a private detective. He had detective business cards printed, rather optimistically claiming 'twenty years' experience'.[70] The point here is not just that young women and men were *playing* detective, but that others *wanted* to believe them, to the extent of giving them credit.

For those who assumed it in reality, the role of female detective could provide an opportunity for self-invention that offered new scope to break the boundaries previously limiting their lives and adopt a more powerful and intriguing persona. This was certainly true of Antonia Moser and of Kate Easton, women who ran their own agencies at the turn of the nineteenth century, competing in newspapers for celebrity as lady detectives.

Antonia Moser, Entrepreneurial Chameleon

Charlotte Antonia Williamson was born in 1856 into a family of inventors. Her father – whose ancestors came from France and Germany – was a successful engineer who designed, made and sold some of the first washing machines. Charlotte grew up in a relatively privileged household in Holborn, where she and her siblings enjoyed education, travel and the London social scene. In March 1882, she married her first cousin, Edward James Clarendon Williamson, who also was a mechanical engineer. Their first child, Margaret, was born in October. Margaret may have been a seven-month baby, conceived on the couple's honeymoon, but it seems quite possible that the twenty-six-year-old Charlotte had fallen pregnant before the marriage. Her behaviour after marriage also suggests a woman who refused to be bound by the niceties of Victorian convention.

During divorce proceedings in 1890, Edward testified that Charlotte had, within eight or nine months of their marriage, announced her intention of going to work as a female detective for Maurice Moser, a well-known former detective inspector of Scotland Yard who had founded his own private enquiry agency in Southampton Street, Strand. Such behaviour would have been highly unusual among middle-class wives with small children, unless they required the additional income that work provided. Her husband objected to the job but did not oppose it, until it became evident that his wife was using the opportunities for absence afforded by her work to exit her marriage.

Edward was also conducting an affair. His wife, who counter-sued for divorce, accused him of cruelty as well as adultery. She would make very public statements in the press about Edward's bad behaviour, accusing him of using a rival detective agency to confect claims about her and asserting acidly: 'To have to support a husband is not always a pleasant task, and I think you have had some slight experience of Mr Williamson's funny little ways of making money.'[71]

During the divorce proceedings, Edward testified that Charlotte had wished to hang a picture of Maurice Moser in the marital bedroom. This intrusion – which, when Edward mentioned it, caused much mirth in the courtroom – was perhaps the most flagrant way in which his wife could declare her sexual preference for her employer and hint that she was conducting an affair with him: 'Mr Kisch [for the prosecution] remarked: "you did not want to have the detective eye always on you" (Laughter.) [Williamson responded:] "No I did not". (Laughter.)'[72]

Edward had employed a disreputable, rival firm of detectives (Henry Slater) to investigate his wife's activities; Louisa Sangster, a female detective in Moser's employment, testified against the couple.

It was this aspect of the case that most entertained the newspapers. Maurice Moser, the arch-detective and successful author of *Secrets from Scotland Yard*, had been hoist with his own petard. 'A Singular Divorce Suit: A Lady Detective Respondent' was the headline in the *Leicester Journal*; 'Mr Moser and his Female Detective' ran the item in the *Jersey Weekly Press*.[73] The case brought under scrutiny the potential failure of the public/private boundary in detective work that had always, newspapers jeered, threatened the modesty of the female detective in particular. Was it not the case, the newspapers seemed to hint, that a wife who left her domestic role to take up spying on others, had embarked on the slippery slope to disregarding the sanctity of her own marriage? Once the decree nisi was granted, Antonia Williamson went to the Isle of Wight with Moser and her children. She took Moser's name and appeared as his spouse in the 1891 census, but there is no evidence that they ever married.

The most remarkable fact in Charlotte Williamson's case is that, undaunted by a very public divorce from Edward in 1890 and a less public (but no less acrimonious) split from Moser in 1892, she continued to work as a self-proclaimed 'detective expert', running her own successful private enquiry agency in the Strand until 1907, when she passed the business to her daughter Margaret.[74] A newspaper reader in 1890 might have suspected that Charlotte's job as a female detective for Moser was merely cover for her affair with him. But, in retrospect, the opposite appears true. The affair may have been the necessary means for Charlotte to learn a fascinating trade that she regarded as her true calling.

True to the entrepreneurial spirit of her family, she reinvented herself as Antonia Moser, happily using the cachet of Moser's name and reputation to bolster her own credentials as a 'detective expert with offices in every city of the world'. She was a committed and open feminist and advocate of women's suffrage, who was happy to announce in public that women made excellent detectives and should consider the detective profession when thinking of possible careers. In January 1913, the *London Evening Standard* published an interview with her. In it, she argued:

> A woman makes as good a detective as a man and often a better. Her instinct and powers of intuition are an asset rather than a hindrance to her in this profession, and her individuality and resourcefulness, unfettered by official training and red tape, are allowed free play at critical moments, and greatly enhance her value as an enquiry agent.[75]

Her interviewer noted that he had encountered male managers of private enquiry agencies who 'pooh-poohed the idea of employing women in this particular sphere', arguing that their 'imaginative' and 'sentimental' tendencies mitigated against the 'rational' requirements of the job. Antonia Moser, citing her twenty-five years of experience as a detective, takes the contrary view, not only asserting women's rational control, but also that *imagination is a strength* in detective work. Men are too hidebound by their police training, which 'tends toward the suppression of individuality', whereas women are more mentally flexible and creative in their approach to the 'unexpected', which often happens in cases where 'carefully constructed theories fall to pieces'.

Antonia Moser asserted that: 'A business woman with a well-trained mind, plenty of common sense, one who is naturally sharp and resourceful, and has, besides, a knowledge of foreign languages and plenty of savoir faire, might enter the business with a good chance of success.' Moser is here not merely speaking of women as occasional employees of agencies run by men, but of the possibility that – like herself – women might run a detective agency as a business. The fact that many women excelled at speaking French and German and other modern languages, as these frequently formed a part of Victorian middle-class female curricula (whereas Latin and Greek were less commonly taught), made them particularly eligible for a profession that had quickly become international in its dimensions. The New Woman is a different kind of detective from her predecessors. She is a kind of envoy, whose cases may involve international trade as well as commercial theft, tracking absconding criminals and disappearing money as it crosses borders and time zones.

In reality, Moser confided to the *Standard*, cases dealing with probate, divorce, misappropriation of funds and thefts are those with which a woman would most frequently come into contact. Men would be more likely to 'shadow' suspects. Occasionally disguise is necessary and situations are involved that require 'great personal courage'; there are also 'times when the comic element is not lacking'. But really it is the 'incessant work' and 'uncertain hours' that form the main discouragement, rather than women's unsuitability for the detective role.

Antonia Moser felt very strongly about women's right to own property, to have financial control of their earnings and to vote. In the *Referee* for 7 April 1912, she complained of women's lack of legal status and enfranchisement and the fact that by law woman is 'not even a parent' – she was not assured of custody of her own children. She argued angrily:

Thousands of women are obliged to earn the living of their children under the most cruel and heartrending conditions, yet Members of the House of Commons cheered again and again when the Bill to give women a legal status was rejected. *Women's demand for the enfranchisement of their sex is both moral and economic. Without the lever of the vote they are unable to demand a living wage*; and they view with horror and disgust the cynical idea that it is open to their sex to obtain by vice what they are unable to obtain by work. The 'maudlin sentiment' expressed by many that woman is to depend upon the 'chivalry' of man instead of justice and 'recognition' is at the root of the world-trouble of to-day. Let man act a manly part toward the other half of creation and cease to enjoy the sight of her suffering. Let him acknowledge that she has both legal and moral rights.[76]

Moser speaks as a working single mother who had assumed responsibility for supporting herself and her family. For her, obtaining the vote is not merely about righting age-old wrongs visited on the property and parental rights of women whose marriages had failed: it is about assuring a fair living wage for all working women. Moser wrote for *Votes for Women*, the newspaper of the Women's Social and Political Union, which campaigned for women's suffrage, on the subject of 'Women Workers and the Vote' (she also advertised her detective services – 'advice free' – in the suffragette newspaper's classifieds).[77] She was vocal about women's right to equal pay for equal work and the effect that the female franchise would have on women's wages.[78] Her detective expertise came in handy at suffrage marches where, as she explained in *Votes for Women*, she was easily able to spot police 'narks' (spies and agents provocateurs) and confront them.[79]

In asserting the claims of women, including herself, to be excellent and 'expert' detectives capable of running their own agencies, Moser was doing more than declaring a profession, thought by many to be disreputable, to be well suited to and stimulating for her female peers. She was asserting a woman's right to seek and know the truth, to escape from vaunted male 'protection' into a situation of financial independence and professional directorship of her own life and business. This was a powerful contention. Indeed, one can say that Antonia Moser assumed the mantle of the detective divorcee, Mrs Percival Flight in *The Lucky Shilling* – that fictional drama of 1888 – and by 1890 had made it a reality. She brings a recognisably feminist flair to the self-invention and self-promotion that becoming a detective allowed women to explore.

Indeed, she was happy to provide newspapers, as Maurice Moser and other male detectives had done, with 'fictionalised memoirs' of

24. *Antonia Moser,* Reynolds's Newspaper *(4 July 1909).*

cases she had solved, which were published as a series, *The Thrilling Adventures of a Woman Detective*, in the *Weekly Dispatch* in 1907. In these self-mythologising tales, which resemble the cases of fictional detectives appearing in newspapers in the same period, Moser frequently portrays herself getting the better of men. In 'The First of the Gold Brick Swindles', for example, she travels to New York and impersonates a widow, Mrs Greatorex, to expose a gang of crooks who are trying to lure an unsuspecting young heir into a foolish investment in a goldmine. The satisfaction of the story lies not only in Mrs Moser's success in arresting the swindlers, but in proving wrong the 'cocksure' male heir who was determined to ignore her advice.[80] Moser's articles show that she was highly aware of literary and dramatic works that involved crime and detection: she cites Dickens, Gaboriau and Victor Hugo, and plays such as *Raffles* and *The Silver King*, when describing the tradition of gentlemen thieves to which one of her marks belonged.[81] She knowingly constructs her detective 'adventures' within a genre that included fable as well as truth.

Image management was important to the success of the female detective, who could compete with her rivals, not only by means of direct advertisement, but through fictive conjuring of the 'exploits' that underwrote her legend. For the reader and potential client, it was not always easy to determine what was real and what was invented, either in the person of the fictional sleuth or the persona of the factual detective: an uncertainty both potentially troubling and intriguing.

The Performative Art of Detection

Kate Easton, whose advertisements competed directly with those of Antonia Moser, considered 'her profession a splendid one for women, but a candidate should be *a first-rate actress*, be able to efface self, possess indomitable pluck, an unshaken nerve, unlimited patience, powers of physical endurance, and excellent eyesight, hearing, and memory.'[82]

Easton herself was an actress before she became a detective. Like Antonia Moser, she was born in 1856, but into a working-class family: she was the youngest of six children of a tobacconist and waterman, who also worked as a stage-door keeper.[83] The family had close links with the theatre. Her brother became a 'professor of music' and her niece, Madeleine Lucette (who was close to Kate in age), was a highly successful Victorian actress and playwright, whose plays included detective characters.[84] In 1881, aged twenty-four, Kate described herself in the census as an actress. In 1901, living in Great Russell Street with her eighty-two-year-old mother and widowed cousin, Hannah Edwards (sixty-three), Kate, underreporting her true age by over a decade as she would continue to do until her death, still described herself as a 'vocalist and actress', but in truth she had not made a great success on the stage. She would attain much greater renown in her self-chosen role, as the manager and star of her own detective agency.

Easton learned how to 'efface self', but not in the manner of the Victorian domestic angel who put the needs and wishes of her family ahead of her own. Instead, she became, in her own capitalised words,

'KATE EASTON, THE LADY DETECTIVE' who undertook personally 'matters requiring a woman's tact and delicacy', but who also carried a gun. By 1895 there were twenty-seven different London private enquiry agencies listed in Kelly's Directory alone. Agencies had to differentiate their services from one another, emphasising their unique selling points. Easton's advertisements routinely appeared next to those of five or six other agencies in the *Morning Post*, including those of Justin Chevasse, 'private investigator to the aristocracy', and Harrison Ford, a detective in Piccadilly who specialised in divorce.[85] In this marketing context, to inhabit the persona of a 'Lady Detective [who] Knows not Fear and can Shoot Straight', as one newspaper would describe her, was to profit from the image of the female detective that Easton would certainly have encountered in melodrama on the theatrical stage of her youth. Fiction fed reality, in turn allowing clients to perceive themselves more heroically: not as merely snooping wives or suspicious employers, but as fearless warriors facing down skulduggery. Easton's agency, in Shaftesbury Avenue, was in a building that today houses rehearsal rooms for theatrical productions.

Easton was a feminist, who participated in the suffragist campaign of 1911 that encouraged women to spoil their census forms or refuse to submit their data. As they 'didn't count' fully as persons, they would refuse to be counted.[86] Like Moser, she used magazine appearances to build her detective persona, thrilling readers with tales of impostors and how to 'track and trap' them. When it came to actors, it took one to know one. In describing her cases, she naturally tends to emphasise her skill, endurance and bravery. In reality, of course, many of her cases were as sordid as those of Emily Oxley and other detectives employed by spouses who wanted a divorce. In 1909, Easton was cited in the divorce case of Francis and Violet Wigglesworth.[87] Mr Wigglesworth, when he separated from his wife, first employed a male detective, W. James of Walham, to shadow her and obtain evidence of Violet sleeping with her lover. But, when it 'became

25. *Kate Easton*, Reynolds's Newspaper *(13 August 1905).*

necessary to dispense with' James's efforts, Wigglesworth turned to Kate Easton, who proved much more effective – succeeding in getting her assistant, Mrs Bardrick, into position as a resident in Ennismore Avenue, Chiswick, where (as a lodger who was 'on familiar terms' with Violet Wigglesworth) she observed the suspected couple in flagrante delicto. Tellingly, W. James, disgruntled at being taken off the case, had warned Mrs Wigglesworth that her husband was having her watched. Female detectives had to contend not only with difficult clients but with male rivals putting a foot out to trip them.

In 1911, Easton sued one of her former clients, Mrs Ruth Hitchcock of Knightsbridge. Easton had undertaken the work of having Mr Hitchcock followed to uncover his suspected infidelity.[88] The shadowing failed, however, when one of Mr Hitchcock's former servants realised that Mr Hitchcock was being tailed and put him wise, spoiling the surveillance operation. Mrs Hitchcock argued that Easton had underperformed; Easton responded that the leak was purely accidental. Easton won her claim for her account to be paid. The Hitchcockian case, however, is a salient reminder that much female detective work was more *Kramer vs. Kramer* than *North by Northwest*. Easton succeeded in getting her name known by astute theatrical publicity, emphasising her more glamorous role as a 'Lady Detective' who could find missing persons and restore missing documents. But acrimonious divorce cases remained her bread and butter.

In the 1898 musical farce, *Bilberry of Tilbury*, the detective Stella Dashwood is the leader of both an all-female detective agency and The Elysian Girls, a theatrical troupe in which her 'renowned lady tecs' dance and sing. Their double lives, on stage and on the case, enable them to detect the sexual infidelities that their clients wish investigated. The knowing manner in which the farce deals with the relationship between theatre and detection is suggestive not only of the fact that theatre-goers at the *fin de siècle* knew of female detective agencies but also that actresses and detectives might sometimes be the same people.

The performativity of female detection was part of its appeal to clients – and, perhaps, also to women considering entering the profession, who were given a licence to reinvent themselves.

Henry Simmonds's detective agency was situated at 29–30 King Street, Cheapside. His advertisements boasted that 'Simmonds' Lady Detectives personate any character in life'.[89] He also hinted that he had 'rendered secret services and obtained valuable information for European and foreign Powers, newspapers, politicians, sportsmen, financiers, & hundreds of the principal trading firms in London, and throughout the world'. Such advertisements suggested the thrilling possibility that female detectives were everywhere: their universal ability to become whatever person they were required to act as could serve as a means to infiltrate any political setting, business or diplomatic context. William Pierrepoint, head of a rival agency in Chancery Lane, similarly stressed that 'his staff of Lady detectives has been his success. They move in all circles from the highest to the lowest.'[90] Whether it was often true or not, the fantasy of the female detective as a character who could go anywhere and 'pass' for anyone stimulated the market for enquiry agencies as well the market for fiction. The two traded on one another – deriving mutual benefit.

When George R. Sims in 1897 invented the character of Dorcas Dene, a lady detective who has been an actress and brings her remarkable powers of impersonation to bear on her detective work, he was drawing on knowledge of Kate Easton, Dorothy Tempest and other actresses who moved between these interlinked professions. Sims was a playwright, who knew the world of London theatre intimately, penning melodramas and burlesques. He must surely have seen a production of Colin Henry Hazlewood's *The Female Detective* at some point in his career, observing the success of the central character's multiple quick-change act, which Dorcas Dene replicates. Sims was also a journalist who wrote regularly for London newspapers, and took a personal interest in the police, becoming a close personal friend of Inspector Macnaghten of the detective department. Sims's career nicely illustrates the confluence of writing, performance and detection in the nineteenth century. Dorcas Dene's exploits are, of course, imaginary, but they recall real cases. One of the most horrific cases she solves is that of Judkins Barraclough, a millionaire who is, his aristocratic second wife suspects, keeping a terrible secret. Dorcas tracks Judkins to an abandoned house, where he has imprisoned his first wife in a cage and is feeding her only brandy drugged with chloral, attempting to produce a 'natural' death that will leave him free from prosecution for bigamy. Judkins has been bitten by his first wife, who is kept in a state more animal than human. Dene discovers:

> The centre of the room was entirely occupied by what looked like a huge wire cage. Wire netting nearly six feet high was stretched from side to side of the room on ropes which were fastened in the walls by iron rings ... In one corner of the cage ... covered over by a scarlet blanket, lay a woman.[91]

The scene bears obvious resemblances to Jane Eyre's discovery of Rochester's maddened and degraded first wife, Bertha Mason, in Charlotte Brontë's novel of 1847. But it is also linked to a real case. Edward Charles Judkins appeared in the papers in 1896 charged by his wife with adultery. He had been keeping (though not caging) a lover, the actress Gladys Knight, in an apartment owned by a comic actor, Mark Storey, for over a year. A witness for the prosecution, Mrs Overden, affirmed that Ms Knight sent out washing as 'Mrs Judkins'. Overden had hunted down letters whose handwriting proved the adulterer's guilt. Sims would have known about this case through his many connections to the theatre.

Edward Charles Judkins, in keeping a 'second wife' in a second home, had not, of course, committed a crime as startling as that of Judkins Barraclough, but the interplay of newspaper-serialised fiction by Sims and newspaper reportage in the Judkins divorce case is symptomatic of the way in which bigamy plots in fiction became a mode of dramatising the sexual double standard in marriage and the way in which husbands, whether violent or not, frequently did leave their wives 'confined' or 'driven to drink' through abandonment and abuse. Dorcas Dene liberates both Judkins's first wife (literally) and his second one (from the cage of an unhappy marriage). The female detective is, whether in real life or on the page, always a 'character': her role in combatting crime carries the symbolic weight of fantasy.

Henry Slater chose to make his fleet of 'lady detectives' a particular selling point in the newspaper advertisements with which he flooded the zone in the 1890s and early 1900s, often taking a full column in the 'public notice' section, in which he inserted up to eighteen different notices recommending his agency.[92] In one ad, headed 'YOUNG LADY DETECTIVES', he boasted: 'MR HENRY SLATER can arrange for any character in life from his Staff of Female Detectives, from a crossing sweeper to a princess.'[93] Slater was the enquiry agency equivalent of a theatrical impresario. His advertisements conjured up an extraordinary spectacle: an 'Army' of 'Lady

Cyclist Detectives'. Slater boasted that, for the last seventeen years, he had never lost a divorce case and the secret of his success was his decade-long use of female agents. He claimed to be able to send women of 'all ages and sizes', rather as if he were supplying fashion models instead of investigators. Describing himself as 'the world's greatest detective', he made sure that his agency, situated at 1 Basinghall Street 'near the Bank of England', was familiar by its ubiquity in taking up entire newspaper columns, which suggested its size and scope. His marketing, which successfully made him a house-hold name, shows the role of imagination and the importance of attention-seeking even in undercover work.

Potential clients for detective work would typically find them-selves using a telegraphic address – among them were 'INQUISITOR, DESPATCH, TOUCH' – to make initial contact with an agent. Like all telegraphic messages, their enquiry was translated into morse code to be passed as a tapped signal along the telegraph wires and re-transcribed into words at the detective's end. Applicants sending a telegram to an enquiry agent must already have felt as if they were participating in a detective drama. This sense of theatre was enhanced by the fact that advertisements for enquiry agencies often appeared on the same pages as theatrical notices.

In fact, Slater was as much of an impostor as his 'army of lady cyclists' was a fiction. He went by many different names – George Tinsley, Captain Brown, Captain Scott – and had worked as a pawn-broker's assistant, a solicitor's clerk and a snake-oil salesman, before settling into the role of private dick.[94] His flair for hype and flagrant disregard for the niceties of the law had, by 1890, already caused him to be investigated for fraud, and in 1904 would land four of his men in jail, when they were found guilty of fabricating incriminating evidence in a divorce case. Judge Darling, at the Old Bailey, opined that Slaters should be 'stamped out' as it 'was not an agency for the legitimate detection of crime but an agency which was perfectly prepared to go to any lengths to prove offences which had never been committed provided sufficient money was paid'.[95] As detectives go, Slater was not a successful artist but a successful framer.

Slaters was an egregious example of an agency prepared to create rather than investigate plots. Yet the world of the private enquiry agency generally drew attention to the potentially fictive nature of identity and the extent to which both detectives and clients played a 'role' that had to be interrogated. Stories of female detection, whether they appeared as newspaper reportage or serialised fiction in periodicals, highlighted the extent to which women might be 'acting' in all their domestic and social activities, concealing the intrigue and misery that formed what Wilkie Collins in *Basil* (1852) called 'those ghastly heart-tragedies ... acted and reacted, scene by scene, year by year, in the secret theatre of home'. Female detectives underscored women's ability to inhabit different personae, whether they were playing characters of diverse ages and nationalities or simply negotiating the boundary between their private and professional identities. These stories also foregrounded the extent to which what might previously have been written off as low-value domestic activity (chatting, watching the street, waiting on social superiors, paying social calls, shopping) could also be well-paid professional surveillance. Indeed, the doctrine of gendered 'separate spheres', where women were sequestered in the sanctum of private, domestic life while men issued forth into public, professional spaces, was challenged by the detective business in multiple ways. Female (and male) detectives undertook their professional work largely in the private realm. That work exposed the truth that domestic space was frequently insecure, violent and unhappy; that both men and women often pursued different lives, identities and avocations in different spaces; and that marriage, far from offering peace and harmony, was often a battlefield that combatants had only very recently been given the legal power to leave.

In the modern information economy of Victorian Britain, women would play an increasingly central role. The relationship within newspapers of real-life cases, serialised fiction and advertisements for goods and services, including private enquiry agencies, showcased the ways in which the female gaze could be monetised – attracted to look, to read, to covet, to buy. The female detective's gaze was ambiguous. On the one hand, it was empowering, a symptom of a society in which women were gaining increasing freedom to travel, to make their own judgements and to gain their income professionally in ways that allowed them considerable choice, intellectual stimulation and responsibility. On the other hand, it was potentially cruel and distressing, a symptom of a society in which women were paid to hound and denounce other women, to injure their future prospects and (as readers) to pry into the sexual and financial transgressions of those whose circumstances were often less fortunate than their own. This discomfiting tension is one reason why 'the female detective' remains such a powerful headline throughout the latter half of the nineteenth century. In accepting the invitation to look, we are complicit in the work of private detection and the moral compromises it involves.

Victorian newspaper readers liked to imagine themselves as detectives and the detective looked back at them from the pages of the newspaper, connecting the world of crime, of human curiosity and of social injustice. Journalism normalised the female detective as a fact of life. In the 1890s it would idealise her as an agent of change.

5

POLITICAL PIS
Newspapers and the New Woman Detective

My sole object is to get at the truth.[1]
Elizabeth Burgoyne Corbett, *Behind the Veil or Revelations of a
Lady Detective* (1893)

What lies on the opposite side of *Truth*? If this were a Victorian riddle, you might guess *Fiction*.

But if this were a map of London in the 1890s, the right answer would be the Westminster Detective Agency. On the opposite side of the road from the offices of the liberal journal *Truth*, the Westminster Detective Agency was the partner organisation of the magazine and was funded by the same Liberal MP, Henry Labouchère. Its agents, who included female detectives, broke stories such as the shocking forgery of the 'Parnell Papers', which sought to implicate Irish MP Charles Parnell in the Phoenix Park murders: the politically motivated assassination of two English officials in Dublin. Advertisements for the agency appeared in *Truth*; political exposés in *Truth* derived from the agency's investigations. Snoops and scoops crossed and re-crossed the street. Their proximity highlighted how blurred the line might be between private and public investigation, criminal case and broader social enquiry.

The close relationship between journalism and detection was visible throughout the map of Victorian London. Catherine Louisa Pirkis, creator of fictional female detective Loveday Brooke; Florence Marryat, creator of fictional female detective Jane Farrell; and George R. Sims, creator of fictional female detective Dorcas Dene, all published novels with F. V. White at 31 Southampton Street, just off the Strand. When visiting her publisher, Marryat may well have bumped into detective Maurice Moser on the stairs. Moser's famous detective agency was based at number 31 in the very same building. These authors, hurrying along Southampton Street, would have passed the offices of the *Million*, which emphasised in its pen-portrait of Moser (who was also an author) that he was 'within a few doors' from the newspaper's office and that 'most of the sensational stories of the last years' had emanated from his agency. Pirkis, in visiting her publisher, would also have passed the Southampton Street offices of George Newnes, publisher of *Tit Bits* and the *Strand Magazine*, where Conan Doyle's Sherlock Holmes stories appeared in print.

The nexus of periodical publishing and detective agencies around the Strand in London made the linkage between one kind of literary investigative work and another obvious. Several of the lady detectives of *fin-de-siècle* fiction (Lois Cayley, Dora Myrl) have careers as journalists that lead them towards detection. As Myrl breezily remarks: 'Within the last year I have been a telegraph girl, a telephone girl, a lady journalist. I liked the last best.'[2] The heroine of *Jennie Baxter: Journalist* (1900) is a newspaper columnist who takes the place of a Pinkerton's detective on the trail of some stolen diamonds.[3] Loveday Brooke's fictional detective agency is in 'Lynch Court, Fleet Street'. The *Ludgate Monthly*, which published the Loveday Brooke stories, was at Mitre Court, Fleet Street. The location of Loveday Brooke's first case, at 'Craigen Court', is also reminiscent of the address of the real detective Cooke's offices at 9 Craig's Court, Strand. Cooke's

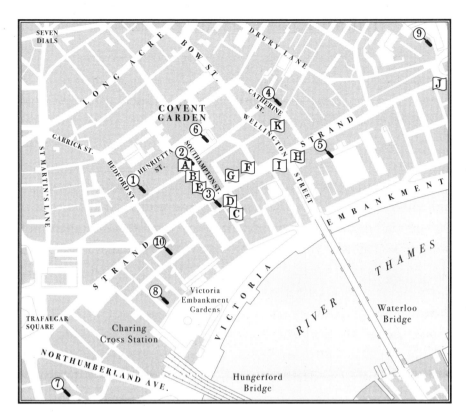

Detective agencies

1. Steggles and Darling,
   22 Henrietta Street
2. Maurice Moser,
   31 Southampton Street
3. Harris, 319 Strand
4. Attwoods (moved from
   6 Catherine Street to Wellington
   Street, Strand, 1887)
5. Granger-Stark, 150 Strand
6. The National Detective Agency
   (a fake agency), New Inn
   Chambers, Wych Street, Strand
7. Cooke's, 9 Craig's Court
8. Ward, 22 Buckingham Street
9. Morgan's detective agency,
   5 and 6 Clement's Inn, Strand
   (1909)
10. Antonia Moser,
    Dane's Inn Chambers,
    37–38 Strand (1905)

Publishers and newspaper offices Ⓐ

A. *The Strand Magazine*,
   8–11 Southampton Street from 1892,
   (published Sherlock Holmes stories)
B. F.V. White, 31 Southampton Street
   (published *Dorcas Dene, Detective*)
C. Tinsley Brothers, 16 Catherine Street,
   Strand (published *The Moonstone* and
   Eleanor's Victory)
D. G. Vickers, 3 Catherine Street, Strand
   (published *Revelations of a Female
   Detective*)
E. *The Million*, 8–11 Southampton Street
F. *The Globe* (offices on 367 Strand, burnt
   down 1892)
G. *The Sketch*, 172 Strand
H. *The Illustrated London News*,
   198 Strand (1895)
I. *The Illustrated Sporting and Dramatic
   News*, 148 Strand (1884)
J. *The Graphic* (from 1890 *The Daily
   Graphic*), 190 Strand (at least 1885–1903)
K. *All The Year Round*, 26 Wellington
   Street, Strand

*Map of Detective agencies, publishers, and newspaper offices in Victorian
London.*

claimed to be the oldest private detective agency in London. It is likely that Pirkis read the advertisements for detective agencies that appeared so regularly in newspapers of the 1880s and 1890s and based her fictional agency around the listings.

'Investigative journalist' first appeared as a coinage in 1890; the 'detective reporter' who embedded themselves in a location, posing as a penniless person to obtain admission to a workhouse, as a madman to obtain entry to a lunatic asylum, or committing a minor offence to spend time in a prison, was a Victorian role that both women and men pursued. Readers were hungry for direct experience of uncomfortable and dangerous situations: the 'semi-detective business' of reportage straddled a border between pioneering socio-logical study and sensationalist stunt journalism that traded on brief explorations of working-class life by middle-class slummers. Elizabeth L. Banks became famous as a 'stunt journalist' of this kind. Posing as a crossing-sweeper, flower-girl or housemaid, she informed readers minutely of the hardships and sensations of people in these jobs.[4] Banks, as a female 'detective reporter', was taking a deep (or shallow) dive into marginalised female experiences that, in acquiring the status of memoir, the moral frame of truth-seeking, and the dangerous frisson that accompanied real-time physical vulnerability, attracted readers who would normally avoid personal acquaintance with 'low life'.[5]

Newspapers and magazines were, not coincidentally, where serial-ised detective fiction flourished. As Sam Saunders has explored, the burgeoning Victorian periodical press, with its established interest in crime and readers' desire to penetrate 'private spaces, moments, and relationships' associated with crime, gave rise to new literary forms, including 'social exploration journalism' (which showed readers around criminalised locales), 'police memoir fiction' (cases loosely based on the 'experiences' of real professional investigators) and wholly invented detective stories, which often shared the same week-by-week case format as memoirs and described themselves as the 'experiences' of a

26. *Elizabeth L. Banks poses as a housemaid in* Campaigns of Curiosity:
Journalistic Adventures of an American Girl in London *(1894).*

named sleuth.[6] Female detective heroines became commonplace in the 1880s and 1890s, from the *Illustrated Police News* to the *South Wales Echo*, the *Fife Advertiser* to the *Jarrow Express*. With the rise of the 'New Woman', who was characterised as independent, educated and active in professional life, the female sleuth became a symbol of women's penetration into areas once considered unsuitable for virgin eyes. She took on a more visibly political role as a trailblazer. Just as Kate Easton and Antonia Moser were using their personae as real female detectives to assert women's rights and capabilities, women writers were asserting power to unmask social hypocrisy, corruption and exploitation through the medium of fictional female sleuths.

The golden age of female detection is often conceived of as the 1920s and 1930s, when Agatha Christie's Miss Marple and Dorothy Sayers's Harriet Vane sweep into view. But this golden age arose on the foundation of sedimentary rock laid down in the last two decades of the nineteenth century. Recent criticism has chipped away at the layers of forgetfulness that obscured these strata, but many seams remain relatively unexcavated. Here, I am taking a fresh look at late Victorian detective fiction by three women that combines journalistic observation with political activism.

For these three women authors – Elizabeth Burgoyne Corbett, Florence Marryat and Catherine Louisa Pirkis – the periodical press is their core model of investigative work. It is where they get their early writing experience and source stories for fiction, and is often an essential element in the plots they construct. But, still more importantly, the periodical press offers a journalistic mode of reading female investigation as social enquiry, whose primary task is to expose public inequity rather than merely private iniquity. Their female detectives point to male discrimination against women and to systemic rather than local injustices. They become figures who not only celebrate the possibility of women's professionalism, energy and effectiveness in a taxing career: in succeeding as sleuths, Dora Bell, Jane Farrell and Loveday Brooke also herald more expansive political enquiries into money, marriage and morality.

Elizabeth Burgoyne Corbett: Following the Money

'Why work hard when there is no necessity? You have established your claim to rank amongst the clever women of Society. What more do you want?'

'Money. That's what I want.'

Elizabeth Burgoyne Corbett, *The Marriage Market*

Elizabeth Burgoyne Corbett (1846–1930) was a successful nineteenth-century journalist and novelist. Her *Secrets of a Private Enquiry Office* (1891) sold, by her own account, 'hundreds of thousands of copies', becoming a standard title in Routledge's Hearth and Home Library. She began writing in 1874, aged twenty-eight, for the *Newcastle Daily Chronicle* and became a prolific and versatile writer of novels and plays that cross genres, exploring everything from children's literature to social satire and science fiction. As a journalist whose stories were widely syndicated across multiple periodicals, Burgoyne Corbett was, by 1901, reaching an audience of over a million readers. Her two series of Dora Bell adventures, published from 1892 to 1894, introduced the character of a professional female detective, whose exploits graced the pages of regional newspapers, from the *Leeds Mercury* to the *South Wales Echo*, the *Fife Free Press* and *Exeter Flying Post* to the *Jarrow Express* and the *Cork Weekly News*. Dora's stories are many times shorter than Sherlock Holmes's, which typically occupied 7,000–9,000 words in the sixpenny *Strand* magazine, whose richly illustrated monthly format was designed to appeal to the aspirational middle classes. The first series of ten Dora Bell adventures are around 3,500 words each, the second series 1,500 words each: nowadays they might even count as flash fiction. Situated on the Saturday page of these penny and halfpenny papers, alongside recipes and ideas for entertaining children, they were aimed at a time-poor, cash-strapped readership, particularly of women.

Detective Dora is an ordinary, attractive young woman, with a mother, a young sister Nellie, who is thinking of following her into the profession, and a love interest in the shape of her detective colleague, Adam Henniker. The fact that Dora and Adam work together on equal terms is unusual in early detective fiction. The agents of Bell and White's firm are, like male and female Victorian journalists, working together as a team or family to produce results that expose the truth. Dora's father doesn't appear at all (we assume he is dead), but her youthful uncle is happy to admit his clever niece to the detective firm. There seems a degree of female wish-fulfilment in this. Instead of toasting muffins or embroidering slippers for a stern male parent, Dora works for money for her fun young uncle – a much more independent position. If she marries Adam, her future husband will know and respect her as a colleague.

Dora Bell's cases, given their compact frame, are not complex mysteries that allow for searching character development, teasing clues and multiple red herrings, but their very briskness points to the quotidian, commercial nature of Dora's profession. Dora takes her career seriously. She learns Pitman's shorthand and insists on taking a £50 course in hairdressing to become a convincingly professional lady's maid. She works as a housekeeper while investigating whether the servants are robbing Mr Flowers, a solicitor, of money and plate. (They aren't. It is their paranoid, somnambulist employer who has been 'stealing' his own goods by night.) Dora is always *businesslike*. She opines:

> The individual who chooses to become a detective must be prepared to be brought into contact with almost every phase of life, and with all classes of humanity. At one time the detective's life is full of excitement and adventure. Anon it acquires the subdued flavour of the commonplace, while the mounting of only one rung in the limitless ladder of time may suffice to introduce duties which are little less than loathesome to many natures. But even very distasteful duties may in time become semi-congenial to an ardent follower of the profession who is businesslike enough to mark a stern line between the necessities of work and the inclinations of leisure.[7]

Dora also poses as a greengrocer's assistant, a nurse and, in 'The Stolen Child', as a slum-sister with the Salvation Army, living in London's poor East End. In this case, Burgoyne Corbett gives us a glimpse of the social problems of the slums, their 'exorbitant rent', alcoholism and child abuse. The Salvation Army demands that its sisterhood 'beg' for money by using the 'slum-card' and selling their paper, the *War Cry*; this money is then redistributed, allowing them few funds for their ministry. This story suggests that Burgoyne Corbett had direct experience of the Salvationists and their working methods. Like an 'embedded' reporter, Dora Bell observes East End residents. She departs as soon as she has found the child, whose theft from its middle-class parents is pure melodrama. Yet Burgoyne Corbett invites her readers to be curious about how the Salvationists operate, with their dependence on unpaid or poorly paid female labour.

Burgoyne Corbett's fiction is deeply preoccupied with money. It considers transactions and the relationship between capital and labour. She often uses the character of the female detective to explore the injustices of an exploitative capitalist system.

Elizabeth Burgoyne was born in 1846 in Wigan into a working-class family; her father was a 'forge hammer man' and she was raised in Warrington among neighbours who were mechanics, weavers, shirt-makers and file-cutters. She spent some of her childhood in Germany and used her fluency in German to translate commentary on the exploitative working conditions of industrial Sheffield from a German point of view. Aged twenty-two, Elizabeth married an engineer, George Corbett, who at first worked as a steam engine fitter, then took berths on shipboard, where he tended to the engines of steam ships sailing around the world. George's repeated and long absences and the relatively low pay his job commanded meant that Burgoyne Corbett was, for much of her adult life, functioning as a single mother of three children and primary breadwinner.[8] Her own accounts of what she was paid, revealed in her long and dismal series

OUR NEW SERIES,

THE ADVENTURES OF
Dora Bell, Detective.
BY

MRS GEORGE CORBETT,

Author of "Secrets of a Private Enquiry Office,' &c.

WILL COMMENCE IN

THE FIFE FREE PRESS
ON

SATURDAY, 6th January, 1894.

27. Advertisement for Elizabeth Burgoyne Corbett's The Adventures of Dora Bell, Detective *in the Fife Free Press & Kirkcaldy Guardian (1893).*

of begging letters to the Royal Literary Fund, provide a sobering record of the realities of Victorian publishing and the disparities been an author's public reach and their income. No wonder that her eyes were fixed firmly on financial injustice.

Burgoyne Corbett was a feminist and a socialist. These political beliefs infuse her writing with a distinctive interest in women's work, women's rights and in their financial precarity. In 1886, Burgoyne Corbett published an article, 'Our Women Workers – Suggestions for Winter Recreation', in the *Newcastle Daily Chronicle*.[9] In it, she proposed that working women should have a recreational club with its own library of books and periodicals of interest to women, such as *The Governess*, *The Dressmaker*, *The Lady* and *The Queen*. The club she imagined would provide a safe, affordable cultural space where women could enjoy their evenings and free time without having to negotiate the male gaze. There was already a Free Library in Newcastle, to which – Burgoyne Corbett complained – women contributed as taxpayers, but where they often were made to feel uncomfortable as readers. Victorian men of different social classes had a variety of all-male spaces: from gentleman's clubs in St James to Freemason's halls, professional associations and working-men's clubs. Women workers deserved a clubroom of their own.

Burgoyne Corbett signed the article 'by a working woman', showing that as a writer she felt solidarity with other working women, from seamstresses to shopworkers to mill hands. Her article also recognised domestic labour as labour: married women are 'so literally workers in the true sense of the term', she asserts, that they have 'no time for recreation'. In 1886, Burgoyne Corbett wrote perspicaciously in the *Chronicle* about the Married Women's Property Act and the uneven way in which its legislation was interpreted across the country. She cited examples where workhouse guardians had judged that women were still obliged to support husbands financially from whom they had been legally separated for years. Nonetheless, she celebrated the removal of the disability whereby a wife formerly 'would only have found every penny of her earnings confiscated by a bad husband without the slightest redress for her grievances from anyone'. Now they retain their earnings, women have an incentive to train for a profession and every woman with 'natural pride' will wish 'rather than occupy an inferior or dependent position' to 'qualify herself for earning money'.[10]

In April 1889, Burgoyne Corbett appears, wearing spectacles, in a pen portrait of 'Contributors to the Newcastle Daily Chronicle'. Described as 'a Newcastle authoress of considerable note', she is one

1.—Mr. C. H. Stephenson. 2.—Mr. N. E. Robson. 3.—Mrs. A. Paterson Martin. 4.—Mr. Robert Dunn. 5.—Mr. William Yellowly. 6.—Mrs. E. Corbett. 7.—Mr. John Wilson. 8.—Miss Hildegard Werner. 9.—Mr. John Oxberry, Junr. 10.—Mr. Walter B. Thomas.

28. 'Contributors to the Newcastle Daily Chronicle', Newcastle Weekly Chronicle *(1889).*

of only two female writers in the group of ten. (The other woman is Hildegard Werner, a Swedish musician, conductor and journalist.) There is something pleasing about the fact that they are portrayed like a deck of cards: the editor refers to them as a 'family'. This community of authorship had many benefits. The *Chronicle* published Burgoyne Corbett's letters on political topics ranging from why competition among retailers led to underpriced matches and hence starvation wages for match girls to why Queen Victoria, who levied taxes on her people without spending money to improve their lot, might not deserve unquestioning loyalty. The editor's frequent decision to print her letters supported Burgoyne Corbett's voice. In this nineteenth-century social media space, she could not be lightly trolled: she had right of reply to readers who complained that she was 'down on men'.

'Kleptomaniac and Thief'

Burgoyne Corbett's views on money and social justice permeate her detective fiction. In 'Kleptomaniac and Thief', a Dora Bell adventure that Corbett published in April 1892 in the *South Wales Echo* and elsewhere, Dora is invited by the manager of Wimpley & Co., a department store in Jermyn Grove, to investigate persistent thefts from its counters. There are a number of regular 'kleptomaniacs' among its wealthy female customers, the manager suavely explains, but the staff are aware of these ladies and deal with the problem by simply adding the expense of the stolen item to the kleptomaniac's monthly account, which is invariably paid without comment. When they don't know which kleptomaniac is responsible for abstracting a certain item, they have an elegant solution – they charge them all.

The problem that has led to Dora's summons is that there is a new and as yet unidentified kleptomaniac on the loose in Wimpley's. Dora's job is to identify them. She patrols the department store and her suspicions at first fix on a lady who swipes a piece of lace. But the shop assistant signals that this wealthy lady is a known offender, so can be ignored. Dora then spots another possible mark. The unidentified kleptomaniac turns out to be a *man*. He is the wealthy son of a stockbroker, about to be married to an aristocrat. Wimpley's is perfectly satisfied with Dora's information and no action is taken against him; he will presumably be billed *post facto*, without comment, like other valued customers. While Dora is in the store, however, a small girl is caught stealing a bun. She wails piteously that it is for her mother, who is ill and starving. But the child is disbelieved, prosecuted and sent to a reformatory for three years. Dora visits the starving mother and finds her dead. Burgoyne Corbett's comparison of the innocent child, who steals out of dire need but is condemned by society, with the bachelor whose needless depredations are winked at, was highly topical.

The word 'kleptomaniac', which first appeared in print in 1861, was by the 1890s sufficiently well understood by ordinary readers to be used without explanation in newspapers. For example, in 1896, Mrs Sarah Henney, 'a fashionably-dressed, ladylike person', appeared at Marylebone Police Court charged with robbing Whiteley's in Westbourne Grove and other London department stores of items whose value totalled over £100. The *Evening Standard* reported that the lady's husband had private means and held a good appointment. Mrs Henney 'was not an ordinary thief', as she locked up the items she stole in boxes rather than reselling or using them.[11] Two relatives, 'public men, holding good positions' stood bail and undertook to 'look after' her. She was discharged. It was evident to the public reading these cases that the treatment of theft by the wealthy differed from the treatment of poor people; it was treated as a forgivable neurosis precisely because it was not actuated by need. As a journalist, Burgoyne Corbett must have studied newspaper reports of such cases and drawn on them in her detective fiction. Wimpley's in Jermyn Grove is clearly a version of the real Whiteley's in Westbourne Grove.

Other periodical writers examined the same question. James McLevy, among his serialised detective stories set in Edinburgh, included 'The Kleptomaniac and the Diamond Ring' (1888), where Mrs Makepeace, a professor's wife and persistent kleptomaniac, is falsely accused of stealing a ring. The ring was, in this instance, stolen by a 'common thief' employed as an assistant jeweller. As Detective McGovan comments: 'in a rich person this weakness is called a disease, and grandly labelled kleptomania; in a poor person that same disease is briefly called "tarry-fingered". The tarry-fingered one, if caught, is often sent to gaol; the kleptomaniac is usually pitied, and bought off by her friends.'[12]

Despite this assertion, McLevy's story displays little pity for the shopman thief, who is a well-known lag. In McLevy's works, criminals form a distinct community, usually known to the police for a previous conviction. Burgoyne Corbett, by contrast, is outraged on behalf of the poor child in her story, who steals to save her dying parent.

Corbett often makes her detective stories a vehicle for reflections on social and financial injustice. In 'SWE-E-EP!', Dora Bell investigates a theft from a disreputable character, 'Mr Davison', who poses in high society as a generous and amiable host of lavish parties but is actually, under another name, the owner of half a dozen money-lending enterprises in the West End. Davison uses his parties as a form of bait, to lure in aristocrats who wrongly trust his advice and can be persuaded to patronise the loan sharks Davison recommends – who are, in fact, avatars of himself. Davison's premises are robbed by a 'common thief', who breaks his leg when coming down the chimney to grab some jewels (which have been pawned by an aristocrat, and so do not technically 'belong' to Davison either). Dora poses as a charity nurse to access the thief, who is feverish and delirious so doesn't notice Dora's presence; she secures and returns the missing jewels. No criminal prosecution is brought. The story poses a broader question about which man is the more dangerous con-artist: the high-society loan shark or the tarry-fingered sweep. How, indeed, should one define theft, when usury by the wealthy abstracts much greater sums than shoplifting by the poor?

Similarly, in 'A Pattern of Virtue', Burgoyne Corbett uses detective fiction to investigate capitalist exploitation that is also ruthless seduction. Dora happens upon a suicidal seventeen-year-old on Westminster Bridge and talks her down from the edge. Lucy Markham is a country girl who, having been orphaned, came to London to seek work as a shopgirl. She was promised marriage by her employer, Mr Collinson, and naively believed his honourable intentions when he set her up in a villa in St John's Wood, only realising belatedly – due to the snide comments of a servant – that she was now in the position of a mistress and would never be able to marry or regain a respectable position. Dora's reaction is swift and sure. She digs dirt on Mr Collinson, who passes as a 'pattern of virtue' in public life but has played this trick on many women before. Dora uses the damning information she holds on him to force Collinson's hand. She effectively blackmails him, demanding as the price of her silence that Collinson allow Lucy to leave him and that he fund Lucy's education for five years. Collinson complies and Lucy proves to have a 'talent for operatic composition'. She is, Burgoyne Corbett tells us, 'talented, industrious, and ambitious, . . . when her five years of study are ended there will be another star added to our galaxy of genius.'

Fallen women in Victorian literature conventionally stay down. Even if they have been seduced due to their excessive innocence, they die, nobly, as in Elizabeth Gaskell's *Ruth*, or painfully, as in Hardy's *Tess of the d'Urbervilles*. Burgoyne Corbett, *au contraire*, does not permit her wronged teenager to plunge into the Thames. The female detective ensures that, instead, her star will ascend indefinitely. Lucy is not auditioning for the part of Mimi; she wants to be Puccini. Blackmailing the villain is, of course, morally questionable as a detective practice (as is nursing sick burglars without a nursing qualification). That is, however, not the point in the Dora Bell adventures: Dora assists women who have been cheated to get their own back. As Burgoyne Corbett commented in the pages of *The Women's Penny Paper*, a periodical written, edited and published entirely by women:

I have seldom written anything in which I have not taken the opportunity of airing some of my views regarding the consequences meted out to erring women, in opposition to the popular treatment of equally or more guilty men. Until lately, however, it has been very uphill work to fight against social usages. I remember when a few years ago I published a three volume novel, entitled

'Cassandra,' a writer in the Academy [. . .] expressed his astonish-
ment at the idea of 'anyone, much less a lady, having the bad taste
to make an open allusion to such a subject as man's immorality!'[13]

Burgoyne Corbett does not let guilty men off the hook and neither
does Dora, her secret agent. In another story, 'Levying Blackmail',
Mr Smithson, who has been preying on innocent women, forging love-
letters that appear to be in their writing then blackmailing them for large
sums of money to prevent a scandal, is dog-whipped in a very graphic
fashion until he lies, 'a moaning, bleeding mass upon the floor'. Men
administer the whipping, but the female reader looks on with Adam
Henniker, whom Burgoyne Corbett gives the line: 'shall I confess it? – I
thoroughly enjoyed seeing him writhe and shriek under the lashing . . .'[14]

As Inspector Macnaghten, Chief of the CID, remarked in his
reminiscences of late-Victorian London:

> The amount of blackmail levied in the Metropolis is stupendous,
> and is the unsuspected cause of many a suicide and voluntary
> banishment from the country. Many gangs of blackmailers have
> reduced their damnable profession to a fine art, & when they have
> tasted blood and got their claws into a victim, they will never
> leave him till they have sucked him as dry as a squeezed lemon, or
> till death releases him from a life not worth living.[15]

Macnaghten cited the real case of a gang of blackmailers who targeted
wealthy widowed ladies; actresses were also regularly targeted by blackmailers at the stage door.[16] Burgoyne Corbett draws on topics of current
newspaper debate to supply her with ideas for cases, many of which
involve women exploited by unscrupulous men. Her imagined, graphi-
cally violent retribution against the blackmailer takes the predatory idea
of financial vampirism and reverses it to make the male culprit bleed.

Indeed, there is an element of retribution against exploitative
capitalists in many of Burgoyne Corbett's stories. Burgoyne Corbett

had been shamelessly ripped off by publishers as a young writer, particularly by the firm of Swan Sonnenschein, whom she unsuccessfully took to court. In 'His Last Victim' (one of the *Secrets of a Private Enquiry Office*), she lambasts 'the human vampires who fatten on the last penny they can wring from struggling authors'.[17] Her heroine, a talented but vulnerable young author, is nearly driven to suicide by the debt she incurs when she accepts a contract from a rogue publisher, who makes her pay ruinous publication costs. The secrets revealed by private enquiry agents in Burgoyne Corbett's fiction are not always, legally, crimes: rather they are social injustices and hypocrisies. Throughout her fiction, Burgoyne Corbett makes the twin suggestions that the very rich are often getting away with murder, and that it is up to women workers to hold them to account.

Readers of Burgoyne Corbett's fiction in a periodical setting would have seen adjacent examples of real-life women detecting crime. In the *Fife Free Press*, an advertisement for the Dora Bell Detective Stories serialised in the newspaper appears on the very same page as a story about a bigamous Kirkcaldy man arrested when his mother-in-law detected him. His suspicious female relative followed him 'home' to the second wife, whom he had unblushingly married in the same church as the first.[18] The Dora Bell case 'The Mysterious Thief' appears in the *South Wales Echo* in March 1894, immediately succeeded by real-life commentary on 'The Grafton Street Murder', detected by a woman who became suspicious of a fellow lodger after hearing an argument in the apartment below; she stayed up all night and followed bloodstains to discover the murdered body in a corded trunk. The appearance of the Dora Bell stories in a newspaper setting was a reminder of women's constant proximity to real crime.

Playing Men

The youthful characters, Messrs Bell and White, who found the private enquiry office in Burgoyne Corbett's best-selling 1891 *Secrets of a Private Enquiry Office*, are male, but they employ a female detective (later identified as Dora) to assist them. Significantly, some of the cases with which the private enquiry office deals involve women who are playing men, in one sense or another. In 'The Polish Refugee', Count Feodor Plotnitzky teaches French, German and the violin to a host of pupils. He has perfect manners and is 'bewilderingly handsome', with 'a moustache so perfect in its size, its shape, its neatness, and its glossy blackness, that it is the admiration of one sex and the envy of the other'. He is also a wonderful teacher, according to the headmistress: 'the most capable teacher I have ever had in the school. The progress his pupils make under his tuition is perfectly miraculous, when compared with the results of lessons by former tutors. His terms are rather high, but his abilities more than justify their exaction.'[19]

The detectives are hired to investigate the mysterious Plotnitzky by a baronet whose wealthy daughter, Mabel, has, like 'the majority of his young lady pupils', fallen madly in love with him. The baronet doesn't oppose Mabel's wish to marry Plotnitzky, but he wants to know more about the man who has infatuated her, seemingly without having given the heiress any encouragement.

Of course, the mysterious Plotnitzky – the perfect man – turns out to be a woman. Feodore has taken the position of private tutor to support her mother, an aristocratic widow whose husband died leaving her penniless. Feodore is given an honourable filial motive for professional cross-dressing. But the female reader cannot help but ruminate on the fact that when 'passing' as a man, the woman can command a much higher rate of pay: the rate her teaching evidently deserves. She is also enabled to write cantatas and have them produced by August Manns (a real contemporary musician) in concerts at the Crystal Palace, a feat substantially harder to achieve as a woman. Being a man might in one sense be a disguise, but in a professional and artistic sense it enables her to be 'seen'. In creating the character of Feodor/Feodore, Burgoyne Corbett may well have been thinking of Hildegard Werner, her fellow contributor to the *Newcastle Daily Chronicle*, who had been a medallist at the Stockholm Royal Academy of Music, studied in Vienna and Paris and became 'the first lady violin teacher in Newcastle'.[20] Both of Burgoyne Corbett's daughters would also become professional musicians.[21]

It is intriguing that, when Feodore passes as a man, all her female pupils adore her: '"Oh! He is just heavenly!" sighed Miss Philippa Sudds.' Lesbian attraction is real and pervasive in the story. The detective prevents Mabel from marrying Feodore, by elucidating Feodore's 'real' gender. The conclusion is that Mabel's father, the widowed baronet, falls in love with Feodore and marries her himself: heterosexual order is restored and the woman is 'rescued' from any obligation to obtain an income through labour outside the home (surely a huge loss to the teaching profession). Feodore becomes Mabel's stepmother. If Mabel, however, retains any of her same-sex passion for her former teacher, she lies conveniently near at hand for them to be able to satisfy the impulse without scaring the horses.

While (with one or two exceptions) real Victorian female detectives rarely cross-dressed, the ability to cross-dress and pass as a man is essential to the Victorian female detective on stage and in fiction.[22] In Burgoyne Corbett's later detective novel *When the Sea Gives Up Its Dead* (1894), the female detective heroine Annie Cory passes by day as a blonde artist, Una Stratton, and uses cork height-improvers and a moustache to pass by night as Ernest Bootle: both aliases shadow the suspect, Hugh Stavanger, who has framed Annie's fiancé for a diamond robbery. Annie follows the villain to Malta and into a casino at night, exposing herself to an all-male world of drinking, gambling and conspiracy. It is notable that in her new 'Jekyll and Hyde' existence of burning the candle at both ends, Annie's artificially lightened day-side is female and her artificially dark night-side is male. Annie retains 'her masculine clothing, without which it would not have been so easy for her to penetrate unobserved into all sorts of places'.[23] Still more remarkably, her maiden aunt also cross-dresses, takes the

Underground to the docks at night and successfully spies the villain being smuggled onto a ship lying at anchor. Miss Cory is courageous, and also clearly enjoying herself:

'Yes, men generally have an idea that women are of no use,' Miss Cory said, and her voice had such a triumphant inflection in it that her hearers at once found themselves heartened again. 'But in this case they may thank their stars that they have got women to help them.'[24]

The adventure not only leads Annie into grave danger, but – in common with many female detectives of the period – also opens a new world to her: a world of travel, of inhabiting alternative identities (male and female) and having surprising, potentially indecorous experiences, using her courage, social skills and problem-solving abilities without male supervision or restraint. Her suspicions are proven correct; she solves the case and demonstrates her husband-to-be's innocence. He has been framed by the son of his jeweller *employer*. Again, it is capital rather than labour that is responsible for theft. Even though Annie is manifestly in the right, the male judge still tears her case to shreds, as: 'He had read all about Annie's adventures, and had at once dubbed her in his own mind an unwomanly schemer. He didn't like unwomanly women. They set a bad example to others. Therefore an example must be made of them.'[25]

The judge has, presumably, been reading the newspapers and has allowed private prejudice to colour his conviction. It is only when Hilton Riddell appears, the lost brother of Annie's fiancé, that male testimony can convict Hugh Stavanger. Burgoyne Corbett here points to the truth, which she knew well from her own court experience, that justice and male judgment are often poles apart. Female detection is only a fingerpost on the road to equality.

Burgoyne Corbett's feminist anger is most explicitly expressed in *New Amazonia* (1889), a science fiction novel in which the author falls asleep and wakes up 600 years in the future: in a prosperous, healthy and just nation (formerly known as Ireland) entirely governed by women. The cities of this new state – which still seems strikingly modern – are named after women; its transportation systems involve floating rail, powered by clean electricity. Its women, freed from restrictive clothing, poor diet and educational malnourishment, fulfil their destinies to become wise leaders, scientists, translators and economists. These beautiful, short-haired, culotte-wearing, vege-tarian female citizens are almost seven feet tall and extremely fit. They have discovered the secret to living to be centenarians, in perfect health. A Victorian man appears so physically, intellectually and morally puny to them that they mistake him for a child. They cannot believe that it was historically the case that women laboured under the burden of unequal marriage and property laws and that women were not granted equal pay for equal work. In New Amazonia, divorce is readily accessible and fault-free, but male cheating within marriage results in instant banishment. Burgoyne Corbett asks:

'I suppose crime is occasionally to be met with in New Amazonia?'
'Sometimes; but very rarely. There is very little incentive to crime here; when it does occur, we accept it as an indication of a diseased brain, and forthwith use our best efforts to cure the disease.'[26]

The fantasy of *New Amazonia* allows Burgoyne Corbett to fully explore the view that crime is the product of social malaise, which a caring, woman-led society could eradicate.

The New Woman detective of the 1890s is a symbol of what women can discover if they interrogate the status quo, and what they can become if they are sufficiently intrepid. Energetic and fit in mind and body, she is peripatetic and flexible, and enjoys her work and her manifest success in performing it. The *Spectator* in 1893 described the lady journalist and the female detective in pitying terms, imagining the former as a pale and harried figure subsisting on cucumber sand-wiches and the latter as a victim of exploitation in a society where British respect for privacy has been replaced by French spycraft.[27] *Fin-de siècle* feminist detective fiction responds with positive images of healthy, modern young women whose profession is physically, intellectually and financially empowering.

Florence Marryat: Detonating the Marriage Bomb

Where Burgoyne Corbett's feminist detective fiction follows the money, Florence Marryat's lights a fuse under marriage. *In the Name of Liberty* (1897), the novel in which Marryat introduces us to a female detective involved in a high-risk counter-terrorism operation, is so surprising that, as Marryat expert Catherine Pope put it, 'Reading it for the first time in the British Library – my eyebrows kept disappearing over the back of my head.'[28] It shocks from the first pages, where the middle-class protagonists, Maurice Farrell and his wife Jane are depicted as starving in their rented accommodation due to Maurice's unemployment.[29] Indeed, at first this thriller looks as if it might be a piece of investigative journalism or a George Gissing novel of social criticism set in the London slums. Jane is weeping over the body of their baby son. Poverty has starved him to death. Florence Marryat had suffered the lacerating experience of giving birth to a baby with a cleft palate, who died due to her inability to feed her. This subject therefore could not be more emotive, for writer or reader.

Maurice Farrell has been sacked from his job as a journalist for a Conservative weekly, because the editor discovered he had been writing freelance articles for a Socialist paper. He has been black-listed: he cannot now publish journalism. Financially desperate, he is lured to join a secret society of anarchists whose leaders, Denis and Robert O'Brien, are also Irish Fenians. The O'Briens offer him a big payout if he will accompany their sister, Aileen, to Chicago on a dangerous mission to break imprisoned Fenians out of jail. Maurice accepts. He sends an explanatory letter and £20 to his wife. The Brotherhood, however, suppresses the letter and Jane proudly refuses the money; she assumes her husband has left her. Forced upon her own resources, Jane at first works in a milliner's shop, then accepts the suggestion of a policeman, who is a childhood friend, that she should become a female detective.

Jane joins the Criminal Investigation Department's anti-terrorist team and proves to have a brilliant eye for security. She is posted to the London riverside house of the Earl of Innisfale, attending social events to identify intruders and possible entryways for a terrorist attack. In this edge-of-seat thriller, the previously impoverished, isolated and famished Jane achieves a professional life where she is well fed, well dressed and socially valuable. One reviewer objected that the 'very ordinary' Jane could not have accomplished this singular transformation, but the modern reader cannot help but feel that, like Florence Marryat herself, Jane begins to bloom once her husband is out of the way.

Meanwhile, Maurice has returned to London and, spotting Jane in her finery about to enter a carriage, is disgusted by her transformation, assuming that she is a 'kept woman' with a wealthy lover. Jane, in turn, accuses him of infidelity; he was observed (the police have told her) boarding a ship to Chicago with Aileen O'Brien as if they were man and wife. Jane refuses to tell her husband about her professional identity as a detective. The circumstances may be far-fetched, but the impasse between the couple is realistically raw. Marryat calls attention to the sexual double standard.

The novel's climax is shocking. Maurice, in despair after fighting with Jane, accepts the 'black lot' given by the anarchists that commits him to bomb the Earl of Innisfale's household during a party. Jane, in her counter-terrorist role, is stationed in the garden, watching the river for a possible attack. She spots Maurice in the dark, wrests the bomb from him and throws it into the goldfish pond, where it explodes (harmlessly to humans, though fatally to the goldfish); Jane allows Maurice, however, to escape before her police colleagues can arrest him.

This tussle over the bomb between the female detective and the terrorist husband dramatises the struggle over marriage – the anger between the neglectful man and the suspicious woman – in the most violent possible manner. Marryat explodes the tension in this couple's bad marriage in a 'controlled' way: nobody gets killed. But the scale of the threat is palpable. Maurice may not be directly responsible for his baby's death; he may not kill the earl (who, in a romantic plot-twist, turns out to be his long-lost father), but as a terrorist-husband he is only prevented from inflicting mass casualties by the detective-wife who stands in his path.

Marryat's novel, despite its rejection of political extremism, conveys a specifically female rage. Jane Farrell's CID codename is 'Madame Delacour'. This echoes the novel *Belinda* (1801) by popular Irish novelist Maria Edgeworth, in which the central figure, Lady Delacour, also attends masquerade balls and bears two terrible secrets: suspected breast cancer and estrangement from her husband. Although Jane saves Maurice, preventing his assassination attempts and restoring him to his father, the Farrells' marital reconciliation is as fake as Maurice's lost-heir backstory. The real end to *In the Name of Liberty* is where Nora, a poor Irish girl who has been seduced and abandoned by the Fenian Denis O'Brien, runs after her lover to prevent his terrorist attack on Parliament. The bomb explodes, blasting Nora and her unborn child to eternity. In this novel, the victims of male terrorism are women and children – and bombs are a metaphor for the routine violence men do to them.

When Jane subsides back into her marriage to Maurice, the modern reader cannot help feeling disappointed. Order has been restored and female anger has returned to a state of repression. Maurice, during his attempt to free fellow anarchists, is reported to have cross-dressed: in Chicago, he 'changed clothes with [Aileen] on more than one occasion'.[30] Marryat was likely here drawing on real-life events: Michael

Sheehy, a wanted Fenian, had in 1867 escaped from America in women's clothes. Cross-dressing is a sidenote in the plot of *In the Name of Liberty*, but it is typical of the sidelong view the novel takes of masculinity. Maurice's missions look tawdry beside his wife's bravery.

Like Burgoyne Corbett's female detective fiction, Marryat's stories featuring a female sleuth contain explicit social critique. *In the Name of Liberty* is set within the world of journalism and politics, revealing writing as inherently political. Marryat must have followed the anarchist cases reported in the papers in the 1890s, when anxiety about dynamite plots in London, Vienna and Barcelona kept public attention focused on the threat of a terrorist outrage, where perpetrators might be male or female. In 1894, the young anarchist Jacob Polti was arrested after being found with bomb-making equipment in his room. The newspapers reported that a female detective had led to Polti's identification and arrest:

> a female detective was brought into the house to watch the man. Her reports to the detectives made them renew their determination not to let Polti out of their sight. The woman had, when Polti was out, taken a tour of his rooms and found, as she said, some liquid in bottles, many letters, and lots of Anarchist literature.[31]

The police subsequently denied this story, but their wording left open the possibility that the 'information received' that had led to his arrest proceeded from a female source.[32] Polti was condemned. The day after the trial, Polti's nineteen-year-old wife died in childbirth. This case may well have suggested to Marryat the possibility of women's involvement on both sides of her terrorist novel. Women were also reported to have been involved in capturing Fenian terrorist suspects.[33] *In the Name of Liberty* was serialised from January to April 1896 in the *Belfast Weekly News*, where its discussion of Irishmen in London seeking retaliation against aristocratic absentee landlords would have been especially topical. *In the Name of Liberty* may be an anti-terrorist novel, which links Fenians with dangerous anarchism, but its explosive plot reveals marriage (like Ireland) to be a divided and unequal state where absentee landlordism can lead tenants to revolt.

Sensation Novelist and Celebrity Divorcee

Florence Marryat (1833–1899) was born into literary notoriety and marital discord. She was the daughter of Captain Frederick Marryat, a distinguished mariner whose novels of seafaring life, particularly *Mr Midshipman Easy* (1836), won him popular acclaim. His marriage, however, to Catherine Shairp, who bore him four sons and seven daughters, was bitterly dysfunctional. The couple separated and Florence became an early example of a common modern phenomenon: the child who shuttles between estranged parental residences, witnessing

29. Florence Marryat holding a dog (1888).

her mother's fight to obtain maintenance money and her father's exasperation at a woman who, from Dickens's description, seems to have been violent and unstable:

> She had no interest whatever in the children; and was such a fury, that, being dressed to go out to dinner, she would sometimes, on no other provocation than a pin out of place ... fall upon a little maid she had, beat her till she couldn't stand, then tumble into hysterics, and be carried to bed.[34]

This anecdote suggests barely repressed fury issuing in physical attack; in Florence Marryat's novels, angry mothers do hit their daughters.

Unsurprisingly, Florence escaped when she could, but bolted from an unhappy childhood into an equally unhappy marriage. Her husband, Thomas Ross Church, was an ensign in the 12th Madras Staff Corps; she journeyed to the Malaysian island of Penang to marry him and thereafter spent seven years 'in exile' in India and Burma. She caricatured the scenes she encountered in articles for a magazine, *Temple Bar*, to which she contributed under the name Gup, the Anglo-Indian word for 'gossip'. Like Burgoyne Corbett, lonely and increasingly dependent on making her own money, Marryat became a journalist as her marriage began to collapse. She would later write to her daughter Ethel: 'My darling, you do not know half of what I have suffered, and I pray God you may never know.'[35]

In 1860, aged twenty-seven and heavily pregnant, Marryat left Ross Church, returning to England with her children, where she began writing novels, fast and furiously, to earn money to support her newly independent existence. She became the editor of a successful magazine, *London Society*, a journalist, actress and producer. Marryat was immersed in the theatrical world of the 1880s and 1890s: she may well have seen plays featuring a female detective – perhaps *The Lucky Shilling* (1888), where a female detective confronts her husband's crimes.

From the start, Marryat's novels were critical of the institution of marriage. They are page-turners, unafraid to explore issues, including female genital mutilation, vivisection, rape, elective single motherhood, domestic violence and – perhaps most shockingly – the power and strength of female sexual desire. As the *Pall Mall Gazette* sniffily but perceptively remarked in 1880, the 'energy in her work' is sustained 'by a certain rebellious and hostile attitude which she appears to have adopted towards the world and its social institutions'.[36] Having experienced first-hand, both in her parents' case and in her own, domestic violence and the legal disabilities under which unhappily married women laboured when they tried to re-establish themselves socially and financially as independent citizens, Marryat wrote fiction that expresses deep anger about society's neglect of women's rights and needs, and the sexual double standard that sanctions male infidelity while stigmatising extra-marital female sexual experience.

Like Burgoyne Corbett, she penned a futuristic fantasy in which women ruled and men were marginal. 'What Shall We Do With Our Men?' is an astonishing monologue of 1893 – addressed to women only – that Marryat performed in the persona of Electra Thucydides, Senior Wrangler of St Momus College.[37] Electra is speaking 'in 1993' and her words 'are conveyed by means of telephonic communication to above 200 female audiences'. In effect, Marryat pictures herself lecturing by Zoom call. The pleasure of her monologue as Electra (a dramatic protagonist associated with female vengeance) involves surprising reversals. Professor Thucydides notes that women have long been known to be the Higher Sex and female philosophers have debated whether men have brains, or souls at all. Men have recently been admitted to government, but only to the Lower House, alongside gorillas and chimpanzees. There had been public hand-wringing in the second half of the nineteenth century about 'surplus women', who remained unmarried. *Hearth and Home* ran a regular column, 'What to do with our Daughters'. Marryat's 'What Shall We Do With Our Men?' put the boot in, on the other foot.

Perhaps the most electrifying suggestion in her futuristic fantasy is the Marriage Lease Act, which has improved marital relations:

> Since the New Marriage Lease Act has happily passed – constituting marriage a civil contract (it used at times to be a very *uncivil* one) dissoluble at the option of the female partner only, at the expiration of 3, 5, or 7 years: the husband to be given up in tenantable repair & all damages, whether by crockery, fire irons, or other implements of domestic warfare, made good or paid for . . .[38]

Women in 1993 (in Marryat's fantasy) can lease a man like a piano and send him back if he doesn't stay in tune. Marryat's fiction is similarly confronting on the issues surrounding male and female relationships: the battle of the sexes is often literal in her work. The insufficiency of marriage, its inequalities and latent violence, is the shocking truth her female sleuths unmask.

Detecting Infidelity

In her accomplished short story 'The Countess Sorrento' (1898), Marryat again introduces the figure of the female detective. In this tale, however, the female detective is not the heroine. Mrs Thompson is an experienced private female detective, working for Mr Frobisher's 'secret enquiry office', which 'boasted of having lady detectives planted from Siberia to Siam'.[39] Mrs Thompson, the detective, alias 'Countess Sorrento', is despatched to a boarding house in Earl's Court. She is tasked with 'befriending' a woman suspected of being unfaithful in marriage, to expose her infidelity. As we have seen, this was a common situation for real female detectives. Like the 'Countess Carina', who had falsely befriended Gertrude Barrett when that young woman had taken lodgings in Earl's Court while waiting for a formal separation from her abusive husband, the 'Countess Sorrento' is posing as a confidante, but is in fact a ruthless operator who hopes to expose her victim's romantic life. Almost certainly, Marryat had read about Ellen Lyon, who was jailed in 1895 for attempting to procure Barrett; like Lyon, the 'Countess Sorrento' receives her comeuppance.

In Marryat's story, the female detective's intended victim is, in fact, gaming her. 'Mrs Percoral', the woman in the guesthouse whom Mrs Thompson is paid to expose, is *herself* a female detective, hired by Mr Thompson to obtain evidence of his wife's infidelity for his own divorce suit. Drunk on the champagne with which she plied Percoral, Mrs Thompson inadvertently gives away the name of her own lover. The result is 'public disgrace – infamy – ruin!' She has 'fallen into the pit which she had digged for others'.[40] Again, Florence Marryat may well have been inspired to write this story by newspaper accounts. As we have seen, Charlotte Antonia Williamson, the female detective, was caught *in flagrante delicto* with Maurice Moser in 1890 by a female detective from Slaters, a rival agency employed by her husband. Marryat picks up on the centrality of adultery to private detective cases and satirises the 'cat and mouse' game as in fact a seedy marital struggle for control of the narrative of legal fault. She knew this battle intimately at first hand, having struggled with her first husband through lawsuits in which she was obliged to sue for control of her marriage settlement, her earnings and custody of her children.

Marryat, defending herself against reviewers' charge that she exaggerated in her fiction, noted that 'the most unlikely scenes depicted . . . have happened, and are drawn from life; it is a remarkable fact that those incidents in my novels which have incurred most abuse or ridicule at the hands of the public press, have invariably been those gained from the same source.'[41]

Marryat specifically mentioned newspapers who devoted 'leading columns' to 'police court adventures', showing that she read court reportage. Detectives and their dubious methods of obtaining evidence in adultery cases preoccupied newspapers of the 1890s. George Augustus Sala, a fellow journalist, playwright and friend of Marryat's, observed that:

These detectives, whom I ruefully confess to be, under the present conditions of our social scheme, all but indispensable, are ubiquitous. The sunburnt gentleman whom you meet in a boarding house, and whom you have reason to believe is H.B.M Consul at Alcochafada, in the Spanish Main, may be a detective. So likewise may be that fascinating Marchesa Truffatore, the black-eyed beauty whom you met at that nice little dinner at the Hotel Lucullus, and who sang those little Venetian songs so sweetly after dinner ... Your acquaintance with the Marchesa ripened into friendship at Monte Carlo; yet be not surprised if you come across her some day in the witness-box at the Royal Courts of Justice, and if you find her acknowledging while she is being forensically dissected by Mr. Bullyrook Q.C. that she has long been engaged by a private detective agency, and that her real name is Jane Runt.[42]

Sala explores the social duplicity (not only in terms of class identity, but also sexual availability) that the 'detective' abets and the way in which women encountered abroad, at hotels, may be honey traps, seducing the unwary guest into familiar conversation or other kinds of intercourse.

In both of her works featuring female detectives, Marryat uses the existence of this profession to explore the 'double life' that women and men may lead within marriage. As Beth Palmer rightly identifies, performativity is central to Marryat's conception of identity in general: the self is not born but constructed, a 'contingent cluster of theatrical roles'.[43] The sexual affair and the detective job are equivalent kinds of doubling, which may involve cheap guest houses, disguise, role-play and learning lines. Although the protagonist in 'The Countess Sorrento' doesn't attract much sympathy, the setting neatly contextualises marital disappointment and infidelity as a ubiquitous modern reality, where the point is not so much who sins as who wins. Her female detective characters choose work over a dissatisfying domestic situation. These stories are not primarily about 'solving' crime. Their drama is not that of the hunt, the clue, the jigsaw that finally reveals the villain's face. Rather, they position the female detective in a paid role as a social observer; they confront the relationship between power and self-invention. The result in each case is a change in the state of a marriage, but the investigation relates the shortcomings of the State to the condition of marriage itself.

Catherine Louisa Pirkis: Women's Undercover Power

Catherine Louisa Pirkis, who also wrote detective fiction in the 1890s, has received more recent critical attention than Burgoyne Corbett or Marryat, but her stories' fascination with newsprint, languages and codes remains under-explored.[44] Pirkis was a contributor to periodicals, a prolific novelist, and wrote song lyrics for musical theatre. She preferred to appear in print as 'C.L. Pirkis'; some reviewers assumed that her work was written by a man. Her female detective, similarly, lives a quiet life of observation and deduction, her professionalism tacitly asserting that a woman is equal to the many deceptions with which society seeks to mystify the unwary. As Adrienne Gavin points out:

> Just as her creator insisted on 'C.L. Pirkis (not "Miss"),' Loveday Brooke is careful that it is her professional life that becomes part of the public record, not her private life. By maintaining her independence, keeping her personal life inexorably private, and demanding to be judged for her work alone, Loveday achieves what many contemporary women, including writers, were trying to achieve: respect for professional achievement instead of categorisation or restriction based on gender.[45]

Like Elizabeth Burgoyne Corbett and Florence Marryat, Pirkis was engaged in a variety of political debates. She was a notable campaigner against vivisection and for animal rights, a campaign that informs her fiction, particularly *Jack: A Mendicant*, a book about a dog who is stolen and sold for medical research. The proceeds from sales of this work, which attracted positive notice from Queen Victoria herself, directly funded the National Canine Defence League, of which Pirkis was a founding member. Pirkis's espousal of animal rights brought her into the social ambit of Frances Power Cobbe, a powerful feminist who, as we have seen, argued in 1888 for the official introduction of women detectives to British police forces, stimulating widespread public discussion of this issue. Pirkis was likely aware of this debate and of Power Cobbe's advocacy for female detectives.

MRS C. L. PIRKIS

The lady whose portrait is reproduced above may not be known to you—you may never have heard of her before—but if you will read carefully what follows you will derive some information about her.

Mr. Pirkis is a novelist of some repute, being the author of "Wanted, an Heir," "A Very Opal," "Saint and Sybil," "Judith Wynne," "The Road to Ruin," "The Experiences of Loveday Brooke," and other characteristic works.

30. *Catherine Louisa Pirkis,* Evening Telegraph *(1896).*

Pirkis was also secretary of a group who in 1894 petitioned the Czar of Russia on the plight of Polish refugees. Her husband Fred, with whom she shared her campaigning zeal, was described at his death as 'a powerful influence in the Liberal party'.[46] Like Burgoyne Corbett, Pirkis found the medium of 'letters to the editor' of periodicals a good route to airing her views: from slang and colloquial English to poor housing design and suburban sprawl, to the inadequate protections of copyright law.[47] Pirkis's engagement with public opinion through the medium of periodicals is mirrored in her series of detective stories, which, appearing in the *Ludgate Monthly* among news articles, also test hypotheses and question social assumptions.

Pirkis's detective heroine, Loveday Brooke, first appeared in 1893. She is a single, professional woman who is well established as a trusted operator within the private detective agency – Ebenezer Dyer

31 & 32. Family photographs of Catherine Louisa Pirkis (1871).

of Lynch Court – for which she works. At a little over thirty years old, Loveday Brooke is a more mature woman than many of her 1890s counterparts in serialised fiction. Pirkis resists the reader's desire to picture her by saying that she is best described in 'a series of negations': 'she was not tall, she was not short; she was not dark, she was not fair; she was neither handsome nor ugly'.[48] If women are usually described approvingly or disapprovingly according to the male gaze, Loveday is described instead as a gazer: 'Her one noticeable trait was a habit she had, when absorbed in thought, of dropping her eyelids over her eyes till only a line of eyeball showed, and she appeared to be looking out at the world through a slit.' Like Jane Eyre, she dresses unobtrusively in 'Quakerish' black. Loveday is depicted in self-consciously closed terms. She is the oyster of PIs.

Pirkis's heroine redefines Victorian spinsterhood as active, daring and useful. She is quick, professional and crisp in her exchanges with colleagues, clients and suspects. Satisfyingly, she consistently proves her male colleagues wrong. As her employer remarks: 'the idea seems gaining ground in many quarters that ... women detectives are more satisfactory than men'. The superiority of the private detective to the plodding policeman was an established trope from the early days of detective drama. Where the detective is a woman, however, this superiority has an added frisson. It advertises a woman's superior rationality and powers of objective deduction: qualities of which many Victorian men still denied women were capable. It is notable that when commending the Loveday Brooke stories as 'full of thrilling incidents', reviewers connected them with articles in the *Ludgate Monthly* that praised real-life 'Famous Women', such as Ellen Terry, who had become successful writers as well as actresses.[49] *The Queen* listed *The Experiences of Loveday Brooke*, which had just been translated into Danish, in a column, 'What Women Are Doing', that also featured Florence Nightingale's recent paper on sanitation in rural India.[50]

Loveday Brooke's cases are rooted in the environment of journalism, in ways that consistently emphasise the connections between periodical writing, reading and professional detection. Indeed, in 'The Ghost of Fountain Lane', we learn that even when she is on holiday in Brighton, Loveday's table is 'strewn with newspapers, memoranda, and books of reference'; the sea view doesn't interest her: 'I shut my eyes to it, fasten them instead on the daily papers, and set to work.'[51] The policeman who visits her conveys the case via journalism: 'the inspector took a newspaper-cutting from his pocket-book and read aloud'. In this case, Loveday draws a surprising connection between the apparently prosaic mystery she is investigating (the theft of a blank cheque cashed for £600) and a 'supernatural' newspaper story about a Napoleonic ghost making a sensation in London. The police are inclined to suspect the victim's overspending wife. But the real perpetrators of the fraud are men: leaders of a millenarian sect who are cheating their followers out of donations via mesmerism. It is Loveday's ability to connect two seemingly unrelated newspaper stories that enables her to discover the truth.

In 'The Black Bag Left on a Doorstep', the first Loveday Brooke mystery to appear in the *Ludgate Monthly*, the solution similarly arises from acute analysis of newsprint. Loveday Brooke has presented herself at Ebenezer Dyer's private enquiry office, having read in the newspaper of a major case: 'Lady Cathrow has lost £30,000 worth of jewellery, if the newspaper accounts are to be trusted.' Her employer assures her that the newspapers are 'fairly accurate this time'. The story's opening at once signals that the periodical – such as the one we ourselves are reading – is a source of important information, but information we must read *closely*. It will not *always* be accurate. The reader is, from the start, aligned and allied with the detective, who keeps her eyes open for clues, in the shape of untoward stories that appear in the press, and must assess their reliability.

The 'obvious' suspect in the Craigen Court robbery is a French housemaid, who is so distressed at being suspected that (like the maid in Wilkie Collins's *The Moonstone*) she attempts suicide. Brooke sees past the prejudice that frames female domestic servants as the likeliest criminal actors in domestic thefts. The thief of Lady Cathrow's jewels left a facetious message, 'To be let unfurnished', scrawled in chalk on the door of the safe he rifled. Brooke connects this message with a separate story that appears in the newspaper: about clerical garments discarded with a humorous note. She reconstructs the series of events whereby a 'visiting clergyman', who dropped in for Christmas Eve dinner at Craigen Court, purloined the jewels then left his disguise on a doorstep.

It is important that it is Brooke's facility as a reader that enables her to nab the thief. She recognises the shared identity of the stealer and the man who dumped the stole by analysing the handwriting, vocabulary and style. Like a modern profiler-cum-graphologist, Brooke traces the criminal from his 'voice' and signature; in identifying him, she utilises knowledge of joke books and cabmen's vernacular. She recognises the throwaway, chaffing style as young and male. Pirkis's fiction is fascinated by the local varieties of language. In her novel *Judith Wynne* (1884), two women engage in linguistic battle:

> Bryce answered with a roulade of sibilant Welsh, to which Judith returned fire with a round of easy French ... Bryce replied with ... a cannonade of consonants ... Judith ... sent back a succession of short, jerky Scotch phrases ... a string of Gaelic gutturals ... 'It's grand to have so many languages at the tip of one's tongue,' she said.[52]

Pirkis also had multiple languages on the tip of her tongue: her family included several eminent Sinologists. Catherine Louisa Pirkis's husband Frederick and his two brothers, George (married to Catherine's sister Susan) and Albert, had all joined the Royal Navy and fought China during the Anglo-Chinese wars of the 1850s. While Frederick returned to Britain and retired after his marriage, his brothers remained in China, becoming heavily involved in consular relations and studying Sinology. Catherine's nieces and nephews (two of whom Catherine adopted after her sister's early death) would have grown up speaking some Chinese as well as English.

Well-educated middle-class women in late nineteenth-century Britain were often better schooled in modern languages than their male counterparts, who learned Latin and Greek. Pirkis's detective stories, typically for New Woman fiction, show Loveday Brooke's linguistic fluency in French, German and Italian – and her familiarity with different kinds of slang and professional jargon – as a distinctive advantage, enabling her code-breaking and code-making abilities.

Newspapers are everywhere in Loveday Brooke's 'experiences'; they are constantly highlighted as a means both of overt and covert communication. In 'The Murder at Troyte's Hill', 'a newspaper sent down to Mr Craven by his wife was folded so as to direct his attention to the shipping list'. This is done to signal to her husband that their son – a suspect in the case – has sailed to Natal. In 'The Redhill Sisterhood', Loveday (who is being followed and finding it hard to shake the men who are tailing her) sticks her newspaper out of a train compartment window to signal to Inspector Gunning where she is. The periodical becomes a flare, a 'tell'. The villain in this tale poses as a newspaper journalist for a Newcastle paper: 'I am a bit of a literary man myself, and sometimes figure as a reporter, sometimes as a leader writer.' In fact, he is nothing of the kind, as Brooke immediately recognises by her astute reading of his conversation and behaviour. He is trying to play her, to direct her attention towards the wrong property and the wrong suspects: a religious order of women. In gothic novels, no-good nuns are very often the culprits. Here, *au contraire*, the female philanthropists are innocent. The burglaries are being committed by an organised gang of men, of whom the ersatz journalist is a member.

Loveday is the true investigative correspondent here. She writes some deliberately misleading words – 'Wooton Hall is threatened tonight – concentrate attention there' – on a card that the villain will take to the inspector. She writes in invisible ink, *between the lines* of the false message to tell her employer where her real suspicions lie: 'North Cape will be attacked tonight'. A telegram in cipher sent by Loveday earlier in the day has primed the police to hold the card to the fire to make the invisible ink appear. The outward signifier is empty; the apparently blank space contains the real message. Reading between the lines is here a literal as well as a figurative strategy for understanding communication as a form of fencing, with its thrusts, parries and feints.

Missing Women and Not Seeing Them

Pirkis is fascinated by the ways in which cover and content can be misread. In the Loveday Brooke mystery 'Drawn Daggers', the daggers depicted on empty envelopes sent to Mr Hawke from Ireland seem to signify a Fenian threat. He reads them as aggressive, male terrorism – their repeated appearance an escalation, a warning of impending attack. But their real coded meaning, deduced by Loveday Brooke, is quite different. The cards are female communications, from the young woman whose strange disappearance Brooke has been hired to investigate. The intended recipient of their meaning is not the 'somewhat infantine' Mr Hawke, but the woman whom the writer of the envelopes has hired as a body double to take her place. Loveday correctly deduces that Miss Monroe, an heiress despatched from Peking to England, was determined to marry against her father's wishes and hit on a clever exit strategy. She would disembark early and wed her fiancé, while paying another woman of a lower social class to impersonate her for a time in England in the house of the Hawkes, who had never seen a photograph of her. The succession of 'daggers drawn' on the envelopes (the arms of the Irish family into which Miss Monroe has married) indicate the completion of the heiress's elopement scheme. Once the last communication has been received, the body double can safely disappear. The 'daggers drawn' are not in fact openly hostile in a conventionally masculine sense: 'drawn' in the sense of unsheathed or uncovered. Rather they are 'drawn' in the opposite sense of ciphered – deliberately closed. The parallel substitutions in this story between the heiress and the 'empty cover' of her body double, with the 'empty cover' of the envelope, which mystifies and threatens the male reader because the expected content (a letter for him) is absent, suggest the idea of women as themselves 'covers', for hidden messages that are often invisible to the untrained eye. The male detective typically misses the message because he fails to recognise the way in which society obliges women to communicate through absence.

Often in Pirkis's detective stories, we meet with women who have run away. As we have seen, in 'Drawn Daggers', Miss Monroe absconds from a ship so that she can marry the man she desires, free of her father's interference. In 'Missing!', Irené Golding absconds from Langford Hall, wishing to reconnect in Italy with the mother she had supposed was dead and fearful that her father would forbid their reunion if he knew. (This plot repurposes that of one of Pirkis's earliest novels, *Disappeared from Her Home* [1877], in which a young woman similarly 'vanishes', but is in fact visiting her disgraced and socially erased mother.) In 'A Princess's Vengeance', Lucie Cunier seems to have disappeared 'as completely as if the earth had opened to receive her' but has actually married quietly to avoid the attention of an unwelcome suitor. None of these women is missing, from her own perspective. It is only male society that is missing them, as a result of their own ingenuity and independence. These plots, unravelled by a woman, point to the lengths to which women are obliged to go to be themselves and to free themselves. It is striking that both Florence Marryat and Elizabeth L. Banks also wrote novels in this period in which women fake their own deaths in order to get on with their lives. Female disappearance, followed by the assumption of a new identity, is a plot device from the sensation novel that is treated with a new level of sympathy in late Victorian fiction. As Elizabeth Carolyn Miller points out, in 'The Murder at Troyte's Hill', Pirkis's female detective alone 'recognizes that a daughter, Miss Craven, is actually cross-dressing as her brother, who has left the country'. Women disappear and transform themselves in multiple ways in these stories, drawing attention to the ways in which they – like Loveday Brooke – are living undercover roles on a daily basis.[53]

The first chapter of George Eliot's *Middlemarch* (1871) is entitled 'Miss Brooke' and this was Eliot's original title for her most famous novel, which ponders how a woman can be 'greatly effective' in the world; Eliot's heroine, disastrously, seeks enlightenment and philanthropic power through marriage. C. L. Pirkis's heroine shares Dorothea's surname, but her latter-day Miss Brooke has found a way to be 'greatly effective' while remaining single. Professional agency proves a much more secure route to freedom for women than companionship. Loveday's independence (unlike Sherlock Holmes, she has no sidekick; unlike Dora Bell, she has no love interest) is a strong feature of the stories. It allows her to be mobile, fast, uncompromising and pleasingly opaque.

Appearances are misleading in these stories: men are often responsible where women are suspected; the handsome are guilty, the ugly innocent.[54] Physiognomy is not destiny. The face of things is a poor guide to reality. Reading these stories, we come to see all writing as code and all culture as a form of signalling, where messages may be simultaneously overt and covert, that we are invited to decipher. Newspapers exemplify this code. What appears a genuine advertisement may be a signal from one criminal to another, or a bait to lure the unwary customer into an assignation. (Even in her comic writing, Pirkis employs the misleading newspaper story as a plot device: in her operetta *Tempests and Teacups*, a young man pranks his male elders by sending a letter to the paper 'from a famous expert' that causes them to think their china collection valuable – with farcical results.) The increasing vogue for literary detection and detective journalism points, in periodicals of the 1890s, to the ubiquity of disguise and deception in social life and the investigative powers necessary to penetrate its facades. The female detective primes the female reader, in particular, to recognise the difference between the signal and the message.

Living Language and the Humanitarian Detective

Pirkis's humanitarian views and linguistic interests permeate her fiction. In *Saint and Sibyl* (1882), Pirkis opens dramatically with the cries of a little girl who is being thrashed by her father, who runs a travelling circus, for failing to jump high enough during her act. The girl is rescued by the protagonist, Sebastian Walsingham, a young gentleman artist, who happens to be walking nearby and pays the troupe £5 to adopt the child. Walsingham has a habit of rescuing maltreated and injured animals: we are told that he has brought home a puppy, a monkey, a jackdaw and a kitten that was being hung from a tree. The ethics of Walsingham's 'saving' a lower-class, female child, paying for her release as if she were a slave, are questionable; especially as he will go on to marry the wild and wilful but charming Sibyl at the end of the novel.[55] However, it is intriguing that Pirkis chooses to link the corporal punishment of a working-class girl and maltreatment of animals. In her Loveday Brooke story 'The Murder at Troyte's Hill', the villain will kill a dog called Captain, murder his gamekeeper, then threaten to kill Brooke with a geological hammer. As Christopher Pittard has argued:

the animal on the operating table became associated with the body of the woman . . . and (less frequently) of the working class . . . Pirkis shows the trajectory clearly . . . As Craven confesses to

Loveday, he completes the anti-vivisectionist trajectory by realising that a woman's cry might be the best subject of all: 'I wonder
what sort of sound you would make if I were to give you a little
tap just there.' Here he lightly touched her forehead with the
hammer [...] 'It has only this moment occurred to me,' he said,
now with his lips close to Loveday's ear, 'that a woman, in her
death agony, would be much more likely to give utterance to an
elemental sound than a man.'[56]

The psychopath wants to open Loveday, to see what she is made
of. This resembles a perverse interest in a woman's orgasmic cry:
Craven, in his scientific determination to penetrate Loveday Brooke's
skull, is an intellectual rapist as well as a murderer. Brooke summons
assistance, which – anticipating the attack – she has wisely stationed
outside and avoids having her brain tapped by the mad philologist.
Her defiance of the sinister threat of male aggression not only
signals the author's resistance to false 'scientific' approaches to
animals but also a feminist resistance to men who try to get inside
women's heads.

Pirkis is herself interested in philology, but from a different
perspective. Rather than 'murdering to dissect', she is fascinated by
living language. Whether among humans or animals, she implicitly
advocates humane enquiry that is interested in living subjects rather
than anatomisation. This is reflected in her view of detection not as
a primarily forensic, post-mortem skill (though Loveday does occasionally display this) but as a live social mode of investigation that
has at its heart human sympathy, interview technique and close
observation of inter-class relationships, dress and language.

Public-Facing Private Eyes

Like Elizabeth Burgoyne Corbett and Florence Marryat, Catherine
Louisa Pirkis makes her 1890s female detective a private eye with a

33. *'With His Lips Close to Loveday's Ear', illustration by Bernard Higham in Pirkis's* The Experiences of Loveday Brooke, Lady Detective *(1894).*

public mission. The professional background of all of these women in journalism and their acquaintance with a wide variety of periodicals informs their understanding of crime as a social phenomenon and their invention of female detectives who – whether going undercover, writing shorthand or scanning newspaper stories to research cases – share many of the characteristics of investigative reporters.

Their cases reflect the real historical moment of the 1890s and its debates: mesmerism and money-laundering, kleptomania, blackmail, terrorism, the cat-and-mouse prosecution of married partners by one another for adultery. Loveday Brooke, like Dora Bell and Jane Farrell, not only exposes family secrets, but also wider power dynamics. Their quiet competence constitutes a specifically female, implicitly feminist challenge to the assumptions of those whom they encounter, who doubt their abilities, methods and theories but are repeatedly forced to admit that they are right.

Classic detective fiction has commonly been viewed as a conservative genre: the sleuth 'solves' the crime, returning society to a state of order. But this is not the whole truth.[57] The detective tale can also complicate the reader's sense of who is responsible for anti-social acts, what incites them and who is or is not punished in the criminal justice system, as 'Kleptomaniac or Thief', *In the Name of Liberty* and 'Drawn Daggers' all do. These stories of the 1890s are liberal in their emphasis on middle- and upper-class appropriation as a frequent source of injury for which working-class characters are unfairly suspected.

However, it is also true that the middle-class female detective who comes to dominate the fiction market from the 1890s appropriates a role that had been, from the 1840s, much more often occupied in reality by working-class women. Like the journalist Elizabeth L. Banks posing as a housemaid to file a story about the privations suffered by servants (rather than encouraging a genuine housemaid to tell her own story), the writers of the last decades of the nineteenth century preferred to imagine college-educated, middle-class women exposing the truth of domestic mysteries, consigning working-class characters to minor parts. Middle-class ventriloquism displays class sympathy at the expense of authenticity. The 'lady' detective usurps the 'female' one. This trend towards sleuths from the higher social echelons would intensify as the century wore on with Henry T. Johnson's serial of 1896, *The Scarlet Scar or, the Strange*

THE FAMOUS COUNTESS-DETECTIVE.

34. 'The Famous Countess-Detective', illustration from the serial The Scarlet
Scar or, the Strange Experiences of a Countess-Detective *(1896)*.

Experiences of a Countess-Detective, and Baroness Orczy's *Lady Molly
of Scotland Yard* in 1910.[58]

Likewise, middle-class female detectives of the later 1890s have
their finger on the pulse and their foot on the globe. They are highly

mobile: both socially and geographically. Their travels suggest a cosmopolitanism that can shade easily (and to a modern eye queasily) into imperialism. Lois Cayley, in *Miss Cayley's Adventures*, is a journalist in Italy, shoots a tiger in India and saves a woman she stumbles upon from white slavery in Egypt. Her conquering posture with her umbrella resembles that of Britannia with her trident and a lion at her feet. A Cambridge graduate and embodiment of female energy, Lois trounces the competition in a Swiss bicycle race that was supposed to be only for men. She goes on to save her boyfriend from a mountaineering accident and dispose of the crook who framed her fiancé as a fraudster. She is the sort of cheerful, clever, vigorous woman of whom, in a decade or two, Bertie Wooster will quite reasonably be afraid.

Fantasy female detectives of the last decades of the nineteenth century are also *fast*. Dora Myrl arrives in print on her bicycle, sweeping into view with proto-cinematic sexual energy:

> An audacious toque, with a brace of scarlet feathers stuck in it, was perched amongst thick coiled hair that had the ripple and lustre of a brown trout stream in the sunshine. The short skirt of her tailor-made dress twitched by the light wind showed slim ankles and neat feet cased in tan cycling shoes.[59]

Dora cycles at up to 12 miles per hour to catch a thief. She races on a high-speed train at 50 miles per hour to rescue men who are doomed to be dashed to smithereens if she doesn't reach them in time. Having once worked as a telephone girl, Myrl solves several of her cases by following electric cables. The frisson of electricity created by her presence is that of sexual modernity. Dora Myrl shares her name with Dora Bell in all but two letters. It is hard to avoid the conclusion that McDonnell Bodkin was borrowing from Burgoyne Corbett's serialised creation. Myrl reflects, however, from her shapely ankles to her flirty scarlet toque, a distinctly male gaze. With her

35. *Grant Allen*, Miss Cayley's Adventures *(1899)*.

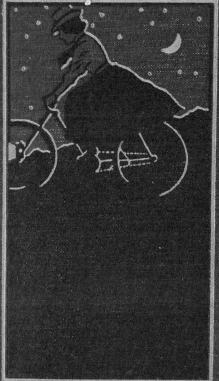

DORA MYRL
THE
LADY DETECTIVE

MᶜD. BODKIN Q.C.

36. *McD. Bodkin*, Dora Myrl: The Lady Detective *(1900)*.

scarlet feather and her trout-stream hair, Dora combines some of the qualities of the hunter and the quarry.

Unlike Dora Bell or Loveday Brooke, who work on a regular basis for an enquiry agency, taking up cases they are given by their employers – as most real female detectives did who performed agency work – Dora Myrl is, from the beginning, self-employed. She decides to be a detective; she becomes a detective. She commands the fee she chooses. Indeed, she commands men in general. As Dora Myrl asks her male companion: 'Will you take your directions from me?' He responds: 'All right. You boss this show.'[60] One of the thrills of these ladies of the 1890s is the picture they present of women telling men what to do, impersonating men, exposing their devious stratagems and overtaking them, literally and figuratively.

The fact that Lois Cayley and Dora Myrl do not work for an employer – they embrace detection as a calling that comes to them – is wishful and remote from the reality of private enquiry for most Victorian women. The caseload of the fantasy female detective, who works in high life and solves high-level cases of poisoning, fraud, grand larceny and child-swapping, bears scant relation to the caseload of the real Victorian female private enquiry agent, whose daily cases were much more likely to involve investigating adultery, probate, writs, suspect employees, trade competition and striking workers. Henry Slater used the tantalising image of 'an army of lady cyclist detectives' to advertise his company, but the reality of his business model was framing spouses and co-respondents in divorce suits. The fantasy female detective at the turn of the century is a New Woman: capable of pedalling to secure her own getaway, she is a poster woman for female liberation. Like her foremother on the 1860s stage, however, she still constitutes a glamorous picture that covers up the dead wall of reality, its grim landscape of male violence and female social disadvantage; the continued resistance of the police to employing women on regular salaries; and the seedy world of private enquiry agencies that often served women ill, whether as employees or targets.

Nonetheless, the works of Burgoyne Corbett, Marryat, Pirkis and their successors are important and effective in imagining a different future. They create an impression, a desire, an image of the female detective as a powerful modern scourge of social injustice that multiplies and reproduces itself – inspiring imitators. Making the link between women's real penetration into the marketplace of the Strand as the author of scoops and the doyenne of snoops, they situate investigation as a female skill, akin to journalism, of benefit not only to a particular individual family but to society at large, relating individual mysteries to the complex wider political canvas of capital and labour, of terrorism and of misogyny. Their professionally curious heroines, appearing in weekly columns where their suspicions are justified and their detractors trounced, enter the lists of a debate about money, marriage and masculinity that sets women firmly on the trail of equal rights.

6

MRS WARNE'S PROFESSION
Inventing the Female Detective

I appreciate all you have done for me, for my agency, and for all of
Chicago . . . All right, Kate, finish that scotch and let's go grab the
bastard.[1]

John Derrig, *Kate Warne: Pinkerton's First
Lady* – a novel based on Warne's life (2014)

The image, fostered by fiction, of the courageous female detective
as an agent of social justice was inspiring for women seeking
new powers. But it also had unforeseen consequences. The fusion of
desire with reality altered published accounts of real women detectives, whose lives were most acceptable when read along the lines of
their fictional counterparts. This is especially true of 'Kate Warne':
an icon of American detection whose story is a mixtape in which
documentary and fantasy meet and merge.

The persons we imagine are often more compelling than those we
know. 'Kate Warne' may, in this regard, be the most successful undercover agent of all time. She was certainly one of the most influential
figures in convincing the public of the respectability, even nobility, of

sleuthing as a profession for women. Yet the magnetic field of myth has distorted her history. Like those of other real female detectives, her achievements were filtered through reportage and memoir that favoured exceptional narratives of perilous action, bravery and self-lessness, blurring the moral complexities and routine, organisational and administrative aspects of the detective business.

This chapter considers the relationship between reality and inven-tion in creating 'Kate Warne' alongside the character of the female 'detective spy' in American Civil War fiction and how the legacy of this sensational figure persisted in dime novels featuring women detectives who cross the boundaries of class, gender and sexuality through the 1880s and 1890s. These fictions offered readers a glimpse of new freedoms; yet they created a troublesome template for pioneering American women police detectives, such as Isabella Goodwin, who were breathlessly reported in terms of their fictional counterparts: a narrative that skewed the public view of their work. Encountering these women is tantalising: it means entering a maze of mirrors, which reflect the features that made female detection admirable but often distort the background that made it necessary.

Death of the 'Unknown Lady'

On 28 January 1868, in Chicago, tragedy struck. Snow was driving on the wind, but it was soon joined by sparks and balls of flame. A burst pipe had started a fire above Griggs, a rare book and stationery store in the heart of the city, and before long, several blocks of commercial buildings were engulfed in what would become known as the Great Fire in Chicago.[2] People stood in the street and gaped as flames shot up into the night sky.

That same night, a thirty-eight-year-old woman suffering from pneumonia slipped into unconsciousness, never to wake again. Reputedly, by her bedside was Allan Pinkerton, the forty-eight-year-old Scottish émigré, heavy set and chin-strap-bearded, who founded

Pinkerton's Detective Agency. Deeply shocked by the loss of his protégée, Pinkerton put his formidable power as a storyteller into an obituary for the *Chicago Republican* that would both honour her memory and promote his agency. Kate Warn (her name would only later acquire an e) had, he asserted with characteristic hyperbole, been 'undoubtedly the best female detective in America, if not in the world':

> She was born in the town of Erin, Chemung county, New York
> ... Her parents were honest and industrious people, but being
> poor required the early labor of their children, and the subject of
> this sketch being the oldest, there devolved upon her while a mere
> child, many of the household cares of a numerous family.
> Consequently her privileges for obtaining an education were very
> limited. She was a marked woman among her sex, with a large,
> active brain, great mental-power, an excellent judge of character,
> and possessed of a strong, active vitality. She showed herself well
> fitted to assume the responsibilities and discharge the severe and
> trying duties of the responsible position which she occupied at
> the time of her death—the superintendence of the female portion
> of what is said to be the largest detective organization in the
> world ... she exhibited great kindness, strength of will, and force
> of character, imbruing all who surrounded her with the strict rule
> of moral probity and right she had made her own.[3]

Pinkerton's obituary for Warn was lengthy and emphasised both her effective managerial skills ('head', 'charge' and 'superintendance' are mentioned ten times) and her kindness (mentioned five times). He noted that Warn possessed attributes commonly associated with men in the period: she was firm, decisive, active, with a strong will, and 'subjected everyone who came within range of her mind to her ideas'. Her life was a proof of what women could do: 'she developed that her sex could do much more than had ever before been ascribed to their sphere'.

However, Pinkerton also took time to assert that Kate Warn was a pure woman. She might have followed an unorthodox, even reviled profession and followed no particular religion, but she conformed to the Victorian ideal of womanhood; she was charitable to prisoners, kind to subordinates and 'conscientious in the extreme':

> As the world generally looks at these things at the present time, the very name of detective is synonymous with associations of evil. Still this is not necessary, and so far as regarded the female department under the charge of Mrs Warn was not true. Among some of the earlier investigations with which she was concerned was that of the robbery of the Adams Express Company at Montgomery, Alabama, whereby that company lost about $10,000. After long and careful following up of this case by both the male and female portion of Mr Pinkerton's force, the money was all recovered except $485, by Mrs Warn at Jenkinstown, Penn, nearly one year after the money had been stolen ... She was also 'the lady unknown' who arranged for the sourcing of the sleeping-car berths for Mr Lincoln, Mr Pinkerton, and Mr Lamon, upon the eventful passage of Mr Lincoln from Philadelphia to Washington on the 22d of February 1861. After the breaking out of the rebellion, Mr Pinkerton having been assigned to duty as the head of the Secret Service of the army of the United States, Mrs Warn took charge of the female department at the national capital for that perilous service, and continued at the head of it during the worst years of the war, or up until 1863, when Mr Pinkerton retired from active service for a short interval.

Previously, detectives had been associated with 'evil', but Warn was all moral probity and compassion. Like a queen, a nurse or a soldier, Warn had put her duty to her country and her countrymen first. She was willing to disappear on a personal level, to be what occasion demanded. This was a rebranding of the detective alias as the cloak of conscious virtue that justifies all seeming deceptions as trials in the service of a greater good. Pinkerton attested that she ministered to the poor and helpless, even if they had been fighting on the enemy side:

In 1861 or 1862 when what was then known as contrabands [self-emancipated slaves and those fleeing the Confederate side] were coming so frequently into the Union lines, Mrs Warn was kind to the utmost extreme of her ability, and many of those poor unfortunates who sought a refuge within the lines of the Union army at that time, were indebted to her for her kind attention to their wants. The prison of the district where those parties were confined was frequently visited by Mrs Warn, and the poor and helpless were always cherished and kindly cared for by her.

Pinkerton buried Kate Warn in the private Pinkerton family plot in Graceland. As it did for Elvis, in a later age, Graceland became a sign of her ascension. She transcended her difficult beginnings, like one of the characters in Samuel Smiles's recent bestseller *Self-Help* (1859), which would inspire a new genre of aspirational self-improvement literature. Pinkerton's obituary was not initially widely circulated: it was reprinted in the *Democratic Enquirer* in March and a few other newspapers, then faded from sight, until the story was picked up by a feminist journal founded in New York in January 1868, the month of Warn's death: *The Revolution*, authored by Elizabeth Cady Stanton, Susan B. Anthony and Laura Curtis Bullard, leading lights of the campaign for female suffrage and women's legal emancipation.[4] Kate Warn's death was about to take on a whole new life.

To Cady Stanton and her fellow feminists, Warn was just what the women's liberation movement needed: an example of women's success when they were given the chance to become, professionally, the powerhouses and pioneers the world required. The *Revolution*'s story 'What Women Are Doing and Have Done' follows Pinkerton's obituary closely. However, it takes more time to describe the background to Abraham Lincoln's passage from Harrisburg to Washington in 1861 and why Warn's organisational skills were useful:

> At the time of the passage of Mr Lincoln and suite from Harrisburg to Washington to be inaugurated, the air was crowded with rumours of assassination, and well-organised plots had been laid at Baltimore, the details of which no one sufficiently knew to propose a plan of circumvention. Suddenly an 'unknown lady' appeared and arranged the time of departure, the procuration of sleeping-car berth, and such other precautionary steps as ... her intimate knowledge of the plot and ready judgement suggested. This 'unknown lady', was Mrs Warn.[5]

It mattered in 1868 that Kate Warn had reputedly been part of a plan to save the president from assassination prior to his inauguration in 1861 – because, of course, Abraham Lincoln had indeed been assassinated in April 1865. Retrospectively, it seemed obvious that, had Lincoln been assassinated in 1861, just before he was inaugurated as president, the outcome of the brewing Civil War and the direction of American history would have been irrevocably altered. The 'unknown lady' took on the heroic mantle of the Unknown Warrior (also a Victorian trope[6]) or the 'Lady with the Lamp', as Florence Nightingale had been dubbed for attending to injured and dying soldiers in the Crimea. The fact that Pinkerton's agency had become, during the Civil War, the Union's secret service – operating in the national rather than private interest – helpfully blurred the lines between policing and private enquiry, legitimising the idea of women as police officers with a protective remit of public service, rather than spies hired by dubious private agencies to investigate indiscretions in the bedroom and boardroom. The *Revolution* used Warn's success to argue that women should achieve equal representation in the police force:

Three years ago, in a public speech, we proposed a company of 'Women Police' uniformed and paid by the State, to watch and guard young girls and boys coming to this city. Although the press ridiculed the suggestion, it will yet be done. The above sketch shows how effective a true and able woman is ever found in defending public safety and virtue. If one half our police force were women, many of the evils of our present system would be remedied at once.[7]

The *Revolution* was a relatively small-circulation newspaper with 2,000–3,000 readers, but its words were shared across Victorian social media (the telegraph) all around the world. Hurricane Warn made landfall in the UK in July 1868, six months after Warn's death in Chicago. Over fifty national, regional and local papers in Britain and Ireland copied the *Revolution* article word for word, in part or in full between 9 and 18 July, from the *Illustrated Police News* to the *Sun*, the *Cornish Echo* to the *Renfrewshire Gazette* (Scotland), the *Monmouthshire Beacon* (Wales) to the *Roscommon Messenger* (Ireland). Briefly, Kate Warn went viral.

Kate Warn's obituary arrived in Britain in the middle of the Sensation boom, when strong women and stirring incidents were in vogue and when demands for women's rights, including the vote, were already being made in representations to Parliament. The idea of a smart woman who was both cool and composed enough to deal with violent emergencies and sufficiently saintly to put herself in harm's way to serve the nation was irresistible. The *Lady's Own Paper* politicised Warn's death, repeating the *Revolution*'s line: 'It is often asked, would you make women police officers? It has already been done. A society exists [in America] for the discovery of crimes, conspiracies and such things. The chief of this band was Mrs Kate Warn.'[8]

Directly below this article was one about the salaries of female physicians in New York, New Jersey and Philadelphia: an encouragement to British female readers to marvel at the financial independence of American women doctors. Ida Husted Harper's *History of Woman Suffrage* quoted the *Revolution*'s obituary of Warn when considering whether women in America could become police officers. She noted that the New York legislature in 1868 had voted on legalising prostitution, a move that brought into sharp focus the need for 'woman as police'.[9] In terms of sanitising and glamorising female detection, Kate Warn did more useful work after her death than before it.

Behind the Veil

But who was Kate Warn(e) really?

The truth is that we know remarkably little about her. Most of what we do know is filtered through the lens of Allan Pinkerton: a man who was a known fabulist and self-publicist, whose famous logo of an open eye ('we never sleep') was invariably turned to the main chance. We do know that her name wasn't Kate, and that much of what Pinkerton wrote about her is either false or misleading.

The lady who became famous as 'Kate Warne' was born Mahala Ann Warn, the daughter of Israel Warn and his wife Elizabeth Hulbert, in Erin, Chemung County, New York State. She became known in her family as 'Angie Mahala Warn', a name she retained in private life until her death. Pinkerton dramatically depicts this family as numerous, poor and uneducated. Again, this isn't entirely true.

Warn's father, Israel, was a blacksmith in Chemung, who moved west across country to become a farmer in Nelson, Illinois. In the federal census of 1860, he reported his real estate at $5075 and his personal estate at $495 (collectively worth around $200,000 today). This was not wealth, but neither was it grinding poverty. Kate was the eldest girl of nine siblings. The census, which asked about education, notes that the Warn children went to school – boys and girls alike – at a time when this was far from inevitable. Only an aspirational, financially stable farmer would send his girls to learn to read and write when they could be of practical economic value tending animals and crops, and doing the endless physical labour of a homestead, from washing to childcare, sewing to cookery. Angie Mahala certainly reinvented herself to become a detective, but hers is not quite the Cinderella story that the silver-tongued Pinkerton made it appear.

Warn's grandmother, Mahala Brooks, came from Connecticut: she was the daughter of Abigail Goslee and Josiah Brooks, a corporal in the Revolutionary Army who received a pension for his service during the War of Independence. The Brooks were a respectable, established local family, descended from some of the first colonists in the area in the seventeenth century. The wider Brooks clan comprised a number of families who were deeply embedded in the north-east coast. The Hulberts (who were connected to the Brooks by cousinage) were also landholders in a small way in Glastonbury, Connecticut. These were people with servants, steadings, history. After Josiah Brooks's death, most of the family relocated westwards, to New York State, including Warn's grandmother, whom she would have known growing up, and her uncles and aunts. It seems that the family lost status in this period. Elizabeth Warn, Angie Mahala's mother, became ill. Perhaps it was then that the eldest daughter of the family felt the need to go out to earn her keep in the city.

By 1850, it seems, Angie Mahala had already left home, presumably to work, so her twenty-one-year-old silhouette is not visible in the 1850 census. By the time of the 1860 census, however, she was back at the homestead with her sisters, Lucy and Belle, and brothers Henry and George. This was likely because they had just buried their mother, Elizabeth. Her father did not mourn long: with pragmatism or relief, Israel remarried to the family servant, Dianna Campbell, and started a second family. In the 1860 census taken eight years before her death, Angie Mahala Warn appears without a husband. In 1861, 'Mrs Kate Warn' appears in the Chicago City Directory as 'wid

George' [widow of George], living at 285 West Adams Street. But there is no evidence that Angie Mahala married between 1860 and 1861 or at any other time. She did not change her maiden name. It appears on her will and on her death certificate.

George H. Bangs, one of Pinkerton's other 'right-hand men', also lived on West Adams Street, at 333. This accommodation was provided by Pinkerton for his operatives, who worked out of the office. Such arrangements helpfully blurred the line between personal and professional life. If Angie Mahala Warn and Allan Pinkerton were lovers as well as associates, as others suspected, then there were discreet means and places for them to meet. Frank Morn notes that: 'on several occasions critics, even within his own family, claimed that Pinkerton kept concubines and was having a love affair with Warne. After his death women vanished from the agency, probably because of the overt policies of his sons, who suspected their father's philandering.'[10]

John Stewart has established that Angie Mahala's three sisters – Lucy, Belle and Kitty – became sex workers and successful bawdy-house owners in Chicago and then in St Louis, Missouri. He argues that two of her sisters also at some point worked as agents for Pinkerton: he identifies Kitty as 'Hattie Lawton/Lewis', a key operative.[11] It stands to reason, then, that Angie Mahala was aware of sex work and it is quite possible that she also engaged in it. Pinkerton always claimed that he met 'Mrs Warn' when she appeared at his office, seeking employment, in the spring of 1855 (when she was twenty-five). This is not entirely consistent with his claim that, in 1868, she had been working as a detective for about fifteen years (since 1853). It may be that Angie Mahala did present herself at Pinkerton's office, but the story of a mid-Victorian woman applying for a detective job that does not yet exist is dubious.

Pinkerton says in his obituary of Warn that he, like a demure young woman approached by an eager suitor, refused her untoward proposal before finally accepting it on mature consideration:

Up till that time, he had never dreamed of employing females, and even then could not realise how they could be employed without a strict regard for the prejudices of community. After several interviews, however, Mrs Warn succeeded in convincing Mr Pinkerton that the innovation could be realised, and she entered his service.

He wanted it to seem that he had never considered employing women as detectives: that the proposition was unheard of. (In his later fictionalised memoir *The Expressman and the Detective*, he would claim that 'it was the first experiment of the sort that had ever been tried'.[12] This was untrue; in the 1850s women were already being employed in the UK both as private enquiry agents and as detective searchers by the police. As an expatriate Scot, Pinkerton may well have known this.) It may be that Angie Mahala did solicit Pinkerton, but in a way that was unfit for the pages of hagiography.

Pinkerton presents 'Mrs Kate Warn' as a respectable figure wearing the weeds of widowhood, who has entered the workforce to support herself in the absence of the husband who would normally have done so: but Warn's dead husband was probably a beard, a veil that allowed her to behave with the freedom accorded to sexually experienced, mature, financially independent women – who did not need a chaperone and could travel alone. Such liberty permitted the female detective to do her work. According to Pinkerton, Warn specialised in playing widows and women with absent husbands: Mrs Imbert in the case of the Adams Express robbery, Mrs R. A. Potter in the case of the 'somnambulist and the detective'. It is telling that in the former case, Pinkerton gave Warn the alias of a famous fraudster and bigamist, Jules Imbert (itself an alias for George Day); Pinkerton had solved this case at the beginning of his relationship with Warn. Pinkerton, then, makes Warn in imagination the widow of a crook, casting her in a piece of detective theatre that alludes to the storyworld of crime. For a seasoned and habitual fabulist such as Pinkerton, who brought his narrative skills to his work, the invention of 'Mrs Kate Warn' was a small step.

As 'Mrs Angie M. Warn', Warn's name was regularly printed on the front page of the *Chicago Tribune* between 1861 and 1866 as someone who had letters waiting for her, unclaimed, at the Chicago Post Office. Many Victorians who didn't have a regular postal address or wished for privacy collected mail from the central post office. But the fact that until a couple of years before her death, 'Mrs Angie Mahala Warn' was directing her mail to the post office, where she was sometimes unable to claim it, strongly suggests that she was directing family to write to her under one cover, while using the other (Kate Warn, or sometimes Mrs Cherry or Mrs Barley, or MB or Raisins) as her professional alias. Ms Warn didn't want everyone who knew her to know where she lived or what she did. Her sisters, too, are notable for the number of different names they travelled under. Sex work and detection had some features in common in the period: they both required discretion and encouraged reinvention.

It is unlikely that we will ever know how Angie Mahala Warn and Pinkerton really met. But a telegram sent by him to her during the Civil War, when they were both working out of Washington as agents of the hastily assembled secret service, is suggestive. Pinkerton's code-name during the war was General E. J. Allen. He writes to Warn: 'Kate Allen two eighty eight I st Washn I shall probable [sic] leave here Tuesday evening direct for Washn Robert will be with me if I make connection I shall be home Saturday morning Joan not well Allen Pinkerton'[13]

The fact that Kate is to be found at Pinkerton's Washington address (288 Eye Street) is significant here. Also, he does not say he will be back: he says he will be 'home'. That is the kind of information one relays to an intimate, as is the state of his wife's health. Tellingly, Kate is not Mrs Barley here or Mrs Cherry or Mrs Warn. She is Kate Allen. If Pinkerton is E. J. Allen, this strongly insinuates that Kate is his partner. In the Civil War payroll, Pinkerton is first and Warn is second to be listed. Her funeral was held from Pinkerton's Chicago home and he acted as her executor. That they were intimate partners as colleagues cannot be doubted; given Pinkerton's other known adulteries, it is a reasonable supposition that they were intimate in other ways. Pinkerton's warm admiration for Warn, expressed in his appreciation for her appearance as well as her professional talents, is evident in all his later, dramatised accounts of their detective adventures.

Allan Pinkerton would capitalise on Warn's story in his prolific and imaginative 'true crime' memoirs of the 1870s and 1880s. Suddenly, her name acquired an extra 'e', perhaps conferring greater distinction, in the way that Smythe may appear more aristocratic than Smith. In *The Expressman and the Detective* (1874), Pinkerton described Warn as

> above the medium height, slender, graceful in her movements, and perfectly self-possessed in her manner ... Her eyes were very attractive, being dark blue, and filled with fire. She had a broad, honest face, which would cause one in distress instinctively to select her as a confidante, in whom to confide in time of sorrow, or from whom to seek consolation. She seemed possessed of the masculine attributes of firmness and decision, but to have brought all her faculties under complete control.[14]

In *The Spy of the Rebellion* (1883), Warn is

> of rather a commanding person, with clear-cut, expressive features, and with an ease of manner that was quite captivating at times, she was calculated to make a favourable impression at once ... She was a brilliant conversationalist when so disposed, and could be quite vivacious, but she also understood that rarer quality of humankind, the art of being silent.[15]

Here, 'Kate' – while rather tall and 'commanding', with 'fiery' eyes – is praised in a manner that aligns her with the *beau idéal* of Victorian womanhood: her commanding ability to charm is only matched by her ability to listen: to be a patient, silent sounding-board for others' words.

In his adventure narratives of the Civil War, Pinkerton describes all his female operatives in romantic terms. 'Hattie Lawton' is conjured thus: 'Her complexion was fresh and rosy as the morning, her hair fell in flowing tresses of gold, while her eyes, which were of a clear and deep blue, were quick and searching in their glances.' In remaining with her pretended husband, the spy Timothy Webster, until his execution, Lawton's courage and tenderness are likewise praised: 'No patient ever had more careful nursing, or more tender consideration than did Timothy Webster, from the brave true-hearted woman who had dedicated her life and her services to the cause of her country and its noble defenders.'[16]

Pinkerton's deployment of the women in his force using multiple aliases extended to casting them posthumously in the role of saints and saviours. He was determined to show that while detection was generally a 'black art' and detectives often worse than the criminals they pursued, his agency was on the side of the light:

> The employment of female detectives has been the subject of some adverse criticism by persons who think that women should not engage in such a dangerous calling. It has been claimed the work is unwomanly; that it is only performed by abandoned women; and that no respectable woman who becomes a detective can remain virtuous. To these theories, which I regret to say are quite prevalent, I enter a positive denial.[17]

Pinkerton's positive denials should make us question what he gains from his account of Kate Warn's life: what he emphasises and what he omits. The 'purity' of her heroism is designed to serve a narrative that raises the status of Pinkerton's agency, and of detection itself, to an unassailable level of patriotism, self-sacrifice, bravery and compassion. In becoming an emblem of something Pinkerton wished to project, Kate Warn, the 'unknown lady', fades into a tasteful haze of ideality.

The most famous and often-quoted example of Warn's heroism as a detective is her arranging a sleeping car in the night train of 22 February 1861 that bore Abraham Lincoln from Philadelphia to Washington. Pinkerton, Warn and Lincoln's friend and bodyguard Ward Lamon were on this train. The transport from Harrisburg to Philadelphia and thence to Washington, whisking the president elect through Baltimore in the early hours of the morning, was arranged in secret – replacing the original plan for Lincoln to speak in Baltimore en route to his presidential inauguration – in order to circumvent a suspected plot to assassinate Lincoln, either by scuppering the original train on which he had been expected to travel, or by attacking him when he exited it.

Ward Lamon, in his *Life of Abraham Lincoln*, made no bones about Pinkerton's manipulative role in persuading Lincoln that he needed protection. He had this to say about the journey:

Mr Lincoln soon learned to regret the midnight ride. His friends reproached him; his enemies taunted him. He was convinced he had made a grave mistake in yielding to the solicitations of a professional spy . . . He saw that he had fled from a danger purely imaginary, and felt the shame and mortification natural to a brave man under such circumstances.[18]

Several newspapers scoffed at the story of Lincoln's hasty retreat to Washington:

There is not one scrap of evidence given that any such plot for the assassination of Mr Lincoln or for his harming in any way existed except in the brains of these very smart detectives. The whole burden of the story is the industrious manoeuvrings of these astute and busy officials in imposing upon the minds of Mr Lincoln's friends and himself the idea of some terrible impending danger – a plot . . . without a single plotter to be seen, recognised, pointed out or named to this day.[19]

Was there really ever a credible threat to Lincoln in Baltimore, or did Allan Pinkerton use his powers of persuasion to create a situation of benefit to his agency, where he was in charge of the president's movements (much to the disgust of Lamon) and could claim credit for 'saving' him from a plot that was merely a rumour? It may be that Pinkerton was gunning for the job of head of the secret service more than any assassin was gunning for Lincoln in Baltimore in 1861.

Certainly, Pinkerton entered immediately into a publicity campaign in 1861, when news of Lincoln's sudden flight was reported, gathering witnesses to testify that to him, Allan Pinkerton, belonged the glory of the hour and not to John A. Kennedy, the head of the New York Police. Pinkerton accumulated letters from all those involved and had them printed in the newspapers: he even self-published a booklet of witness statements corroborating the role of the Pinkerton agency in removing Lincoln from danger. Pinkerton's emphasis, then, in his 1868 obituary of Warn, upon her heroic role as 'the lady unknown' in the train adventure was of a piece with his staging of this story as a dramatic *coup de théâtre*. Pinkerton was reputedly involved in the Underground Railroad, freeing black slaves by bringing them north to safety and citizenship. It is striking that the story of Lincoln's 'rescue' from South to North has many of the same characteristics to that of a rescued slave: he is smuggled out to freedom, under a shawl and an assumed identity, by a white woman who pretends to be his sister.

What we know about Warn's part in the arrangements for Lincoln's journey to Washington highlights her organisational role as a go-between and an efficient administrator for Pinkerton. She brought news from Pinkerton to Norman Judd (a future minister in Lincoln's administration), arranged a future parley between them, secured tickets in the night train from a railway official in a private meeting and met Lamon, Lincoln and Pinkerton at the train door, ushering them into their compartment.

Modern accounts of the journey, keen to thrill, depict Warn sitting with a gun ready to defend Lincoln from assailants while he slept. This is fantasy. Lamon records that all four passengers lay in their berths, with Pinkerton rising from time to time to check on their progress. Lincoln was, in any case, not really in any danger once he had boarded the train from Philadelphia to Washington, because nobody but a handful of his own protectors knew he was there (he was supposed to be still in Harrisburg), and the telegraph wires to Baltimore had been cut to prevent word getting out. Modern insistence on Warn, disguised as Lincoln's 'sister', sitting up and tending him through the night is reminiscent of similar depictions of Florence Nightingale sitting with wounded men in the Crimea. Nightingale was a statistician and social reformer, an early adopter of the pie chart, whose central achievement was organisational: she brought rational analysis to the deployment of field hospitals. But, like Warn, she is commonly staged as a nurse-cum-saviour in time of war, a 'Lady with the Lamp', combining bravery with tenderness.

None of this negates Warn's effectiveness as a pioneer Pinkerton employee and superintendent of his first female detective department. But the mythic qualities that Pinkerton attributes to Lincoln's escape and Warn's daring part in it as the 'unknown lady', in a story that he re-told and embroidered decades later, are designed to serve his own reputation. As S. Paul O'Hara points out in *Inventing the Pinkertons*, the agency played a central role in enforcing both capitalist objectives and state power in the later nineteenth century: its less palatable activities included strike-breaking, quelling industrial unrest by spying on union leaders and enforcing the rights of property: 'If corporate managers were the "visible hand" of the market, the Pinkertons were the market's visible fist; they were the shock troops of industrial order.'[20]

The 'folkloric' quality of Pinkerton's fictionalised memoirs, depicting the agency and its detectives in a heroic light, served to distract from their role as enforcers of corporate power and from an often unscrupulous surveillance culture. Pinkerton consistently depicts beautiful female representatives of his agency during the war riding horses, braving danger, supporting their male associates through capture, trial, imprisonment unto death, and saving the Union side from new engines of destruction by smuggling plans of submarines through enemy lines. Like the French Resistance *avant la lettre*, these daring women make the female detective spy into a figure of romance, whose noble aim of victory over evil justifies all deceptions and smooths all seeming irregularities.

It is likely that some of the 'fascinating women' Pinkerton deployed during the Civil War to gather information and to pose as wives of male agents were ladies who were willing to travel and to room with male counterparts because sex work had been part of their curricula vitae. Pinkerton aimed to present a morally unimpeachable version of this reality. Working-class women were presented as middle-class ladies, whose virtuous and dignified behaviour under pressure contrasted with the vulgarity and loose sexual morals of the villains whose plots they foiled.[21] The identities of multiple real women are conflated into figures of fantasy. Pinkerton drew on an emergent genre of fiction and 'memoir' featuring brave belles and dashing detectives to magnify his own achievements and burnish the Pinkerton brand.

There is only one known contemporary image of 'Kate Warne', in the collection of the Chicago History Museum. It is a photographic print touched up with watercolour paint, labelled 'Kate Warne 1866'; the spelling 'Warne', not used by Pinkerton before his imaginative detective memoirs of 1874, indicates that the label was probably not created until after Warn's death. The image shows a woman in a full-skirted silk gown, tightly buttoned at the bodice. Her hair is neatly, a trifle primly, pinned up; her centre parting and tight-lipped smile

37. Portrait of 'Kate Warne' (1866).

may suggest the firmness of character Pinkerton identified in Warn, or simply the subject's irritation at standing still. She holds a closed fan in her right hand and the back of a mahogany and velvet armchair in the other.

The image's provenance is as blurry as its medium. It was donated by Ronald P. Cameron in 1927, but there is no record of where he obtained it; the museum contacted Pinkerton but was unable to authenticate whether the print really represented Warn or not. Cameron's note referred to 'Miss Kate Warne' and inaccurately described Lincoln's 1861 journey out of Baltimore 'disguised as a nobleman' with Miss Warne as 'his nurse'.

There is no concrete evidence that it is, in fact, a picture of Angie Mahala Warn at all. It is perfectly possible that the endlessly reproduced image of the world's most famous female detective is as fake as the name 'Kate Warne': a blind behind which the real woman remains opaque, successful in death as she was in life at maintaining her alias. The story of Angie Mahala Warn's work as a detective is the perfect example of fact and fiction blurring like the lines and tones of a photograph overlaid with paint. Indeed, 'Kate Warne' could stand as an emblem for the way in which fiction and reality, truth and desire regarding the figure of the female detective, encounter one another in the Victorian press, becoming at times so (con)fused that they are no longer securely separable. The establishment of the real Victorian female detective as an accepted professional figure patrolling streets from London to Los Angeles owed much to the desire-lines established by fiction; however, the same fantasy routinely misrepresented the lives of real women trying to follow a career that did not often adhere to the lines or deal with the cases sketched in imagination.

Civil War and the Female Detective

The American Civil War offered Allan Pinkerton, and many women who wanted to imagine themselves undertaking daring acts of deception and detection, a moral framework and a practical reason to reinvent themselves. What might once have seemed a cowardly and mercenary act – spying on others – now took on a patriotic fervour and urgency that brooked no opposition. The pages of racy reminiscences (real or invented) frothed with stories of women who had passed as men, who had fought as soldiers, or assumed a bold incognito, stepping into the jaws of Confederate territory to penetrate the secrets of enemy submarines, stymie planned attacks and rescue wounded lovers. Pinkerton had used these stories to celebrate and rehabilitate his agency, giving it a moral authority and scope that made it seem unassailable: a part of national security at the highest level.

For readers, however, particularly female readers, the stories of courageous women detectives told by Pinkerton were part of a broader landscape of Civil War literature where a key pleasure was the battle women were quietly winning to throw off the gendered restraints previously imposed on them. Pinkerton's tales may have had a foundation in fact, but they were also riding the coattails of a trend.

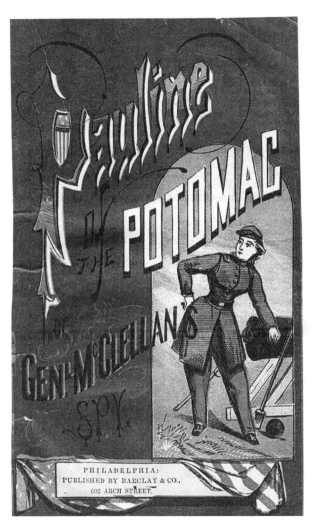

38. *Wesley Bradshaw (Charles Wesley Alexander),* Pauline of the Potomac or General McClellan's Spy *(1864).*

"But in the meantime," replied the fair captor, curveting her horse in the rear of Dallett, and still keeping her revolver leveled directly at him, "you will take up your line of march for Washington. Forward!"   See page 53.

39. Pauline D'Estraye in Turkish dress, frontispiece to Pauline of the Potomac *(1864).*

In Charles Wesley Alexander's *Pauline of the Potomac or General McClellan's Spy: An Authentic and Thrilling Narrative of the beautiful and accomplished Miss Pauline D'Estraye* (1864), the heroine appears on the cover in male uniform, leaning nonchalantly against a cannon. On the frontispiece, she is depicted on horseback in Turkish dress, threatening a man on the ground, who cowers before her as she towers over him. The adventure begins in France, where Pauline, the young daughter of the widowed aristocrat, Julien D'Estraye, helps him to escape the French Revolution and accompanies him to

America. Pauline falls in love with a promising young man, William Fairfax, but accepts her father's decision that she cannot marry her fiancé when Fairfax elects to join the secessionist side in the Civil War. In an extraordinary scene, her dying father dedicates Pauline to America and the Unionist cause, draping the flag like a bridal or nun's veil over her head.

This fatherly blessing helps to excuse what might otherwise seem female impropriety in Pauline's subsequent decision to join the war as a spy, dressed in male attire. Like Joan of Arc, Pauline becomes an embodiment of the purity of nation: her figure upholds the principles embodied in the Union, and the inviolability of the flag.

Pauline swims her horse through rivers and, while disguised as a secessionist, steals a fresh horse from a farmer. She also shoots two male assailants from the saddle, before galloping away. (We are reassured that the men were not mortally wounded.) More conventionally, when tending to dying soldiers on the battlefield, Pauline moistens the lips of all alike, whether Union or Confederate. The author insists his account is based on Pauline D'Estraye's diary reminiscences. However, though her name recalls that of Pauline Cushman, there was no real Pauline D'Estraye and her adventures are mostly pure invention.[22]

Charles Wesley Alexander followed *Pauline of the Potomac* with *Maud of the Mississippi* (1868), a similarly sensational, fictitious sequel.[23] 'Maud' succeeds as a spy, saving General Grant from assassination by eavesdropping, bribing landladies to give her information, and bantering with shop owners to discover intelligence about Confederate conspirators. Like 'Kate Warn', Maud is bent on preventing her male superior from being offed, and herself from being outed. She comes close to death when she steps out from a wardrobe and confronts the conspirators, who threaten to kill her; but her gun and whistle save her.

'Kill her!' hissed Herring, in the excess of his rage; and the eyes of all the villains flashed wickedly at me. The next moment my revolver was out and ready in one hand, while in the other I held a policeman's whistle. I said:

'Gentlemen, as you like: but beside the fact that I have a shot here for each of you, with one to spare, a breath on this call will bring to my help the policemen I took care to have stationed outside.'[24]

Versions of this scene would recur in many female detective dramas. Civil War narratives of plucky female spies had a long life and influence on the American image of the female detective as an action heroine who possessed 'masculine' strength of body and character, knew how to handle a gun and engaged in acts of extreme physical courage, often to save worthy men.[25]

As Alice Fahs comments in *The Imagined Civil War: Popular Literature of the North and South 1861–1865*:

Portraying girls who ran away from home, disguised themselves as men, and even served as soldiers, sensational novels were often energized by plots of transgression against prevailing norms of behavior for women. At the start of the war, such novels provided a means of imagining women's active participation in the conflict. Indeed, one author later admitted that she had been inspired to disguise herself as a man both before and during the war by an antebellum sensational novel titled *Fanny Campbell, the Female Pirate Captain: A Tale of the Revolution*. Drawing on this and other sensational literature, Sarah Emma Edmonds published a highly embroidered account of her wartime adventures in 1864 titled *Unsexed: or, The Female Soldier. The Thrilling Adventures, Experiences and Escapes of a Woman, As Nurse, Spy and Scout, in Hospitals, Camps and Battle-fields*.[26]

It is worth noticing the consistency here between Pinkerton's tales of Warn and Lawton's ability to nurse the wounded, while also acting as spies and scouts, and contemporary sensation fiction that insisted on women's caring role during their transgressive impersonations of male soldiers. Fahs notes that there was a 'circular economy' between sensation 'memoirs' and newspaper reportage, which drew liberally on fictionalised tales, such as that of 'Annie Lillybridge', supposed to have fought in the 21st Michigan Infantry in order to be beside her lover. There were many accounts of Parson Brownlow's daughter (Susan or Martha) defending the Unionist flag and her own honour against Confederate marauders. The highly sensationalised *Parson Brownlow's Book* sold more than 75,000 copies in thirty days in the summer of 1862. Both men and women enjoyed reading these adventures. They combined patriotic pride with a gleeful abandonment of conventional gender roles.

Among the thrilling sensation novels set during the Civil War were several by a British author, William Stephens Hayward, whose name will be familiar to readers of the earlier chapters of this book. Hayward, a gambler, jailbird and prolific writer of racy fiction, found in America inspiration for adventures in which women called the shots. In *The Black Angel* (1863), he depicted strong women aiding the war effort. In the sequel, *The Star of the South* (1864), the heroine, Coralie is imagined on horseback, leading the regiment into battle against male advice:

'Young lady, this is no place for you. Go to the rear.'

Coralie's eyes flashed, and she turned crimson.

'I shall not go to the rear. I shall go to the front.'

... Coralie touched with her gloved hand a small revolver she wore in her belt.

'I will shoot the first man who dares to lay a hand on my horse's bridle,' she said, quietly.

'I will not suffer this. I will return. I will lead my men back.'

'Lead them back, if you choose,' replied Coralie, scornfully. 'I shall go on. Is this a time to talk of going back? Look up the hill;

see how our brave troops are pressed – see how the shot and shell are tearing around them, while they are too weak to charge into and drive back the enemy. Lead back the men, if they will follow you, which I doubt. I will see whether or not they will follow me.'[27]

In this provocative and sexually charged scene, Coralie moves from being a figure to be protected and sent back, to being a figure who threatens to shoot any man who prevents her from leading. Using a phrase ('shot and shell') familiar from Tennyson's Crimean poem 'The Charge of the Light Brigade', she exposes cowardice in her male colleague, as well as alluding to the 'too weak' men who are fighting. It is clear that she rides forward to challenge the men around her as well as to defend the men on the hill. Other chapters are titled: 'Coralie Horsewhips a Colonel' and 'Coralie Captures a Prisoner'. The remarkable plot uncovers Coralie's relationship with a black female servant, who proves to be her half-sister. It challenges racial and class boundaries, as well as conventional gender roles.

From Gunslinger to Gumshoe

Hayward's depiction of feisty female leadership and physical bravery in *The Black Angel* and *The Star of the South* is intimately related to his simultaneous depiction of the female detective Mrs Paschal in his pioneering 'memoir', *Revelations of a Lady Detective* (1864). She, too, is outnumbered and trapped by a band of conspirators, faces execution and has to fight her way out or, like 'Maud Melville', summon assistance at the last moment with a whistle:

> I raised my whistle to my lips, and turning my face in the direction of the river, blew loudly and shrilly upon it. So prolonged was the signal that I only desisted when Zini sprang up the steps, and with one energetic blow dashed it out of my hand . . .
>
> 'Quick! Quick!' He cried. 'She has accomplices without.'

The Secret Band rushed with rapidity down the ladder, and Zini dragged me to the part of the room in which the huge mill was situated. It was a terrible instrument. As an implement of torture and death it was unequalled.[28]

Mrs Paschal's antagonists here are Italian Mafiosi in London, who intend to kill her with an old water wheel, on an abandoned island in the Thames. But the torturing 'mill' has associations with the violence of the Spanish Inquisition and Paschal's attempted prevention of an assassination attempt conjures Kate Warn's Baltimore adventure of 1861. Indeed, Hayward's female detective of the 1860s is, in many ways, a spin-off of her American antecedents. Maud of the Mississippi likes a cigar and is never without a weapon. Importing to Britain an image of a woman with a gun who likes to smoke (she has a cigarette in hand on the cover) and can handle every kind of treachery and physical threat, Hayward made Mrs Paschal a female spy who would look as at home on the banks of the Hudson as in the bank vaults of Belgravia.

In 'The Mysterious Countess', Mrs Paschal regrets that she isn't carrying her gun with her when she is cornered in a secret bank vault by the cross-dressing Countess Vervaine, who is robbing the premises: 'I sighed for a Colt's revolver, and blamed myself for not having taken the precaution of being armed.'[29] It would have been very surprising for any British woman to have owned a Colt in 1864. Mrs Paschal's gun-toting bravery derives straight from the Civil War fiction read and written by the author who created her. Mrs Paschal also reflects, of the cruel countess, who beats her maids in private:

She regarded me as something for which she paid, and which was useful to her on certain occasions. I believe she looked on me very much as a lady in the Southern States of America looks on a slave – a thing to minister to her vanity and obey her commands.[30]

Mrs Paschal has to 'become' a lady's maid to detect the countess's night-time robberies of the Belgravia bank; she also has to pose as a maid to discover how violent the countess is to her social inferiors. What is being detected here is as much class warfare, which Hayward suggestively links to racial oppression in America, as a financial crime.

Here, we see the direct influence of American models of female heroism during the Civil War, involving the patriotic female detective-spy – cross-dressing, straight-shooting, class-hopping – on one of the very first books of British fiction depicting a professional female detective. This is a channel of influence that has largely been ignored.[31] The American 'romance of war' and the 'detective story' featuring brave and daring women are closely allied; both also draw on the stage conventions of sensation drama. Elizabeth Burgoyne Corbett, in the same year that she was writing Dora Bell detective stories, wrote a play, *The War Correspondent*, in which her heroine – who has an eman-cipated black servant, who plays a central role – becomes a blockade runner in the Mexican–American War to save her father from assas-sination. The melodramatic action allows the heroine both to detect a plot to kill her family and to bestride the stage with gun in hand.

As we have seen, early pulp fiction by William Stephens Hayward and James Redding Ware in 1864, involving the female detective as action heroine, swiftly led to theatrical depictions of the female detec-tive from 1865 onwards, as an on-stage protagonist who cross-dressed, assuming multiple characters of various social classes, and who physi-cally pursued villains, often with a gun. Colin Henry Hazlewood's play *The Female Detective* was successfully staged in Britain and then in America in 1865, becoming a staple of the stage repertoire over the next two decades in both countries. Thus Carlotta Crabtree, the American actress, played *The Female Detective* in Boston in 1869, bringing Tom Taylor's adaptation of the play (now called *The Little Detective, or Woman's Curiosity*) back to Britain in the 1880s. Meanwhile, Cameron and Ferguson, a Glasgow and London-based firm, offered in

1887 a 'Detective Library' featuring Redding Ware's *The Female Detective* alongside *The Indian Detective* and *The Yankee Detective*. At sixpence a volume, these were dime novels for the British market. The transatlantic traffic in female detectives of this type thrives throughout the latter half of the nineteenth century, existing in parallel to the emergent genre of more self-consciously cerebral detectives, who can solve a crime at arm's length by means of subtle reading of traits and tells. It is fascinating to see how this popular model of female detection, to which cross-dressing, physical acts of bravery and the upsetting of gender conventions are central, crosses and re-crosses the Atlantic like a successful common species of bird: it migrates and returns.

From Kate Warne to *Lady Kate, The Dashing Female Detective*

Pinkerton's celebrated depiction of 'Kate Warne' – which, as we have seen, hovered between fact and fiction – almost certainly influenced Old Sleuth's dime novels of the 1880s: *Lady Kate, The Dashing Female Detective* (1886) and *The Great Bond Robbery or Tracked by a Female Detective* (1885), whose heroine is Kate Goelet. These novels also build on a longer tradition of action heroines in American popular fiction. The character of the female detective in 'low' literature, in both Britain and America, offered a chance to redefine gender boundaries: brave women were depicted smoking, swearing, fighting, gambling and going where they chose.

Lady Kate, The Dashing Female Detective is an entrepreneur: a 'self-made girl', as the narrator describes her. We are told that she was 'a waif', placed in a charitable institution by her unknown parents as a child, but ran away from it, graduating from crossing-sweeper to newspaper vendor to telegraph operator and thence to a position as a Customs House detective, searching women for items smuggled under their apparel. Kate managed to educate herself and 'had picked up many lady like accomplishments': 'She was a smart, brave, enterprising, beautiful, virtuous young woman, born with great natural talent and wonderful energy of character.' Kate is a working-class heroine who will become a lady in aristocratic terms, as well as a lady detective in professional life.

The female detective of the dime novels is an aspirational figure. She offered readers of cheap fiction, many of whom were immigrants or otherwise stood outside the charmed inner circle of social prosperity, education and secure national identity, a boundary-crossing fantasy that allowed them (albeit briefly) to imagine being both outlaws and insiders, behaving with the physical freedom of a man and, at need, the decorum of a woman. Kate is equally at home in a diamond-studded ballroom, where she can speak French and play the piano, or a low dive, where she plays 'games of chance' and understands and deploys thieves' slang. She is a shapeshifter, for whom class and gender barriers are readily surmountable. She eludes categorisation just as she eludes capture by her enemies. Her aptitude for disguising herself swiftly in any one of numerous personae becomes a physical cipher for her more general and mysterious ability to be anyone she likes. She can both scupper male attacks upon her as a woman and pass visually as a man:

> Kate was a quick thinker . . . [shc] moved a step back, and, as the man reached forth to seize her, she suddenly dealt him a blow that sent him reeling to the ground, and quick as a flash she darted away in the fast deepening twilight . . . A woman disappeared . . . and a man appeared in the pathway.[32]

Kate also uses 'masculine' vocabulary: 'Kate was a woman, but she used a genuine masculine phrase, when she exclaimed: "Well, I'll be hanged if I have not beaten myself!"' During a phase of the plot where she tracks bloodstains, is soaked to the skin in a thunderstorm and falls off a cliff (catching hold of a bush to cling on in a manner that would be made famous by innumerable filmic action heroes), Kate's 'masculine expressions' include 'That's bully for me!' and 'Well this *is* a nice pickle I've got myself into, I must say!' The narrator pretends to apologise for these lapses: 'Excuse us and our heroine, dear reader, but once more Kate fired off a man's declaration, by exclaiming: "Well, I'll be blamed!"'[33] In fact, the story clearly relishes these lapses. Like Kate's prowess in other 'masculine' skills, such as 'games of chance' (poker and billiards), firing a gun and knocking opponents out cold, her free use of language is a form of empowerment that is designed to tickle the female imagination as much as the male one.

The Dime-Novel Detective Has It All

Garyn G. Roberts, Gary Hoppenstand and Ray B. Browne assert that the primary audience for dime novels was adolescent males.[34] Christine Bold also suggests that 'dime novels were a male-dominated genre' in terms of 'publishers, writers and fictional formulas'.[35] But the advertisements at the end of *Lady Kate, The Dashing Female Detective* tell a different story. The ads include a plug for *The New York Monthly Fashion Bazaar*, drawing attention to Munro's Bazaar Pinned Paper Patterns, and *A New Book for Ladies Cutting-out and Dressmaking* – a title also published by Munro, who issued the Old Sleuth detective titles. The publisher clearly expected women who made dresses and enjoyed fashion to enjoy the 'dashing' exploits of a woman who cross-dressed in a matter of minutes, used male slang and routinely knocked men to the ground. Rebecca S. Wingo notes that the audience for dime novels was huge: 'Standard orders for dimes were 60,00 to 70,000 copies, and publishers often reprinted new editions on a near monthly basis.'[36] Both working-class and middle-class readers relished these books. From their repeated tropes, one can readily gain a sense of the satisfactions offered by female detectives in the late Victorian dime novel. The 'unmasking' scene, where a detective who appears to be a man is revealed to be a woman, is a key reveal. There are also frequently scenes where the female detective suffers sexual harassment, only to surprise her assailants with her superior physical prowess in knocking them down. Modern women who have been catcalled or worse while out on the street will readily identify with Victorian women's glee when the male harasser is given his comeuppance. The cross-dressing detective here is a vector in a civil war that is not between North and South but between men and women as autonomous sexual agents.

Kate is the foremother of comic-strip heroines, superheroes who change in an instant behind a bush or in a telephone box, who concuss their attackers, leaving them dazed on the floor wondering where the blow came from. Her chops are less intellectual than karate:

> 'You appear to be the boss, miss.'
>   'I am.'
>   'And you proclaim war?'
>   'I do.'
>   The man drew a pair of handcuffs and seized hold of Gordon.
>   The next moment he lay in the road.
>   'We will go now', [Kate] said to Gordon.
>   The thing had been done so quickly Kate's companion hardly realized what had transpired.[37]

Here, Kate is saving from arrest one of two half-brothers who are frequently mistaken for one another. It adds a frisson that his name is George Gordon – the same as Lord Byron's – but that he prissily disapproves of Kate's career: 'such an unlady-like profession'. The novel roundly scotches this assertion and the male figure who is threatened by the idea of strong women, despite needing one to save him. The fluidity of social class and gender Kate displays are parallel forms of wish-fulfilment in a character whose detective ability to track or 'pipe' others is only equalled by her 'self-made' ability to channel multiple identities.

Similarly, in Old Sleuth's 1898 dime novel *Gipsy Rose, the Female Detective*, the gender- and class-fluid heroine transcends the limits of her poor, obscure origins and her femininity to pass as a male

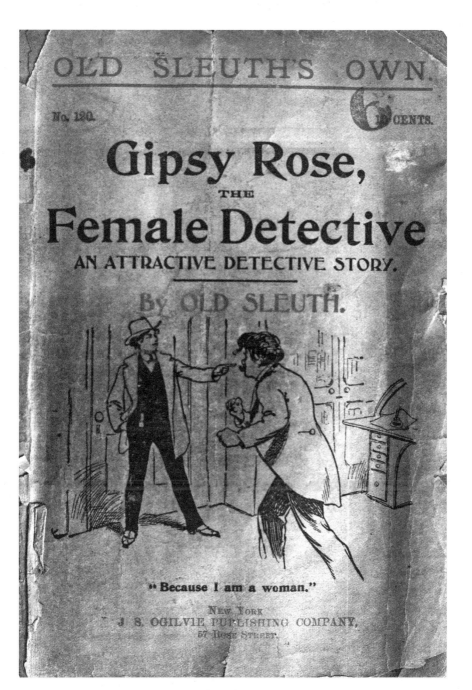

40. *Old Sleuth*, Gipsy Rose, the Female Detective *(1898)*.

professional. Rose is an expert typist, who can be 'placed' in suspect firms by the detective agency that employs her. Typically for this kind of fiction, Rose is summoned to aid a young lawyer in the case of a child who has been kidnapped. The lawyer refuses to countenance working with a woman and dismisses her out of hand, so she returns in male disguise, fooling him completely.

The lawyer is attracted to his female co-worker, but she insists upon maintaining a business relationship, naming her financial terms and refusing to satisfy his curiosity about her antecedents.[38] She keeps wrongfooting him with her successful disguises (for example, as an old beggar woman) and calls him a 'muffin'. Her acuteness in solving the kidnapping case contrasts with his inexperience. Gipsy Rose will end the novel married to the lawyer who at first refused to work with her: her ability to bamboozle him and best him in business bodes well for her power to shape the terms of their marriage.

The Female Detective as Queer Hero

Extraordinarily, in *Cad Metti: The Female Detective Strategist* (1895), another dime novel, the female detective 'Cad' and her detective sidekick and romantic partner Oscar 'Dudie' Dunne can actually *pass for one another*, taking one another's place in a relay manoeuvre to foil the plot against them by organised crime bosses who are money-laundering and masterminding civic corruption in New York. Dudie is strong but 'of effeminate appearance', while Cad

> could make her living on the stage as a marvel. She is a great musical genius. She can sing or dance, she can fence or wrestle like a man. Her strength is extraordinary, and as a pistol shot she is the champion woman of the world; and when it comes to quickness, nerve, cunning, and courage she cannot be excelled.[39]

A 'dude' in American slang of the 1870s and 1880s is a dandy, an effeminate, fastidious city dweller. Oscar, the *dude* of this story, cross-dresses just as his female 'pal' Cad (conventionally a word for a male scoundrel) does. The story experiments with gender fluidity, allowing the reader to take pleasure in a 'strange, weird girl' heroine who can pass for a messenger boy and 'flit from place to place like a shadow'. The wider work that the idea of the detective is doing in this kind of story is to legitimise shape-shifting as a practice that serves rather than undermines the security of the state and its innocent inhabit-ants. What might otherwise seem illicit or improper about gender-fluid behaviour and appearance is endorsed, as it is necessary to evade the murderous antics of millionaires who have 'posed before the public for twenty years' as pillars of society but have been systematic criminals, undermining public safety. As Pamela Bedore has shown, such gender-fluid characters appeared in multiple dime novels, and included 'Gay Gus, the lady detective' (1883) and 'Nina, the lady detective' (1888).[40]

In these Victorian popular fictions featuring female detectives, women and men can pass for one another, support one another and also work together – without losing affection or the possibility of marriage. The *raison d'être* of these fictional female detectives is that they can at one and the same time win men romantically, beat men physically and be men socially. Tantalisingly, they offer a full range of gender positions or masks, to be donned at will, which also hint at different sexual roles that might be occupied, not exclusively, but voluntarily, in relationships that allow for 'detective' elements: role-play, suspense, combat and unmasking. The force of this popular 'pulp' image of the female detective, however improbable her extreme abilities and social trajectory, had real impact on the social scene in America and on the journalistic environment in which the activities of female detectives (including those occupying this role in their imaginative lives) were reported.

Gender Fluidity and Self-Invented Female Detectives

'Female detective' became, by the 1880s, a sign under which gender fluidity and resistance to conventionally gendered behaviour could trade. It created a performative space for experimentation along the fault-line of fiction and reality whose 'detective' play allowed for querying and queering the given or constructed nature of gendered and sexual identity.

Nellie King, known as 'the female detective', was arrested in 1887. She had 'borrowed' a horse and ridden it astride into the town of Frankfort, Dakota, wearing a fetching outfit that, significantly, combined a cowboy's duster coat, pale, tight trousers, women's boots, braceleted wrists and a .38 calibre revolver tucked into her belt. When she removed her cap, her hair fell loose about her shoulders. Posing in the role of a female detective, she claimed to be on the trail of a horse thief. This ruse allowed her to stir up a great deal of attention, 'mashing' (flirting with) men, while stressing the urgency and importance of her mission. She carried a certificate from the Northwestern Detective Association. This persuaded some locals to help her. Eventually, however, it emerged that she was faking. (She had only gained this certificate as a result of an affair with the owner of this agency and it conveyed no real authority.) In Aberdeen, another Dakota frontier town, Nellie falsely claimed to be working for Kingsford Detective Associates of New York City. Newspaper reporters, equally impressed by her glamour and outraged by her deceitful antics, continued to follow Nellie King's exploits. In an interview with the *Indianapolis Sunday Journal*, Nellie was reported as saying:

> Yes, I had rather a gay time in Dakota, but I did nothing that was really criminal . . . I made up my mind to have a little sport if I had to get it all up myself. In the language of the city, I resolved to paint the country about there a vivid hue . . . I made a dandy-looking boy-man, too . . . Did I get arrested! Yes, several times;

but I had a picnic with the officers who pulled me. I scared the whiskers off their faces in many instances with my revolver.[41]

It is easy to imagine Mae West playing Nellie King, who broke the bounds of gender decorum in dress and behaviour in ways that, by her own account, made women 'real mad' and 'sort of paralyzed' men. Over a decade of public opprobrium and press delight, she appeared in bar-room fights, kidnapping allegations and was labelled the 'Cowboy Queen', as well as 'the Female Sleuth'. One headline memorably read: 'She Steals Two Horses, a Man's Clothes and a Young Man Too'.[42]

Jerry Kuntz has convincingly argued that Nellie suffered from a mood disorder, possibly bipolar syndrome, that produced manic sprees in which she indulged in wild, attention-seeking behaviour that struck inhabitants of the frontier towns she visited as alternately entertaining, sexy, disreputable and shocking.[43] Nellie had left home aged nine to join a travelling theatrical company. Her career included periods of sex work and violent physical attack by at least one man. During a wild and difficult life, she became addicted to morphine and cocaine and died sadly young. It is intriguing that she chose to impersonate a female detective to act out one of her fantasies of self: a dashing horseback role in which she 'made an entrance' not to be forgotten. She may have encountered stage performances of 'the female detective' or cheap literature that attracted her to the role, with its customary cross-dressing and powerful implications of well-armed pursuit of male villains. There is a pathos to Nellie's story, which has such a compulsive element of drama to it. Nellie insistently cast herself as the heroine of her own life, but police officers, while they rarely kept her in jail, tagged her as a troublemaker and lawbreaker. She died of an overdose in 1899, aged only thirty-six.

In 1886, the *New York Mercury* printed details of Essie Livingstone, a female detective from Williamsburg who, it claimed, had previously worked as a professional clog dancer. Swapping one form of performance for another, after separating from her husband, Essie began wearing male clothes and acting informally as a sleuth:

> She is short of stature, with a well rounded figure and dark brown eyes. She wears her hair cropped short, and when dressed in men's clothes looks prettier than in dresses. She is about twenty-four years old and has been masquerading as a man for about two years. When she first started out in masculine clothes she was detected by Detective Glori. He was about to arrest her, when she told him if he would let her go she would give him the clue to a burglary which was just at that time mystifying the police.[44]

I have found no evidence that Essie Livingstone existed in real life. It matters most that readers in America and in Britain *wanted* her to exist: a female sleuth who is even more attractive, to both sexes when dressed as a man. Essie is an independent, cross-dressing woman who proves to be more than a match for a clothes-stealing criminal, 'Joker' Long.

While lesbianism is not specifically implied in Essie's abandonment of her husband, it is certainly a subtext in an 1888 article in the *Worcestershire Chronicle*, 'Miss Flynn Smoked Cigars'. Walter Dillon Trenchard of West Kensington was brought before a magistrate, accused of using threatening language to his wife, Alice. Trenchard was also accused of striking Alice and pulling her hair while she was in bed. In his defence, Trenchard submitted that Miss Flynn was residing in the house, sleeping with Alice and 'keeping her from him'; he also complained that Miss Flynn was wearing his dressing jacket and smoking his cigars, swearing, and that she annoyed him by 'smoking around the house in a semi-nude state'. Miss Flynn, whom the reporter described as giving evidence 'in a loud tone of voice', joked in court that she was a 'female detective'.[45] The husband's jealousy of Flynn sleeping with his wife and usurping his 'masculine' privileges suggests not just irritation at an unwelcome guest but outrage at a sexual rival. 'Female detective' here has a frisson of innuendo.

This is also true of the story of Luvena Mabry, the 'only female detective in the South', who was reported in 1889 to be a moonshiner's daughter, hired by police to investigate illicit stills. Like Essie Livingstone, Mabry is described in erotic terms designed to attract male and female readers alike: 'Lorena is a flaxen-haired, cherry-lipped girl of twenty-five, with a form like Hebe.'[46] Like Livingstone, she is described as dressing in male attire to accomplish her investigative work: 'attired as a handsome male book-peddler'. In Mabry's story, however, there is a twist; she has 'mashed' a young woman to the extent of proposing marriage to her:

> In one of my trips into Cherokee ... I made quite a mash on a sweet young lady and I am now engaged to marry her ... I had to play the part of a man up there and I went in male attire. This young girl took to me at once and I could not shake her off. So I just made love to her after the most approved style.[47]

To some readers, this story (appearing as news, but probably confected) of the 'female detective' may simply have raised a smile. For others, its coded suggestion of lesbian romance may have raised an eyebrow. The habitually cross-dressing, role-playing persona of the female detective in the Victorian theatre and dime novel offered exciting possibilities to those who liked to imagine a gender-fluid self, or same-sex romance. The idea that such women existed in real life, as these newspaper reports claim, was tantalising.

Detective work naturally suggested aliases and the possibility that women existed whose professional and gender identities were not what they might appear to be at first blush: that they might 'pass' differently in different contexts. The resulting frisson was different from that generated by a male detective character: the woman who transgressed the social and sexual limits considered proper for women, to serve the wider ends of social justice, was erotically and morally confusing. In America, the imaginary female detective character was more likely to be an outlaw. She was more likely to carry a weapon. In a land where frontiers were still being improvised and negotiated, characters like Nellie King, who throve on self-invention, exploited the uncertainties of new settlement towns to create a sensation as cowboy detectives whose relationship to law and order was as sketchy as it was gripping, existing between male and female conventions, law-breaking and law-enforcement, fact and fiction.

However, the idea of the cross-dressing detective was not confined to American newspapers. In Ireland, the *Derry Journal* in 1880 printed 'A Detective's Story', which recounts how a man and a woman are alone in a train compartment 'on an English railroad'. Suddenly, the gentleman says: 'Madam, I will trouble you to look out of the window for a few minutes: I am going to make some change in my wearing apparel.' She replies politely, turning her back upon him. When she looks again, she is surprised:

> When the lady turned she beheld her male companion transformed into a dashing lady, with a heavy veil over her face.
>
> 'Now, sir, or madam, whichever you are,' said the lady, I must trouble you to look out of the window, for I also have some changes to make in my apparel . . .
>
> To his great surprise, on resuming his seat, the gentleman in female attire found his lady companion transformed into a man.[48]

The man who has turned into a woman, confesses that s/he has robbed a bank. The woman who has become a man announces that s/he is a detective, who has been trailing her/him, and claps the cross-dressed thief in handcuffs.

The 'detective story', here, touches upon more than robbery and its pursuit. It raises the erotic question of concealed identity, particularly the possibility of 'criminal' desires that society conventionally disallows. The cross-dressing fictional detective allows for the possibility of sexually ambivalent and gender-curious practices as well as picturing women 'wearing the trousers' in the workplace. Such fictions are imaginatively enabling, yet, like many fantasies of empowerment, they also gloss over the everyday realities faced by women detectives working in the streets, on the docks, in hotels, boarding houses, stores, buses and trains in nineteenth-century Britain and America.

Exceptionalism and the Real American Female Detective

As we have seen, there were substantial numbers of real female detectives in the second half of the nineteenth century. Some of them worked with police departments; a greater number were employed by private agencies. In America, they performed work very similar to the work that they performed in Britain.[49] These women were routinely viewed in fictional terms. For example, Mary Holland, a Methodist minister's daughter who ran the Holland Detective Agency, became a world expert in fingerprint evidence and co-edited the professional magazine *The Detective* with her husband, was transformed in Hugh C. Weir's stories of *Madelyn Mack, Detective* into a single woman with 'a mass of dull gold hair' who is sometimes presented 'lying flat on her back on a tawny leopardskin'.[50] The work they did was also distinct from that of their fictional counterparts. They were often employed to convict other working-class women, whether fortune-tellers or sex workers, adulterers or shoplifters.

Women were essential to gain access to places where crimes occurred that male police officers and private detectives couldn't easily penetrate. Backstreet abortionists, for example, were targeted using female detectives. In March 1894, no fewer than sixteen midwives and 'malpractitioners' were arraigned in New York and fined sums ranging from $500 to $2,000 as a result of the work of Grace Fox, a private detective hired by the Society for the Enforcement of the

Criminal Laws.[51] In 1884, the eighteen-year-old Maggie Andarise was 'employed by captain McCullagh of the 16th Precinct' in New York to bust an opium joint in Elizabeth Street by posing as a customer and buying opium. Twenty-nine female junkies appeared at the Tombs Police Court, pale and haggard, ranging in age from seventeen to twenty-seven years, their dresses covered in whitewash from the cells.[52] Today, we might see Maggie as a plant or informant, rather than a 'detective', as the New York Times dubbed her, but these roles shaded into one another. Isabella Goodwin, a police matron from 1896 who became a detective sergeant, was given her first big job in 1898 by the NYPD: breaking a 'women's pool room on West 24th Street' – an illegal horse-betting ring – by infiltrating it. 'No man could get in there so they sent for me,' she recalled. She would go on to detect fraudulent palmists, spiritualists, hypnotists and surgeons, usually by posing as a client.[53]

Female detectives' work was frequently in embedded, undercover roles, enabling police and private agencies to gain access to fraudsters, blackmailers and other professional crooks whose connections police guessed but who could not easily be identified and convicted. The detective's job was particularly to encourage women connected to the suspects to speak freely. As Allan Pinkerton put it in one of his rare moments of accuracy: 'They are expected to win the confidence of those from whom information is desired, and to lose no opportunity of encouraging them to talk about themselves.'[54] In 1874, Mrs Holton of Pinkerton's agency was credited with having discovered the whereabouts of Robert L. Dudley, an extensive mail-robber and forger.[55] Mrs Holton befriended Mrs Dudley's sister, Alice Sheridan, patronising the store where she worked and watching closely when she dropped letters in a public mailbox. These letters, written using an alias, led the police to the Dudleys in Boston.

As they did in Britain, American female detectives worked in trains – identifying railwaymen who did not charge or record the proper fare. In 1866, it was reported that they were regularly travelling the New York railroad. In 1859, the *Chicago Times* objected to this 'infamous system':

> It may not be known to the many excellent men officiating as conductors upon the railroads ... that a well dressed seductive-looking female is employed by a detective agency to take items against them ... She takes her seat in the cars, and, on being asked for her ticket she says she had neither money nor ticket. If the conductor sympathises with her ... she makes a note of the circumstance, gets the conductor's name ... and daily reports to headquarters.[56]

Such vilifications of the ruthless female railway detective, flirting with the guard to secure free passage, then turning him in to the authorities as a corrupt employee, contrast markedly with Pinkerton's heroic depiction of Kate Warne solving the Adams Express robbery and whisking Lincoln to safety on the night train.

From 1865, women worked at docks as customs detectives, identifying smuggled fabric and goods carried under women's clothes: this was not merely a matter of small personal items but a way in which professional and commercial agents evaded large amounts of tax, sometimes using immigrants as 'mules'. Female detectives were employed by department stores to detect shoplifting; hotels to detect and deter grifters who would not pay for their rooms; and even at parties, to make sure that guests did not make off with other guests' property. They were, by private agencies, frequently deployed in divorce suits and cases of sexual misconduct, and in cases involving disputed wills, inheritance and probate. Strikebreaking was among the commercial jobs they covered; and corporations in the United States, as they did in Britain, hired female detectives to identify employees and trading partners whose honesty or loyalty they suspected.

It was relatively rare for female detectives to be involved in murder cases. But we shouldn't assume, therefore, that women's detective work was inherently less difficult or valuable than men's. The commonplace reality of nineteenth-century policing, in America as in Britain, is that most crimes are strongly associated with poverty: petty theft, street swindling and confidence trickery, prostitution, drug and alcohol abuse, abortion and concealed births, domestic violence. Often, it was this routine work that led women – like their male counterparts – to become sufficiently experienced to handle more international and more 'public' cases. They developed relationships within the community: their street-level knowledge of persons and places counted. Women police detectives were appointed in significant numbers after 1910 but this appointment was sometimes merely a formal recognition, with title and salary, for the detective work they had been doing for decades. This was certainly the case with Isabella Goodwin.

Isabella Goodwin, Detective from the First

Isabella Goodwin was officially appointed a detective sergeant in the New York Police Department in March 1912, an achievement reported in many newspapers. However, Goodwin noted that she had been working for the police since 1896 – for almost *sixteen years* – when she was finally pronounced a detective and given a detective's salary. Previous to her official recognition as a detective, she was a police matron. She estimated that in those sixteen years she had tackled some 500 cases. She was also swift to remark, when interviewed by journalists in 1912, that although they were reporting her as a singular phenomenon – 'New York's Only Woman Detective' – there were many women working for the NYPD at that time: 'People in general do not seem to know that we already have 70 women connected with the police department.'[57]

The case that brought Isabella Goodwin to public attention was that of the 'taxicab bandits' – a group of professional thieves who in February 1912 committed a violent armed robbery on a taxi carrying

NEW YORK'S ONLY WOMAN DETECTIVE

Mrs. Isabella Goodwin Has Just Received a Raise in Salary for Helping to Solve the Taxicab Mystery—She Tells in an Amusing Way How She Has Caught Fakirs and Confidence Men—Has Been Interested in More Than Five Hundred Cases.

41. Isabella Goodwin, 'New York's Only Woman Detective',
Greene County Herald *(1912)*.

bank employees who were ferrying $25,000 between banks. Goodwin used undercover skills to expose the crooks. She posed as an old Irishwoman seeking work in the Bowery, a poor neighbourhood. Having taken lodgings in a house frequented by girlfriends of some of the suspects, Goodwin kept her ear to the ground, discovering who was 'shedding money like a canary does feathers in the moulting season', and winkling out the truth by encouraging the disgruntled former lover of mobster Eddie 'The Boob' Kinsman to tell all.

Born Isabella Loghry in 1865 to a hotelier and restaurant-keeper in New York's Greenwich Village, Goodwin attended elementary school but had no secondary education. She had, however, the advantage as a detective of being a working-class woman, one of six children, from a neighbourhood that knew the realities of poverty, addiction and sex work. The Loghry family was already in Pennsylvania in the eighteenth century, but the name is Irish – from Leinster – and Isabella's brother's name, Sullivan Hardy Weston Loghry, suggests that her Irish roots were not far from the family's surface. It is therefore no accident that Isabella Goodwin was able successfully to play a poor Irishwoman working as a dishwasher in the Bowery in order to gain intelligence about the taxicab bandits.

This case attracted notice because the robberies had already caused a sensation in the papers, due to the sums involved and the perception that 'the detective bureau and the Pinkertons and the Burns agency were all talking about how soon they would have the taxicab bandits . . . under lock and key . . . and failing, signally, to get clues'.[58] According to the Chicago *Day Book*, Goodwin asked for a week off work, deciding to track down the thieves on her own account. In other versions of the story – including a 'true crime' thriller *The Great Taxicab Robbery*, published later the same year – there was a planned collaboration, with different divisions of the police department working in tandem to capture the robbers when they returned to New York.[59] Having compromised her safety by descending into New York's underworld to secure vital evidence in the case, Goodwin was rewarded with a raise that more than doubled her salary, from $1,000 as police matron to $2,500 as detective sergeant. The story as reported by the *Day Book*, 'Women's Scheming Gets "Taxicab Bandits"', became one about men being 'beaten by a woman', as if the case were a race and Mrs Goodwin (like Miss Cayley in Grant Allen's *Miss Cayley's Adventures*) had, by means of female cunning, beaten her opponents to the finish line.

Other papers compared Mrs Goodwin to Conan Doyle's famous sleuth: 'Here is a real Sherlock Holmes who has been instrumental in the capture of hundreds of lawbreakers, without smoking a single pipeful of tobacco.'[60] Patronisingly, her appearance was frequently mentioned as a matter of surprise – she was 'small, plainly clothed, neat looking' or:

> Mrs Goodwin wore a fetching hat of blue straw tied down with a smart lace veil, a costume of bright blue cloth and satin pumps and immaculate white kid gloves . . . She looked all the world like a society matron ready to take her limousine out for some afternoon tea.[61]

In this way, her 'feminine' dress was implicitly contrasted with the 'masculine' work she undertook. Journalists were always swift to mention that Mrs Goodwin was both the widow of a policeman (John Goodwin) and her son was a detective sergeant: her contribution to crime-fighting had been both professional and respectably maternal: 'With all her skill as a detective, Mrs Goodwin is nothing but a woman and a mother, and she has the prettiest homes imaginable . . . Her daughter, Miss Margaret who . . . runs the household, is a winsome girl of nineteen, pretty as a picture.'[62]

The fact that her daughter was training as a detective was less frequently noted. (Intriguingly, Isabella's sister Rose seems also to have been a detective, suggesting that, in this family, women were expected to work and that they developed a talent for detection.) The *Greene County Herald* article got the shape of Goodwin's family wrong: she had six children – five boys and a girl, though two of her children died in infancy.

One sees a constant desire in reportage about Goodwin to glamorise her life and work by focusing on cases in which the public was at risk from pitiless swindlers. The female detective's art can thus be presented as morally unimpeachable. For example, Goodwin in 1912 arrested the 'seeress' Madame Vesta la Viesta, who had promised that Goodwin's romantic wishes for future marriage would come true and invited her to bestow 'soul-kisses' on men who attracted her. The *Day Book*'s article about this arrest lingers on the louche cynicism of Vesta and the inappropriateness of a woman of fifty channelling 'soul kisses'.[63] Vesta finishes her consultation by saying 'the charge is five dollars, please'. 'The charge is disorderly conduct,' Mrs Goodwin responds, 'showing her star.' The newspaper's knowing pun hints at respectable women reproving women who sell sex – even imaginary sex.

Goodwin, like Ann Lovsey in Birmingham, England, specialised in prosecuting fake fortune-tellers; she also pursued crooked clairvoyants, hazardous hypnotists and quack doctors. This was a common job for female detectives working with the police in this period. Exposing a suspect surgeon or purveyor of risky pills is obviously a work of public importance. Yet fortune-tellers, while they may have defrauded clients in a literal sense, also opened up a figurative space in which marginalised women could disclose their dreams and be granted hope of their fulfilment. Perhaps that nebulous pleasure was worth the money. The press, however, keen to sell a story that resembled the threats and get-aways of detective drama, praised Goodwin's 'nerve' when escaping from 'gypsies', who reportedly attacked her with long knives when she sought to arrest fortune-teller Mary Merindo in East New York: 'Isabella Goodwin, New York's only woman detective, engaged in a desperate battle today with a crowd of infuriated gypsies while trying to arrest. She was saved from serious injury only by the arrival of reserves ... Mrs Goodwin, however, clung to her prisoner until [their] arrival.'[64]

Goodwin was in 1911 also reported to have convicted fortune-teller Patience Stanley, 'queen of the gypsies'. Clearly in New York in the early twentieth century, fortune-telling had an ethnic and cultural dimension, and its suppression was understandably resented by communities who felt betrayed by these detentions. Goodwin's arrests contrast markedly with Old Sleuth's imagined *Gipsy Rose, the Female Detective*, *Gipsy Blair: The Western Detective* or Fergus Hume's *Hagar of the Pawnshop*, all of whom bring the mystique of the gypsy, as imagined by those outside the Roma community, to detective romance.[65]

When Goodwin was interviewed about her work, she emphasised its complex social context. She wanted to get female police matrons from station houses out on patrol in parks, playgrounds and cinemas, where they could deal with sex workers and help them out of the profession, perhaps into a trade school: 'how can you expect a girl to be good on an empty stomach'.[66] She also mentioned strikes and the fact that women police would struggle to patrol them because these girls may bite, kick or stab officers with hatpins because they are 'are fighting in a righteous cause'. Her phrasing suggests that Goodwin doesn't see women choosing to go on strike as merely a law-and-order issue – a battle for social justice is involved. Goodwin is involved in detection as a community police officer: someone who knows the social problems and deprivations of New York's poorer neighbourhoods. Her ambitions for the police include the expansion of the female workforce. She is enthusiastic about the skills that women can bring to policing:

All of them are women of force of character and some of them, like Mrs Adele Preiss, who was a teacher of languages before her marriage banished her from the schools, are women of great intelligence. They need it, as well as all the tact and sympathy they can muster, for they deal with a difficult class, the women of the streets.[67]

One hears in 'marriage banished her' Goodwin's critique of the way in which talented women were routinely denied jobs once they were married. In police work, the social and sexual experience conferred by marriage and age could be an advantage. Women who had been 'banished' from one profession also knew the economic problem of being a woman who needed work: a knowledge that made them sympathetic to exploited fellow females. When Goodwin married again, in 1922, to Oscar Seaholm, a Swedish-American singer twenty-six years her junior, she told the newspapers that she would neither resign her job nor change her name: 'Why should anyone care whether I have married or not?'[68] The headline nonetheless read: 'Mrs Goodwin, Only Womansleuth, Weds'.

When reporters celebrated Goodwin's detective exploits, they never focused on the social, communitarian and women-specific aspect of her work. Instead, they noted breathlessly that she might be deployed on the Herman Rosenthal murder case, using a telegraphone – new technology for reproducing human voices.[69] The sensational literary image of the detective as a lone wolf, an exceptional character who cracks 'high-value' cases that have foiled others, nailing villains, is so pervasive that it falsifies the gradual and persistent way in which women took on detective work through the last decades of the nineteenth century and the centrality of poverty, homelessness, sex work and sexual exploitation to the problems they were addressing. As Dorothy Moses Schulz notes, the homeless typically spent their nights in vacant police cells and station corridors: 'In 1887, New York City … detained 14,000 women prisoners and received 42,0000 female lodgers for overnight shelter; two children were born in precincts.'[70] The Chicago Police Department in 1893 granted Mary Owens, widow of a Chicago policeman, the title of policeman with powers of arrest. Her duties included 'visiting courts and assisting detectives on cases concerning women and children'. This 'social work' was typical of the way in which female matrons were deployed as detectives by American police in this period: the only unusual factor in Owens's case was that she received pay and rank equivalent to her male colleagues.[71]

Emma Taylor is another good example of a female detective who worked as a police matron in America before being formally recognised in the role of detective within the police. Born Emma Hayman in 1846 into a large working-class family on a farm in Upottery, Devon, Emma had a difficult start in life. Her mother died when she was nine and she took on the care of her younger siblings: at fourteen, she is listed in the census as 'Housekeeper'. She then became a governess. In her early twenties, she decided to emigrate to America and married a ship's carpenter, Thomas Taylor in 1873. They settled in Seattle, where she had two children, Walter and Alice. After her husband's death, Emma became a police matron, from 1893,[72] in the Seattle Police Department. In March 1897, the *Caldwell Tribune* announced, under the headline 'The Female Detective', that Emma, having assisted in the apprehension of two shoplifters and having authority to make an arrest, would henceforth be doing detective work.[73]

The *Tribune* commented that Taylor 'plays the part of Old Sleuth', alluding to the author and fictional detective of the popular dime novels. This is further evidence that real women detectives were being seen through the lens of their literary counterparts. It also supports the idea that women who were working in police departments in America were often doing work – just as Elizabeth Joyes, Ann Lovsey and other women in Britain were doing – that was recognised by the public as detection but was not formally salaried as detective work. In 1898, we find Emma Taylor working with male detectives on an assault case where a fifteen-year-old girl, Emma Back, had been taken to a lodging house and sold for sex.[74] The formal admission of women as police detectives in the early twentieth century built on a generation of experience gained by women, often wives or widows of police officers, who worked in environments where they dealt with the same communities of poverty and deprivation, addiction, abuse and crime as their male counterparts, usually with special attention to the female portion of that community. They encountered more squalor than glamour.

From 'Character' to Actor: Seeing Women Detectives

Allan Pinkerton's hagiographic, inventive and self-serving account of 'Kate Warne', and other women on his staff who also served in Civil War roles, insisted on the female detective's 'womanly' qualities: she was pure, charming, self-effacing and compassionate, nursing and 'saving' men as required, while also possessing 'masculine' virtues. She must be physically hardy, brave, and taciturn, able to lead and to exhibit firmness and strong will. The female detective, in these accounts, had not only to do the work of detecting culprits. As a patriotic icon, she was performing the task of navigating an accept-able path for women to cross into what had formerly been regarded as exclusively 'masculine' territory. She was also sanitising a business whose moral depths were murky. In the other nineteenth-century civil war – the war between the sexes – she was a scout, a spy, a sentinel.

The civil war fantasy of women crossing state boundaries to fight, dressed as men, for their loved ones and their ideal of America was empowering. The dime novel exploits of working-class female detec-tives who can pass as men (swearing, shadowing and flooring villains with a swift punch to the jaw) and equally as 'ladies' – dancing grace-fully, speaking French and playing piano – were liberating for many thousands of male and female readers who wanted to believe in the possibility of a career where social class, gender roles and sexual attraction might be more fluid and malleable than they appeared to those hidebound by convention. The female detective in these tales became a symbol of hidden identity, and of outsider integrity that was eventually welcomed into the heart of the establishment she had helped to save from desperate danger. For a readership where many were immigrants and/or socially excluded from power and position they wished to possess, it was a fable of simultaneous outlawry and cherished belonging. No wonder it caught fire.

These fantasies may at first seem to have little to do with the real work of women in police departments and private enquiry agencies across America in the nineteenth century. Yet fictional poster women for border-hopping, such as Pauline of the Potomac and Lady Kate, the dashing female detective, shaped the desire lines that determined how the careers of early female detectives would be read.

To see the female detective at all in this era, we have had to see her as exceptional: a heroine, a 'character' – akin to Sherlock Holmes or Kate Goelet – risking life and limb in undercover operations to achieve a result in a high-stakes case. She has had to be 'Kate Warne', the world's 'greatest female detective', saving President Lincoln from assassination in a daring night-time mission, or catching bank robbers by disguising herself as 'Madame Imbert', the widow of a famous fraudster. She has had to be 'Hattie Lawson', captured behind enemy lines, refusing to abandon her fellow sleuth, as whose wife she was posing, even unto death. She has had to be Isabella Goodwin, 'the real goods', the 'Lady Cop', capturing taxi-cab bandits from the New York underworld by cunning and persistence. She has had, in short, to be a story that conforms to the literary expectations created by the 'female detective' popularised in nineteenth-century popular fiction and theatre. This wasn't a problem exclusively faced by women. Male detectives also felt the pressure of their fictional counterparts and Victorian police departments groaned under the weight of false expectation created by the detective story, with its ingenious leads, sensational rescues and inevitable apprehension of malefactors. However, in the case of the Victorian female detective it has meant that, for over a hundred years, her very existence as a real phenomenon was doubted and disputed. When her existence was known, as in the case of 'Kate Warne', it was buried under such a load of imaginative freight that the facts of her existence and her work became almost impossible to discover.

In 1865, the *Chicago Republican* was already reporting that 'equal numbers of male and female operatives' worked for Pinkerton's detective agency. As Isabella Goodwin emphasised when she mentioned the seventy female colleagues connected with the New York Police Department in 1912, women detectives did not emerge or operate in isolation. Their work was cumulative and collaborative. It was performed in a context of social and moral complexity and ambiguity. Were the 'gypsy' clairvoyants whom Isabella Goodwin helped to arrest in New York really persecuted victims of a misguided moral panic? Was Abraham Lincoln really in danger from assassination in 1861 or was his midnight ride from Philadelphia an ingenious power-play by Allan Pinkerton to assert his authority to shape the future president's path?

Seeing the Victorian female detective more clearly involves knowing that the photograph we possess has been staged, touched up with paint and may not even show the person it affects to portray. It necessitates looking beyond the crimes the detective 'solves' to interrogate the social desires her persona embodies for her contemporaries and for us and the darker tale of violence, corruption and inequity her figure can neither resolve nor conceal.

CONCLUSION

The history of all times, and of today especially, teaches that ...
women will be forgotten if they forget to think about themselves.[1]
Louise Otto-Peters, *Dem Reich der Freiheit werb' ich Bürgerinnen:
Die Frauen-Zeitung von Louise Otto* (1980)

I began work on this book with a quest: to understand a couple of
mysterious hits. *The Female Detective* and *Revelations of a Lady Detective*, two fictional memoirs of working women detectives published in 1864, had seemed at first like oddities in the popular literature of their day. Once I began looking, however, evidence was
everywhere that real female detectives existed in Victorian Britain
and that the press followed their work with bated breath.

The police were deploying women to perform detective work
from the 1840s, both inside and outside police stations: women who
searched and questioned suspects; identified petty thieves and major
fraudsters; illegal abortionists, bogus mystics and food adulterers –
sometimes participating in risky and controversial sting operations
to catch crooks in the act. They gave evidence in court and helped to

311

secure prosecutions. They witnessed violence and were sometimes victims of violent assault by desperate suspects. Often they were the wives and widows of policemen, their work poorly paid or unpaid. Their presence had been ignored or downplayed as casual or occasional. Yet they were part of the fabric of Victorian policing.

Meanwhile, private enquiry agencies employing women as detectives flourished throughout Britain. Female detectives were crucial assets to these operations, which played a major role in Victorian life in the second half of the century. Often the cases that private enquiry agencies dealt with were compromising; they involved adultery, marital cruelty, blackmail, family feuds and the emotional fallout of the 1857 Divorce Act, whose explosive effect was to blow the walls off the doll's house of Victorian marriage, revealing the violence and misery within. Largely unregulated, the private detective agency was not always on the side of the angels, or even of the client. Yet it offered hope to individuals – many of them women – who had been left in the dark, perhaps seeking a long-absent spouse or child. To the wider public, it offered a licence to imagine women infiltrating any aspect of private or professional life, investigating zones that had been kept from them and discovering truths that were sometimes explicitly, but always implicitly, political. Some enterprising women, such as Kate Easton and Antonia Moser, created and managed agencies themselves: regular newspaper advertisements and 'memoirs' of their exploits created public personae that introduced the idea of the 'lady detective' to a wide audience.

From mid-century, the *idea* of the female detective was a potent lure for readers of the emergent 'detective school' of sensation fiction and for spectators in the Victorian theatre. Women contributed as equals to the early history of detective fiction; but the female detective in these stories is often different from the male, as she is more deeply embedded in the events she investigates and at risk from the malefactors she will bring to justice. In the Victorian theatre, the female detective was a quick-change role that allowed huge audiences to enjoy the spectacle of a woman passing as a man, firing guns, cuffing men in 'bracelets' and eventually taking down villains who represented the entwined domestic and public abuses of male power.

All of these figures had remained, for many years, relatively obscure or altogether invisible to historians and literary scholars. But their existence mattered. Their proliferation in Victorian periodicals, as real-life and fictional accounts of female detection met, connected the literary and the literal worlds of crime, suggesting the possible proximity of detective women in any sphere. The person who took your coat at a party or your order in a restaurant, the housemaid, the shopkeeper, the nurse, the fascinating lady you met on holiday or the person seemingly asleep in your railway compartment: all of these might be sleuths. As the *Echo* observed in 1888: 'detectives saunter about the Reading-rooms of the British Museum. And the other day they caught a reader – a reverend reader too – in the act of appropriating not exactly a whole book, but a portion of one.'[2]

The thought that in a library one might be simultaneously surrounded by books containing detectives and by detectives surveilling potential purloiners of those books emphasised the extent to which all of Victorian society had become a reading room. Active looking and careful reflection to detect plot, alibi, motive was, after all, no different in principle from the skills the female reader might be expected to develop as she turned the page, imaginatively inhabiting the role of Eleanor Vane, Ann Lovsey, Mrs Percival Flight, Kate Easton or Dora Bell.

The literary female detective and the real one developed in tandem, sometimes shading into one another. Fanny Hodson, a self-elected detective journalist and campaigner, became a literal detective in the case of 'baby farmers', working closely with the police in a risky, embedded role, gathering evidence to expose women who neglected and killed unwanted children for money. Actresses such as Kate Easton and Dorothy Tempest, who played roles on stage, reinvented themselves as female detectives who could mimic a housemaid, garrulous neighbour or lady's companion to penetrate real-world secrets.

Too much emphasis on the 'professional' versus the 'amateur' detective has obscured the extent to which, for both Victorian men and women outside the very small number of police who were formally given the job title, 'detective' was a self-defined role (whether for 'Kate Warne' or 'Henry Slater'), involving an invented professional persona and activities that bridged the territories of private and public life. I am aware that this book may set the categorisers among the pigeons. There will always be people who refuse to allow that anyone can legitimately be called a detective unless the title is conferred on them by the police.

The Victorians themselves had fewer qualms. They used the term 'female detective' with considerable freedom to refer to detective searchers and women detectives working for the police outside the precinct (often in practice the same women), to women working for private detective agencies (mostly run by ex-policemen and some staffed by former female detective searchers), to detective journalists whose investigations involved an embedded undercover role (often indistinguishable from the kind of investigation launched by a private agency) and to women who directly pursued criminals on a personal basis.

It is precisely this fluidity that interests me. The new Victorian 'role' of detective was both a symptom and a cause of a rupture in the boundaries that separated the private from the public sphere. Where criminality and those who upheld social order might once have been located by readers and spectators in defined areas and cohorts, it was now evident that these were permeable. The ubiquity of the female detective suggested that the legible signs defining gender, marital status, social class, 'respectability' and other markers of belonging and of hierarchy might easily be assumed. Paulina the 'Countess Detective' in *Illustrated Chips* conveys the frisson of such uncertainty:

'What am I but an actress, always changing my part and my make-up? only the dramas I play in on the stage of life are real. What can you do to repay me, my dear? Only this; when your wedding day comes, send me a piece of cake as a souvenir.'

'Oh, but you must come to our wedding!' said Marian impulsively.

'My dear,' said Countess Paulina, with a smile, 'when that day comes I may be thousands of miles away, or I might be there unrecognised by anyone, for I am often present at society weddings, to keep an eye on pickpockets of both sexes.'

'Do such dreadful creatures ever gain admittance amongst the higher classes?' Marian asked with a thrill of disgust. And Countess Paulina replied quietly:

'Such dreadful creatures sometimes *belong* to the upper classes.'[3]

Permeable boundaries to which the female detective drew attention included moral ambiguity surrounding crime itself. Female detectives enabled Victorians to peer through the gimlet-hole at the sexual double standard regarding male and female infidelity in marriage, the unequal treatment of the 'fallen woman' and her seducer, the 'kleptomaniac' and the 'common thief'.

Stories of strong, fast, action heroines, who could battle the injustices and abuses faced by women and oppressed members of society, had huge appeal for the mass market that emerged in the Victorian period. The idea that there were or could be female detectives allowed authors and the public to voice anger about prejudicial laws that prevented women from keeping their earnings and controlling their inheritances; that allowed men – and sometimes women – to get away with cruelty, desertion and even murder; that allowed the rich and powerful to abuse employees, tenants and the truth. The imagined female detective could behave, and even pass, as a man. She modelled the possibility of smart women working and running their own business. In a period where female ignorance and innocence were often conflated, the female detective asserted the moral and social value of women's right to know. Her existence remains a provocation, inviting us to discover the detective within ourselves: curious to unravel the clues amid the concealments of our environment, to interrogate the bad coin we are handed and, like Jemima Davis pursuing the coiner, demand real change.

However, there are important differences between the fictional and the real detective in the Victorian era. The majority of early female detectives were working class. Many of them were mothers. Most of them did not control their own workload and hours. They worked with others, rather than alone. And the kind of cases they chiefly covered were not murders and bank robberies. They were not always defenders of the oppressed. Nor were their own lives always models of moral propriety. They were extraordinary, but not inevitably heroic.

What we want to be true creates action: the literary and theatrical appeal of detection is an important factor in the development of the profession. But to attend fully to women's history, we need to separate the desire for female ancestors of a particular kind to stand for and stand up for us in the past from our desire to know the truth. There is no ignoring the dramatic attractions of the story of female detection; this book is as much in thrall to it as any. But to me the messy truth is more interesting than a varnished tale. These, our foremothers, led lives as complicated, conflicted and contradictory as our own. They were working things out as they went along, without the certainty of resolution or closure. That is the true business of detection. Much remains to be discovered and some things will never be known. The mysterious case of the Victorian female detective is a suitcase – perhaps stolen, a decoy or a clue in the waiting room of history – that we are only just beginning to unpack.

NOTES

Prologue: The Vanishing Lady

1. Several professional female detectives appear at this moment in British fiction. Another 'first' is Ruth Trail in Edward Ellis, *Ruth The Betrayer or The Female Spy* (London: Dick, 1863). Ruth is the protagonist of a pseudonymous, no-holds-barred serial in which she is said to work both for the police, as 'a female detective – a sort of spy we use in the hanky-panky way when a man would be too clumsy' – and for 'a notorious Secret Intelligence Office, established by an ex-member of the police force', run by Eneas Earthworm. However, there is little consistency to her narrative, in which she is a ruthless villain as well as a spy ('her life up to now would fill a dozen volumes brim full of villany [sic], and treachery, and crime, and horror!') and so it is fair to say that she is as a much a mystery as she is a detective.

Introduction

1. 'Capture of an Alleged Coiner by a Woman', *Reynolds's Newspaper* 15 December 1883, 5; 'The Charge of Uttering Counterfeit Coin', *Barnet Press* 15 December 1883, 6; 'Capture of an Alleged Coiner by a Woman', *Illustrated Police News* 22 December 1883, 1–2.
2. See *Oxford English Dictionary*. This meaning of 'detect' dates from c.1449 and shades into our modern understanding of detection.
3. George Augustus Sala, 'Private Detectives', *Sala's Journal* 20 August 1892, 386.
4. Lisa Surridge, *Bleak Houses: Marital Violence in Victorian Fiction* (Athens, OH: Ohio University Press, 2005), 137.
5. *Bilberry of Tilbury: A Musical Farce in Three Acts by Silvanus Dauncey and George D. Day with Lyrics by George D. Day and Music by Guy Jones* (1898), British Library Add MS 53657 K, 8–9.

1 Searchers and Watchers: Female Detectives Working with the Police 1850–1900

1. 'A Strong-Minded Woman', *Reynolds's Newspaper* 22 January 1860, 7.
2. Haia Shpayer-Makov, *The Ascent of the Detective: Police Sleuths in Victorian and Edwardian England* (Oxford: Oxford University Press, 2011), 81.
3. John W. Reilly, *Policing Birmingham: An Account of 150 Years of Police in Birmingham* (Birmingham: West Midlands Police, 1994), 39 notes that Birmingham had one of the most overworked Victorian police forces: 'On a population ratio for 1883, Birmingham was 1:826, Liverpool 1:482 and Manchester 1:432.'
4. Melville L. Macnaghten [C.B, Chief of the CID], *Days of My Years* (London: Arnold, 1914), 65 comments that in the early days, the policeman's 'educational attainments were sadly to seek . . . His reports were laboured, and his spelling indifferent.'
5. Haia Shpayer-Makov notes that, in 1877, 'the police in Birmingham accorded 16 of their 520 officers the title of detective, in Liverpool 28 of 1200, and in Leeds 11 of 355.' *Ascent of the Detective*, 44.
6. *The Times* (after the *Pall Mall Gazette*) 5 October 1870, 5.
7. *Bell's Weekly Messenger* 7 November 1868, 4.
8. 'Defective and Detective Police', *Reynolds's Newspaper* 19 July 1863, 3.
9. Clive Emsley, *The English Police: A Political and Social History* (Hemel Hempstead: Harvester Wheatsheaf, 1991), 120: 'Several late Victorian police forces had employed "Police Matrons", often wives of station sergeants, to take charge of women prisoners, but in many quarters there remained considerable hostility to the idea of recruiting women police . . . Some of the Voluntary Women Patrols were incorporated into police forces as women police in 1918, and in May of that year Lady Nott-Bower addressed the Annual General Meeting of the Chief Constables' Association on the subject of "Women Police"; but many watch committees and standing joint committees remained implacably opposed to the idea.' *Gender and Policing: Comparative Perspectives* ed. Jennifer Brown and Frances Heidensohn (Basingstoke: Macmillan, 2000), 45 briefly details women's early-twentieth-century admission to the police.
10. Louise A. Jackson, *Women Police: Gender, Welfare and Surveillance in the Twentieth Century* (Manchester: Manchester University Press, 2006), 17 offers a useful page about the 1870s and 1880s background to women's employment in the police. She points out (18) that Edith Smith was sworn in as a member of Grantham Police Force in 1915 – 'the first attested policewoman in the UK' – and that 'a further 148 Women Police Service members were employed . . . between 1915 and 1920'. Chloe Owings, *Women Police: A Study of the Development and Status of the Women Police Movement* (Montclair, NJ: Patterson Smith, 1969), 2 notes that: 'In England as early as the Eighteenth Century, during the hearing on a case in court – *R v Briggs* – there was a discussion of the legality of women to serve in a certain compulsory legal office. One of the judges remarked: "I do not know why a woman should not be appointed as a constable." However a century passed before women were employed in police departments.'
11. There was some official anxiety concerning how women should perform the task thoroughly, yet without offending against decency.

12. 'York City Police', *Yorkshire Herald* 7 May 1892, 2.
13. *Croydon Weekly Standard* 7 March 1896, 7 reproduced an interview with an experienced female searcher at a London police station conducted by a reporter for *Woman's Life*. It contains many helpful details: searchers often had to sit up through the night with female suspects. In this case, payment was fourpence per search and sixpence after 10 p.m.: women were not paid by regular monthly salary for their availability or experience as searchers but only on a case-by-case basis.
14. *Soulby's Ulverston Advertiser* 15 August 1850, 4 described Sarah Elliott, a servant guilty of stealing from her employer. The *Morning Advertiser* 27 December 1859, 7 reported that Joseph Edwards had swallowed no fewer than seven gold coins, hoping to dispose of the evidence, when arrested on suspicion of theft. He moved with such discomfort he was 'like a man upon wires'. *Weekly Dispatch* 28 September 1845, 7 gives an example of attempted bribery.
15. *Daily Telegraph* 3 July 1890, 7.
16. *Stroud Journal* 5 April 1879, 5.
17. 'A Virago', *Willesden Chronicle* 30 July 1886, 6.
18. 'Police Courts', *Morning Advertiser* 9 March 1854, 6.
19. *Belfast Morning News* 27 January 1864, 4.
20. Haia Shpayer-Makov, *The Making of a Policeman: A Social History of a Labour Force in London, 1829–1914* (Aldershot: Ashgate, 2002), 218.
21. Proceedings of the Old Bailey 17 December 1855 ref: t18551217-115. Italics mine: '*Q.* You were employed as a female detective? *A.* Yes.'
22. *Morning Post* 14 December 1855, 7. This newspaper has 'Catton Curtis', but Old Bailey Trials online confirms the defendant's name as Cotton Curtis.
23. Shpayer-Makov, *Ascent of the Detective*, 74.
24. By 1861 Walter had retired from the police force and he and Elizabeth had moved to Bishop's Stortford, a market town in Hertfordshire, where Walter had grown up as the son of a local butcher. The couple, now fifty-two and forty-eight, were parents to Susan Orphah, a little girl of three. Elizabeth would end her days in an almshouse in a relatively rural community similar to the Cambridgeshire village she hailed from, far from the noise, misery and excitement of London.
25. *Bell's Weekly Messenger* 5 July 1862, 7.
26. Macnaghten, *Days of My Years*, 140.
27. Shpayer-Makov, *The Making of a Policeman*, 181, describing matters at the turn of the century, says that policemen's spouses, 'unlike soldiers' wives and the wives of metropolitan force policemen in the early years, were not allowed to have employment'.
28. This view of women had a long history in British policing. See Malcolm Young, *An Inside Job: Policing and Police Culture in Britain* (Oxford: Clarendon, 1991), 193, where Young, a former policeman, explains police culture: 'Women who do breach the boundary to penetrate this masculine world can only ever be partially successful and will often have to subsume "male characteristics" to achieve even a limited social acceptability. Ideally they are best returned to a place outside the system, married to policemen and reconstituted into the domestic sphere. Then, with knowledge and experience of the job's specific

peculiarities, they are able to provide an extremely important but relatively unacknowledged role as "police wife".'

29. In 1860, the average price of sugar was 26 shillings 93/4 pence per cwt. *Sun* 4 May 1860, 7. Details of UK sugar consumption are in Sidney Mintz, *Sweetness and Power: The Place of Sugar in Modern History* (London: Penguin, 1986).

30. John Hollingshead, *Ragged London in 1861* (London: Smith Elder, 1861), 55–7.

31. Ibid., 60–1.

32. 'A Female Detective', *Reynolds's Newspaper* 22 January 1860, 10.

33. 'A Strong-Minded Woman', *Reynolds's Newspaper* 22 January 1860, 7.

34. James Redding Ware (Andrew Forrester), *The Female Detective* repr. (London: British Library, 2012), 143.

35. See 'The Police and the Spy System', *Essex Herald* 12 April 1864, which alludes to the secretary of state calling attention to Major Cartwright's report on secret correspondence between the police and private enquiry offices, whereby the police were leaking confidential information.

36. 'Another Apprehension by Mrs Scott the "Female Detective"', *Newcastle Daily Journal* 27 April 1865, 3. In a similar case in Sheffield in 1873, Elizabeth Rodgers, wife of Inspector James Rodgers, used her initiative to apprehend a female pickpocket (Martha Bell) at the railway station.

37. *Berrow's Worcester Journal* 17 July 1869, 9. In another female sting operation, Eliza Bissell in 1877 was deployed by William Osborne (city detective) to smoke out Robert Clough (18), George Blacker (24) and Edward Slow (26), porters for the textile company Bradbury Greatorex. These men were guilty of stealing 88 yards of silk and velvet from their employer. Eliza was furnished with money and instructed to pose as a customer for the illegally obtained fabric. She successfully caught the men in the act of purveying stolen goods.

38. 'Assault on a Female Detective', *Edinburgh Evening Dispatch* 12 May 1887, 2. The female detective in this case may have been Elizabeth Gordon, wife of William Gordon, Sub-inspector Detective Officer of Police in the Glasgow force.

39. *Kilburn Times* 17 December 1880, 3.

40. R. M. Morris, '"Crime Does Not Pay": Thinking Again About Detectives in the First Century of the Metropolitan Police' in Clive Emsley and Haia Shpayer-Makov eds, *Police Detectives in History, 1750–1950* (Aldershot: Ashgate, 2006), 92.

41. *Bradford Weekly Telegraph* 18 July 1885, 4.

42. The 1881 census shows that Nancy Withers and James Withers (both 43) of 57 St Paul's Road, Bradford, had 6 children: Alfred (19), Frank (14), Ada (12), Louis (9), Cosine (7) and Percy (5).

43. National Archives A47548/35, Sir Herbert Croft letter of 16 November 1892.

44. Ibid.

45. Lovsey was still reporting her occupation as 'searcher' at Moor Street station in the 1901 census. As she was already a searcher there in 1865, this means that she was employed by the Birmingham police for at least 36 years.

46. 'Fortune Telling in Birmingham', *Birmingham Journal* 28 October 1865, 5.

47. See *Chester Chronicle* 29 February 1868, 2.

48. Both Ann Archer and Sarah Rebecca Smith received a prison sentence of one month: a standard deterrent for minor offences, but one that must have caused considerable hardship.
49. 'How to Dispose of a Husband', *Staffordshire Daily Sentinel* 17 September 1877, 3. There were two female detectives in this case, one of whom was likely Lovsey.
50. In London in 1871, Lavinia Jupe, wife of Detective Jupe of L Division, in company with a younger woman, raided the house of Emily Rowell or Royal (45), a fortune-teller in Kennington. They were sent by Sergeant Mullard, who deposed that Mrs Royal had practised her trade for sixteen years, mostly on servants: on Sunday afternoons and evenings up to thirty young women would attend Mrs Rowell's home to 'cut the cards'. The *Penny Illustrated Paper*, which ran the article on the Rowell case, titled it 'Female Detectives'.
51. In March 1894 Grace Fox, a female detective hired by the Society for the Enforcement of the Criminal Laws, gave evidence against sixteen abortionists in New York whom she had tracked down by claiming to require their services. *Indianapolis Journal* 24 March 1894, 1.
52. *Leicestershire Mercury* 12 August 1848, 1. In 1871, the Birmingham police used Harriet Courts, the wife of policeman Abraham Courts, to detect a fortune-teller. The *Birmingham Daily Mail* 12 April 1871, 3 reported under the headline 'A Female Detective' that: 'Some consternation was caused when . . . the witness admitted that the police had set her to lay a trap for the fortune teller and . . . it was not the first time she had acted in the capacity of a female detective.'
53. 'A Fortune-Teller Caught', *Birmingham Daily Mail* 6 June 1894, 3.
54. 'Confession of Murder in Birmingham', *Birmingham Daily Post* 9 July 1873, 5.
55. *Nottinghamshire Guardian* 1 February 1896, 6.
56. Frederick William Park (Fanny) and Thomas Ernest Boulton (Stella) were tried in 1870 after leaving a theatre in drag, and charged with 'conspiracy to commit sodomy'; they were acquitted, but the trial became a key moment in gay history. For their brave and colourful history, see Neil McKenna, *Fanny and Stella: The Young Men Who Shocked Victorian England* (London: Faber, 2013).
57. 'Extraordinary Charge of Embezzlement', *Staffordshire Sentinel* 18 August 1877, 10.
58. 'A Female Detective', *Irishman* 4 March 1876, 567.
59. William Wilmott Dixon, 'Studies from Life', *Chambers Journal* 4 October 1879, 637.
60. *Pictorial World* 23 June 1877, 267.
61. The story that the 'first female detective' in the London police succeeded in capturing a gang of coiners is also told in Inspector Cavanagh's *Scotland Yard Past and Present* (1893), though in his account it is a policeman's wife who is the detective and finds the coiners through information gained from a friend whose lodging house they are occupying.
62. Shpayer-Makov, *Ascent of the Detective*, 157.
63. Fanny Hodson (née Stoddart) was born in Northamptonshire in 1829 to Fanny Woodhouse (who had herself been born in Madras) and William Stoddart, a minister. She married her cousin, Doveton Hodson (an army chaplain), in 1848 at the Cape of Good Hope. Her son was born in Tamil Nadu and her daughter in Naples. I traced Hodson's life history before realising that Ruth Homrighaus had also done so; this information has not to my knowledge

been published. Homrighaus's valuable account of the baby-farming scandal can be found in 'Baby Farming: The Care of Illegitimate Children in England, 1860–1943', unpublished doctoral thesis (2003), University of North Carolina.

64. National Archives MEPO 3/93, Fanny Hodson letter of 1 September 1870 to members of the Metropolitan Police. In notes attached to the letters Captain Baynes and others note that Hodson has 'visited many Houses where Women are taken to be confined and the Children put away for adoption or nursed & c, and to get at the secrets went to Mrs Castle's 164 Camberwell Road under the plea that she was 6 months' "enceinte". Mrs Hodson was present at the trial of Waters at the Old Bailey.'

65. A.B. (Fanny Hodson), 'Baby Farming', *The Times* 14 July 1870, 4.

66. Ibid., 9.

67. 'Assault and Robbery on the Street – Courageous Conduct of a Female Detective', *Dundee Courier and Argus* 14 February 1866, 2.

68. Ibid.

69. 'Illegal Drinkselling and its Detection', *Northern Warder and Bi-Weekly Courier* 16 May 1876, 2.

70. *Birmingham Daily Mail* 17 January 1890,

71. Frances Power Cobbe, 'Detectives – To the Editor of the Times', *The Times* 11 October 1888, 5.

72. *Manchester Weekly Times* 13 October 1888, 4.

73. *Yorkshire Post* 12 October 1888, 4.

74. *Irish Times* 12 October 1888, 5.

75. *The Northern Whig* 22 October 1888, 6.

76. *Newcastle Daily Chronicle* 12 October 1888, 4.

77. *North British Daily Mail* 31 October 1888, 3.

78. *Leeds Times* 11 October 1890, 3.

79. Hallie Rubenhold, *The Five: The Untold Lives of the Women Killed by Jack the Ripper* (London: Penguin, 2019), 15.

80. Figures taken from the Office of National Statistics Census 2021, 'The Nature of Violent Crime in England and Wales: Year Ending March 2020'.

81. See Lucia Zedner, *Women, Crime, and Custody in Victorian England* (Oxford: Clarendon, 1991), 313.

82. *Birmingham Daily Post* 29 May 1888, 8.

83. *Manchester Times* 13 October 1888, 4.

84. This joke appeared in the *Dundee Courier* 6 October 1864, 3, and was widely reprinted e.g. in the magazine *Fun* 8 October 1864, 38, the *Kendal Mercury* 7 December 1867, 4 and the *Preston Chronicle* 6 March 1869, 3.

85. 'Female Detectives – What They Are Fitted for and What They Are Not', *Daily Enterprise* 25 July 1884, 4.

2 Home Truths: Divorce, Domestic Violence and the Fictional Female Detective

1. 'The Nature and Amount of Crime', *Lloyd's Weekly Newspaper* 17 March 1850, 5.

2. Inspector Bucket is married, and Dickens implies that his wife may aid him in his detective role. But the abiding image of the Victorian detective remained for many years that of the solitary male.

3. Among those scholars who have contributed to uncovering this alternative route are Patricia Craig, *The Lady Investigates: Women Detectives and Spies in Fiction* (New York: St Martin's Press, 1981); Anne Humphreys, 'Who's Doing It? Fifteen Years of Work on Victorian Detective Fiction', *Dickens Studies Annual* (1996), 259–74; Joseph Kestner, *Sherlock's Sisters: The British Female Detective, 1864–1913* (Aldershot: Ashgate, 2003); Carla T. Kungl, *Creating the Fictional Female Detective: The Sleuth Heroines of British Women Writers 1890–1940* (Jefferson, NC: McFarland, 2006); Maureen Reddy, 'Women Detectives' in Martin Priestman ed. *The Cambridge Companion to Crime Fiction* (Cambridge: Cambridge University Press, 2003) and Lucy Sussex, *Women Writers and Detectives in Nineteenth-Century Crime Fiction: The Mothers of the Mystery Genre* (Basingstoke: Palgrave Macmillan, 2010).
4. The remark is attributed to Thackeray in Sir William Fraser's diaries. See the *Graphic* 3 June 1893, 638.
5. 'Female Novelists – No. VIII, Mrs Crowe', *New Monthly Magazine* December 1852, 441.
6. See A. James Hammerton, *Cruelty and Companionship in Nineteenth-Century Married Life* (London: Routledge, 1992), 105. Hammerton's survey of petitioners for divorce citing cruelty shows a split of 48 per cent middle- and upper-class, 25 per cent lower-middle-class and 26 per cent working-class claims. Evidently these numbers are skewed by the fact that divorce was still difficult for working-class couples to afford and informal separations were common, but the statistics show that domestic violence and cruelty were by no means confined to working-class homes: a revelation that shocked many Victorians, as did the numbers of women seeking to divorce their husbands, a result that male legislators had totally failed to anticipate.
7. *The Divorce Court* 2 April 1864, 1.
8. Ibid., 2.
9. 'Extraordinary Conduct of a Husband a Day After Marriage', *London Evening Standard* 15 December 1866, 5.
10. Geoffrey Larken, unpublished biography of Crowe, 82, quoted in Ruth Heholt, *Catherine Crowe: Gender, Genre and Radical Politics* (London: Routledge, 2021), 2.
11. Meanwhile, Mabel Lightfoot, a dairymaid who was trafficked to France, finds that the marriage she thought she had made was a sham got up to deceive her: she is the mistress of a nobleman, unable to get back to her family and friends.
12. Catherine Crowe, *Susan Hopley, or, The Adventures of a Maid servant* (Edinburgh: Tait, 1842), 30. It was also published as *The Adventures of Susan Hopley; or, Circumstantial Evidence* (London: Saunder and Otley, 1841): the subtitle is important, because the novel drew attention to the fallibility of circumstantial evidence.
13. Ibid., 173.
14. Sussex, *Women Writers and Detectives*, 46.
15. As Crowe and other authors lamented, there was little protection for authors from such theatrical piracy. T. W. Robertson in 'Theatrical Types No IV,' *Illustrated Times* 13 February 1864, 107 describes *Susan Hopley* as a standard part of the provincial theatrical repertoire alongside *Macbeth*.
16. http://www.rossettiarchive.org/img/f84.1.jpg.

17. Jennifer Carnell, *The Literary Lives of Mary Elizabeth Braddon* (Hastings: Sensation, 2000), 324.
18. Wilkie Collins, *The Diary of Anne Rodway, Household Words* 19 July 1856, 2.
19. *Cheltenham Chronicle* 24 July 1855, 2.
20. Chloe Ward, 'Art and the Plight of the Victorian Seamstress' 2021, https://www.wattsgallery.org.uk/blog/art-and-the-plight-of-the-victorian-seamstress.
21. Anne's diary begins with the entry 'work, work, work', evoking one of the stanzas of Hood's famous poem: 'Work—work—work, / Till the brain begins to swim; / Work—work—work, / Till the eyes are heavy and dim! / Seam, and gusset, and band, / Band, and gusset, and seam, / Till over the buttons I fall asleep, / And sew them on in a dream!'
22. Wilkie Collins, *The Woman in White* (Oxford: Oxford University Press, 1998), 32.
23. Surridge, *Bleak Houses*, 156.
24. Margaret Oliphant, 'Sensation Novels', *Blackwood's Edinburgh Magazine* 91 (1862), 566.
25. The idea that Collins used this case, which he would have read in Maurice Mejan, *Recueil des causes célèbres*, which he picked up from a Paris bookstall in 1856, was originally suggested by Clyde K. Hyder and has been followed by subsequent editors of *The Woman in White*.
26. Surridge, *Bleak Houses*, 139.
27. As Sara Hackenberg explores in '"The Magician of Civilised Life": The Literary Detective in Mary Elizabeth Braddon's Early Penny Fiction', *Victorian Popular Fictions* 4:2 (2022), 63–78, Braddon's early works *The Black Band, The Octoroon* and *The Trail of the Serpent* all experiment with detective figures and 'in these fictions she imagines her detective characters as agents of social equity ... who challenge the social hierarchies, stereotypes, and prejudices that form and undermine "civilised life"' (64). For further discussion of Braddon as a detective author, see Jeanne F. Bedell, 'Amateur and Professional Detectives in the Fiction of Mary Elizabeth Braddon', *Clues: A Journal of Detection* 4:1 (1983), 19–34 and Ann Cvetkovich, *Mixed Feelings: Feminism, Mass Culture, and Victorian Sensationalism* (New Brunswick, NJ: Rutgers University Press, 1992).
28. 'Eleanor's Victory', *Morning Post* 17 September 1863, 2.
29. *St James Chronicle* 4 December 1862, 7.
30. 'Detectives in Fiction and in Real Life', *Sheffield Daily Telegraph* 14 June 1864, 7. 'Pre-Raffaelite' is a common variant spelling of 'Pre-Raphaelite' in the period.
31. Heidi H. Johnson compares Eleanor to Electra and considers the 'detectival function' of Braddon's heroines in 'Electra-Fying the Female Sleuth: Detecting the Father in *Eleanor's Victory* and *Thou Art the Man*' in Marlene Tromp ed. *Beyond Sensation: Mary Elizabeth Braddon in Context* (Albany, NY: SUNY, 2000).
32. Mary Elizabeth Braddon, *Eleanor's Victory* (London: Tinsley, 1863), 216.
33. Ibid., 164.
34. Sussex, *Women Writers and Detectives*, 72.
35. I made the discovery of Redding Ware's dramatisation of Collins early in my research. Subsequently, I discovered Karen E. Laird's excellent account of the adaptation, which she does not link to the author of *The Female Detective*, but does identify as a bold reorientation of Collins's novel. See Karen E. Laird,

'"No Paste-and-Scissors Version": *The Woman in White*'s Stage Debut', *Nineteenth-Century Contexts* 36:2 (2014), 179–99.

36. James Redding Ware, *The Woman in White* (pirated adaptation of Collins's novel), performed Royal Surrey Theatre October–November 1860, British Library Add MS 52997, 17.

37. Ibid., 20.

38. 'Southwark', *Morning Advertiser* 1 December 1848, 4.

39. Redding Ware (Forrester), *The Female Detective*, 127. For the murders, rapidly solved by what Redding Ware calls 'the power and extension of the press', see 'A Woman and Two Children Poisoned in a Cab', *Western Gazette* 14 November 1863, 4.

40. Redding Ware (Forrester), *The Female Detective*, 4.

41. See, for example, Kathleen Gregory Klein, *The Woman Detective: Gender and Genre* (Urbana: University of Illinois Press, 1988), 29: 'it is probably coincidental that these novels were published in the same decade as John Stuart Mill's *The Subjugation of Women*, for Mrs. Paschal and Miss Gladden were no harbingers of change for literary or real women . . . These characters are anomalies; the novels apparently led to neither imitators nor followers'; and Michele Slung, *Crime on Her Mind: Fifteen Stories of Female Sleuths from the Victorian Era to the Forties* (New York: Pantheon, 1983), 25: 'After the appearance of W. S. Hayward's *Revelations of a Lady Detective* and Andrew Forrester's *The Female Detective* in the 1860s, it was over two decades later that the fictional female detective made a reappearance in 1888 with Leonard Merrick's *Mr Bazalgette's Agent.*' In fact, as the following chapter shows, the female detective had a long life on the stage in this seeming interval.

42. *Bath Chronicle* 11 August 1870, 5.

43. *Newcastle Guardian* 20 January 1866, 5.

44. J. Redding Ware, *Passing English of the Victorian Era: A Dictionary of Heterodox English, Slang, and Phrase* (London: Routledge, 1909), 89.

3 Sensation and the Stage: The Victorian Female Detective in the Limelight

1. John Douglass, *The Lucky Shilling: an original sensational drama in 5 acts*, British Library Add MS 53396 D, 13. NB: Throughout, punctuation in playscripts has been lightly edited for clarity.

2. *Dublin Evening Mail* 12 May 1863, 4.

3. Charles Dickens, *Household Words* vol. 2, 25 February 1860, 418.

4. The feats of 'The wondrous Leotard' at the Britannia were advertised in a poster now in the Victoria and Albert Museum, collection number E.4885-1923; for Professor Pepper's spectral illusion, see 'Every Night the Ghost! (12th Week)', *Shoreditch Observer* 20 June 1863, 4. The Lilliputian Velocipedists are recorded as an afterpiece to *Happiness at Home* in June 1871.

5. Mr H. Watson's appearance was announced in the *Clerkenwell and London Times* 17 July 1869, 1.

6. *Dublin Evening Mail* 12 May 1863, 4.

7. The scenery of the play had its own notes in the programme, crediting Hugh Muir and Thomas Rogers for their landscape painting. It was set in a ballroom in Baden Baden, on a lonely moonlit lake, and London on Old Chandos Street.

8. C. H. Hazlewood, *The Female Detective; or, The Mother's Dying Child* (New York: De Witt, 1864), 8. This print version is useful in detailing the original costumes and scenery. The manuscript of *The Mother's Dying Child* submitted to the Lord Chamberlain as an acting copy of the work pre-performance (British Library Add.MS 53034 N) has some script variations.

9. Isabel Stowell-Kaplan, *Staging Detection: From Hawkshaw to Holmes* (London: Routledge, 2022), 50.

10. Hazlewood, *The Female Detective*, 19.

11. Trouser roles were often a part of 'illegitimate theatre', including melodrama. As Jacky Bratton notes in 'Mirroring Men: The Actress in Drag' in Maggie B. Gale and John Stokes ed. *The Cambridge Companion to the Actress* (Cambridge: Cambridge University Press, 2007), 235–52: 'Marcia Macarthy (1808–70) made a solid career in the London minor theatres, where by 1838 she was joint manager of Sadler's Wells with her husband Robert Honner. A small, slight woman with a big voice, Mrs Honner's personal speciality was in energetic boy roles or as women in masculine disguise; one of the more remarkable of the latter was her creation of Margaret Catchpole, in a play by Edward Stirling (Surrey 1845) based on the true story of a working-class Suffolk woman whose cross-dressed criminal career included being condemned to death and then transported for horse-theft but culminated in her becoming a wealthy and respectable Australian matron.'

12. Ibid., 34.

13. Katherine Newey, *Women's Theatre Writing in Victorian Britain* (Basingstoke: Palgrave Macmillan, 2005), 218.

14. *Era* 19 August 1899, 9.

15. The *Illustrated Sporting and Dramatic News* 30 March 1895, 18 claimed that the Britannia was the only house in England that employed a stock company. It also described the Britannia Festivals, held a week before Christmas, where actors, clad in the costume of their most successful character from the preceding season, received gifts from the audience.

16. Ronald Mayes, *The Romance of London Theatres* (1923). Victoria and Albert Museum Blythe House Archive PN2596.L6. This collection also has a mixed programme for *Good for Nothing* and *The Lucky Shilling* at the Standard Theatre in 1888 and for *The Convict or Hunted to Death* by C. H. Stephenson and G. B. Ellis's *The Female Detective* at the Pavilion Theatre 1868, with *The Dumb Man of Manchester or the felon heir* by Barnabas Rayner.

17. Jim Davis, 'Theatres and Their Audiences' in Carolyn Williams ed. *The Cambridge Companion to English Melodrama* (Cambridge: Cambridge University Press, 2018), 85.

18. *Era* 4 June 1871, 11.

19. *The Britannia Diaries of Frederick Wilton* ed. Jim Davis (London: Society for Theatre Research, 1992), 96.

20. Redding Ware, *The Woman in White*, British Library Add MS 52997 B, 21.

21. Cited in *Cambridge Companion to English Melodrama*, 128.

22. Nicholas Daly, *Sensation and Modernity in the 1860s* (Cambridge: Cambridge University Press, 2009), 67.

23. The story of Ellen Hanley was transmuted in Gerald Griffin's novel *The Collegians* (1829).

24. Stowell-Kaplan, *Staging Detection*, 41. As Stowell-Kaplan rightly notes, *The Female Detective* also followed the phenomenal success of *The Ticket-of-Leave Man* (1863), which featured the male detective Hawkshaw. Nelly refers to herself as 'Hawkshaw', clearly imitating this male protagonist.
25. *London Daily Chronicle* 10 October 1864, 2. The newspaper reported that the play was performed with *Jessy Vere, or the Return of the Wanderer* as an afterpiece and, as interludes, 'Louis Lindsay, the Ethiopian grotesque, Mr Jester, the man with the talking hand, and Herr Delfger, the Swiss warbler'. This gives a sense of the varied and international flavour of a night at the Britannia.
26. *Daily Ohio Statesman* 30 March 1865, 3.
27. The British actress Fanny Herring played Flora Langton in America in 1875; the play was still being staged in Britain in the 1890s.
28. George B. Ellis, *The Female Detective or the Foundling of the Streets*, British Library Add MS 53043 H, 5.
29. Ibid., 10.
30. Ibid., 13.
31. Nelly remarks, 'I'm your man (aside) I mean – I'm a woman', 17.
32. Ibid.
33. Ibid., 22.
34. Ibid., 27.
35. Ibid., 24.
36. C. H. Hazlewood, *Happiness at Home*, played at the Britannia Theatre 29 May 1871, University of Kent PETT MSS.H.8 SPEC COLL, 7–8.
37. On a similar theme, the song 'Mrs Holmes Taught Sherlock All He Knew' by Alex Sullivan and Harry de Costa (London: Witmark, 1916) tells us, 'The first month they were married, he forgot to pay the rent, /She only had to smell his breath, knew where the money went.'
38. *Era* 4 June 1871, 11.
39. Hazlewood, *Happiness at Home*, 57, 59.
40. Ibid., 14.
41. Ibid., 39.
42. Joanna Hofer-Robinson and Beth Palmer eds, *Sensation Drama 1860–1880: An Anthology* (Edinburgh: Edinburgh University Press, 2019), introduction.
43. *Era* 22 December 1867, 12.
44. *Era* 25 February 1888, 14.
45. *The Lucky Shilling*, 13.
46. Ibid., 59.
47. *Illustrated Sporting and Dramatic News* 14 November 1885, 6.
48. *Era* 25 February 1888, 14.
49. John Douglass, *The Royal Mail* (1887), British Library Add MS 53383 A, 38.
50. Ibid., 14–15.
51. This scene was advertised as recreating the events of the notorious railway robbery and murder in Netherby, Yorkshire, in 1885. In that real-life crime, three robbers had shot at police and one constable was killed.
52. If Hester cannot prove her legitimacy (birth after marriage) she has no claim to the Gower estate, as bequeathed by Sir Frederick. The villains steal the proof of Hester's legitimate birth. They also discredit Hester by palming off the bad coin on her, meaning her employability is damaged by a criminal record and

she is unable to support herself. Then they try to de-legitimise her as mad. Flight damages his ex-wife by telling Lady Fernleigh that she was his 'cast-off mistress'. Although Mrs Flight was innocent of his earlier marriage, her social status is compromised by his confession. Like the 'lucky/unlucky' shilling, she has participated in an apparent transaction that in fact had no legal value.

53. *Funny Folks* 9 June 1888, 179.
54. *Reynolds's Newspaper* 7 October 1888, 5.
55. *Era* 26 March 1898, 11.
56. Max Goldberg and George Comer, *The Tiger's Grip* (1898), British Library Add MS 53654 L, 49.
57. Ibid., 74
58. Ibid., 26.
59. Ibid., 73.
60. Ibid., 75.
61. Ibid., 24.
62. *Bilberry of Tilbury*, 8–9.
63. See Gail Marshall, *Actresses on the Victorian Stage: Feminine Performance and the Galatea Myth* (Cambridge: Cambridge University Press, 1998), 95.
64. George H. Broadhurst, *The Wrong Mr Wright* (London and New York: French, 1913), 15–16.
65. Ibid., 29.
66. Ibid., 93.

4 Sex and the Female Dick: The Secrets of the Private Enquiry Agency

1. *Bilberry of Tilbury*, 8–9.
2. *Cornubian and Redruth Times* 3 February 1893, 8.
3. *Illustrated Police News* 15 August 1896, 1.
4. 'Girl Detectives in Shops', *Daily Gazette for Middlesborough* 15 April 1889, 3. The article is specifically about arrests for theft, but the idea that women's names should be protected, partly to enhance their usefulness in future cases, was commonplace.
5. 'An Interview with a Man of Mystery', *Pall Mall Gazette* 19 January 1889, 3.
6. 'Our London Correspondent', *Suffolk and Essex Free Press* 30 September 1858, 2.
7. *Morning Post* 4 October 1901, 1. The ad is for H. E. Benson, private detective and inquiry agent. Slaters' ads also named divorce as a leading reason to call them. The fact that some other agencies noted 'we are not just useful in divorce cases' shows how central divorce was to the industry.
8. James Peddie, *Secrets of a Private Enquiry Office* (London: Clarke, 1881), 85.
9. *London Evening Standard* 4 February 1881, 4.
10. 'Lady Detective Knows Not Fear, and Can Shoot Straight', *Lloyds Weekly News* 19 May 1907, 6.
11. Ibid.
12. *Norfolk News* (see also *Morning Post*) 29 May 1897, 1.
13. 'The Action for Adultery', *Cheltenham Looker-On* 26 August 1854, 5–8. Mr Lloyd Evans was formally separated from his wife Sarah and they lived apart.

Nonetheless, he objected to her intercourse with Ansley Robinson to the extent of prosecuting him.

14. 'Court for Divorce and Matrimonial Causes', *Express* 4 May 1860, 4. In the case of *Gath v Gath and Woodward*, Mr Gath had endeavoured to entrap his wife into adultery to secure a divorce using the services of a detective, Duffy, who wrote 'filthy letters' to Mrs Gath, attempting to seduce her. The court granted a divorce; however, costs were not awarded. Sir Cresswell Cresswell, presiding, reproved Mr Gath, noting that under the present condition of the law no other verdict was possible, but that a bill had already passed one house of Parliament that would have produced another outcome.

15. *The Times* 8 January 1875, 1. These two advertisements appeared one above the other.

16. Enquiry agencies that advertised female detectives included: Aylmer's, Henry Simmonds, William Pierrepoint, Ward's, Edgar Wright, the Westminster Detective Agency and Henry Slaters.

17. *Western Daily Mercury* 19 May 1881, 6.

18. *Journal of Commerce* 23 June 1888, 2.

19. 'The Pantomime at the Theatre Royal', *Hull Packet and East Riding Times* 29 December 1871, 8.

20. *North Wilts Herald* 30 May 1870, 4.

21. See, for example, D. Worthington, accountant, estate agent and debt collector, who ran a private enquiry office in Wakefield; James Hawson, commercial accountant, business and advertising agent of Sheffield, who also ran a private enquiry office, and F. Morgan of Ramsgate: 'Trademen's accounts kept and assisted; Private Enquiry Office'. The *Cheltenham Mercury* for 7 January 1882 advertised The Trades' Debt Recovery and Private Enquiry Office: 'Wills and Agreements drawn up. Rents collected on moderate terms. Debts bought for cash, or collected on Commission.'

22. *St James's Gazette* 3 December 1888, 12, which was reporting on a case in the City of London Court that Saturday, where Millicent Lucas had served the summons.

23. Ibid.

24. *Aberdeen Express*, repr. *Funny Folks* 8 December 1888, 2.

25. 'An Interview with a Man of Mystery', *Pall Mall Gazette* 19 January 1889, 3.

26. The journalist wondered if these ladies were ever met with insult or assault; Mr Flowerdew replied no: those being served recognised that someone serving a writ was 'under the special protection of the court' and that to attack them would be an offence. *The Annual Practice* (London: Sweet and Maxwell, 1909) shows that Flowerdews, founded in 1884, became 'Law Accountants and Costs Draftsmen' and 'General Agents to the Legal Profession' as well as 'Law Stationers, Printers and Lithographers'.

27. *East Anglian Daily Times* 24 September 1895, 8.

28. *Lloyd's Weekly* 26 January 1890, 8. See also 'A Female Detective', *Islington Gazette* 8 January 1890, 3.

29. See National Archives divorce file J 77/381/1565. Mrs Bartley, the female detective in the Robins divorce case, was said to have been the wife of 'a retired police constable' who had gone into the private enquiry business. She may have been the wife of Thomas Bartley, a private enquiry officer who testified in a bigamy case at Marylebone in December 1876.

30. Their first adopted daughter died aged only 2 years old. The second, Mary Ann Hardcastle, was 16 in 1891.
31. 'A Female Detective', *Northampton Mercury* 19 June 1880, x. The Married Women's Property Act of 1870 had established a woman's right to her earnings after marriage; the Act of 1882 gave her the right to retain all her property after marriage.
32. Nell Darby, *Sister Sleuths: Female Detectives in Britain* (Barnsley: Pen and Sword, 2021), 84.
33. *The Stage* 26 November 1908, 23.
34. 'Regent Street Palmists in Court: The Evidence of a Lady Detective', *St James Gazette* 1 September 1904, 16.
35. Beatrice M. Craven, born around 1875, was widowed and lived in Hammersmith, London. She worked as a private detective from at least 1911 to 1939. Emma Taylor's story is explored more fully in Chapter 6.
36. 'A Female Detective', *Hampshire Telegraph* 20 October 1888, 12.
37. 'Women as Detectives', *The Queen* 27 October 1888, 33.
38. 'A Lady's London Letter', *Cheltenham Examiner* 8 October 1890, 2. This gossip about a female detective who was a Newnham graduate who 'studied with high distinction' originated from an article in *Tit Bits* in October 1890, in which a lady detective at Moser's agency boasted of her fashionable wardrobe, European travels and £500 a year pay.
39. 'Lady Detectives,' *Hearth and Home* 9 June 1892, 21.
40. 'A Lady Detective's Experiences', *Sketch* 24 January 1894, 30.
41. 'Clara Layt' would prove to be an alias. See p.175.
42. *Music Hall and Theatre Review* 22 December 1893, 10.
43. *Haddingtonshire Courier* 7 October 1898, 2. The local paper reported on the treasures, which were auctioned after Lady Susan's death.
44. Lady Connemara, Petition for Divorce, The National Archives, Kew, Surrey, England; Court for Divorce and Matrimonial Causes, later Supreme Court of Judicature: Divorce and Matrimonial Causes Files, J 77; Reference Number: J 77/431/3142. Lord Connemara brought a cross-suit, accusing his wife of adultery with Briggs, but did not appear in court to defend himself. Lady Connemara's petition was granted.
45. Edinburgh Register House, Document Reference: CS241/3431 Building WRH.
46. East Lothian Archive, Haddington, John Gray Centre, letter books for Coalston aka Colstoun EL568/3. Issues surrounding a 'nuisance' at the Old Mill, rivers and wells, occurred from 1895 to 1896. These letters also show that Hamilton Broun was 'liferenter' rather than heir after Lady Susan's death and that this limited his powers.
47. *Musselburgh News* 24 December 1897, 4.
48. *Liverpool Mercury* 5 May 1860, 4.
49. *Chesham Examiner* 4 June 1897, 5.
50. In America, private detectives were sometimes disallowed from testifying in divorce cases on the grounds that, as they were interested parties, their evidence was insecure.
51. *Bridport News* 14 November 1884, 3.
52. *Barry Herald* 15 June 1900, 3.
53. *New Bloomfield Pennsylvania Times* 3 September 1878, 1.

54. Proceedings of the Old Bailey ref t18950325-334, 25 March 1895 Henry John Clarke. Ellen Lyon. Sexual Offences.

55. *Midland Daily Telegraph* 2 April 1895, 2.

56. There is solid genealogical evidence for the life-paths of most other detectives in this book, but Ellen Lyon(s) is hard to pin down. She said at her trial that this was a name she was 'known by', implying multiple aliases. However, one of the addresses she gave in court, 43 Chandos Road, is very close to Westdown Road in Low Leyton, where the Lyon family of coach-painters and sign-painters resided from 1891 to 1901 and the birth date of Ellen Elizabeth Lyon (6 February 1867) is consistent with the suspect's age at the time of the trial, so this may well be her.

57. 'Detectives in Divorce', *Portsmouth Evening News* 7 February 1895, 4.

58. *Reynolds's Newspaper* 25 July 1852, 12.

59. *Tipperary Free Press* 11 July 1865, 2.

60. *London Evening Standard* 15 January 1894, 2.

61. *Yorkshire Evening Post* 26 May 1892, 2.

62. 'Espionnage as a Profession', *Spectator* 18 February 1893, 13–14. The article suggested that 'boys and girls' were also employed as 'detective spies', being cheaper and less liable to get drunk.

63. *Reynolds's Newspaper* 9 November 1884, 3.

64. *Birmingham Daily Mail* 5 July 1884, 3.

65. 'Mrs Detective Tyler', *United Ireland* 19 July 1884, 6.

66. *Freeman's Journal* 15 July 1884, 7.

67. *Carlow Sentinel* 20 January 1883, 4. The *Sentinel* claimed to be repeating a story first published in the *Limerick Chronicle*.

68. *Philipsburg Mail* 13 December 1894, 1.

69. *Edinburgh Evening News* 12 October 1892, 2.

70. *North Wales Chronicle* 14 July 1900, 8.

71. *Ally Sloper's Half-Holiday* 13 September 1890, 7.

72. *North Devon Gazette* 29 July 1890, 7.

73. In court, Louisa Sangster, who was an employee at Moser's Southampton Street office, gave evidence that she had observed Charlotte and Maurice in bed together. Sangster was born and lived in Marylebone; she was single and nearing 50 when she was called to testify against Charlotte and her employer. The 1891 census shows her living in the Portman Buildings in Lisson Grove; she claims her occupation to be 'builder's clerk'. It is possible that she worked as a clerk after or alongside her time working as a female detective, but it is also possible that she hid her true occupation under this more anodyne job title.

74. Antonia Moser declared bankruptcy in August 1908. See 'Woman Detective's Affairs', *Standard* 28 August 1908, 10. The article stated that her daughter, Miss Margaret Williamson, had 'joined her in partnership in January last, and was still carrying on the business'.

75. *Standard* 4 January 1913, 13.

76. Antonia Moser, *Referee* 7 April 1912, 4. Italics mine.

77. Antonia Moser, 'Women Workers and the Vote', *Votes for Women* 8 August 1913, 650.

78. Antonia Moser, *Westminster Gazette* 14 March 1913, 3.

79. Antonia Moser, 'Police "Narks"', *Votes for Women* 10 April 1914, 4.

80. Antonia Moser, 'The Thrilling Adventures of a Woman Detective: The First of the Gold Brick Swindles', *Weekly Dispatch* 23 June 1907, 6.
81. Antonia Moser, 'A Millionaire as Burglar', *Reynolds's Newspaper* 4 July 1909, 2.
82. *Lloyds Weekly News* 19 May 1907, 6.
83. Kate Easton's father, William Mead Easton, was a 'waterman' when he married, but had a variety of subsequent jobs. Nell Darby describes Easton well in *Sister Sleuths*, but there are some holes in her data. For example, she lists three Easton siblings: Madeline, William and detective Kate, but there were in fact three more surviving siblings: Julia, Sarah and John. She claims there is no 1881 census record for Easton, but this is because the family were mis-transcribed as Eastors. It is this census that shows William's profession as stage door keeper.
84. For example, *The Grass Widow*, which featured a woman ill-advisedly married at 16, who was trying to secure a divorce.
85. *Morning Post* 18 July 1908, 1.
86. For further discussion of this phenomenon among Victorian female detectives, see *Sister Sleuths*, 120–1.
87. *The Times* 24 April 1909, 5.
88. *Globe* 5 October 1911, 7.
89. *Daily Telegraph* 9 December 1908, 24.
90. Ibid.
91. George R. Sims, 'The Empty House', *Dorcas Dene, Detective* (London: White, 1897), 83–4.
92. See, for example *Brighton Gazette and Sussex Telegraph* 7 November 1896, 1.
93. *London and Provincial Entr'acte* 26 July 1902, 12.
94. Slater publicly endorsed St Jacobs Oil, a spurious medicament supposed to alleviate rheumatism, but actually composed of aconite, alcohol and turpentine.
95. *Cannock Chase Courier* 12 November 1904, 9.

5 Political PIs: Newspapers and the New Woman Detective

1. Elizabeth Burgoyne Corbett (Mrs George Corbett), *Behind the Veil or Revelations of a Lady Detective* '1: Miss Kelmersley's Party, and What Came of it', *Montgomeryshire County Times* 5 August 1893, 7.
2. McD. Bodkin Q.C., *Dora Myrl: The Lady Detective* (London: Chatto & Windus, 1900), 6.
3. Robert Barr, *Jennie Baxter: Journalist* was a serial in the *Denison Review*, see episode 2, 'The Diamonds of the Princess', 11 May 1900, 6, in which Jennie gets the better of celebrated detective Mr Cadbury Taylor, a thinly disguised version of Sherlock Holmes.
4. See Elizabeth L. Banks, *Campaigns of Curiosity: Journalistic Adventures of an American Girl in London* (London: Cassell, 1894). These pieces had previously been published as 'In Cap and Apron' in the *Weekly Sun*, and the articles on working as a crossing-sweeper and flower-girl in the *English Illustrated Magazine*.
5. For discussion of the detective reporter phenomenon, see Stephen Donovan and Matthew Rubery eds, *Secret Commissions: An Anthology of Victorian Investigative Journalism* (Ontario: Broadview, 2012). As Shpayer-Makov, *Ascent of the Detective*, 160 points out, there was also 'a web of mutual dependencies between [police] detectives and journalists interested in crime'. The police needed the

press to circulate information that might help bring forward witnesses; the press needed the police to feed them stories. 'So overlapping were their tasks that at times they exchanged roles and crossed into each other's domains' (156).

6. Sam Saunders, *The Nineteenth-Century Periodical Press and the Development of Detective Fiction* (London: Routledge, 2021), 93–4.

7. Elizabeth Burgoyne Corbett (Mrs George Corbett), 'No 230,421' in the *South Wales Echo* 4 June 1892, 4.

8. In 1887, she made the first of many applications to the Royal Literary Fund, noting that 'My husband was a little over six months from July to January totally unemployed. Has now obtained a berth at £12 per month as a marine engineer. I have disposed of occasional articles to Newcastle Chronicle, but have nothing for this month accepted. Our income will henceforth be £144 per annum. Last year it was only £70 including £19 which I received for contributions to Newcastle Chronicle.' This application was rejected due to her 'literary claim' being insufficient. She was luckier in obtaining a grant in 1901, by which time she had published fifteen novels and many serials. Her financial situation had, however, not improved. Her husband, she said, only sent in £56 a year from his seafaring. Her own earnings 'had totalled on average £64 per year for the last 3 years, but were uncertain'. See Burgoyne Corbett, 23 March 1887 application to the Royal Literary Fund, BL Loan 96 RLF 1/2259/1 and Burgoyne Corbett, 1 May 1901, application to the Royal Literary Fund, BL Loan 96 RLF 1/2259/12.

9. Elizabeth Burgoyne Corbett, 'Our Women Workers – Suggestions for Winter Recreation', *Newcastle Daily Chronicle* 3 November 1886, 4.

10. Elizabeth Burgoyne Corbett, 'Husband and Wife', *Newcastle Daily Chronicle* 29 September 1886, 4.

11. *Bayswater Chronicle* 25 January 1896, 5.

12. James McLevy [pseud. James McGovan], 'Experiences of an Edinburgh Detective: The Kleptomaniac and the Diamond Ring', *Dundee People's Journal* 6 October 1888, 4.

13. Elizabeth Burgoyne Corbett (Mrs George Corbett), 'Letter', *Women's Penny Paper* 30 November 1889, 66.

14. Elizabeth Burgoyne Corbett (Mrs George Corbett), 'Levying Blackmail', *South Wales Echo* 21 May 1892, 4.

15. Macnaghten, *Days of My Years*, 127.

16. 'Levying Blackmail on Actresses', *South Wales Daily News* 29 January 1889, 3.

17. Elizabeth Burgoyne Corbett (Mrs George Corbett), *Secrets of a Private Enquiry Office* (London: Routledge, 1891), 127.

18. 'A Kirkcaldy Man's Crime', *Fife Free Press* 30 December 1893, 6.

19. Burgoyne Corbett, *Secrets of a Private Enquiry Office*, 91.

20. Werner was also a composer; the founder, leader and conductor of the all-female Mignon String Orchestra; and gave popular lecture series on Scandinavian music.

21. Both Burgoyne Corbett's daughters, Minnie and Lilian, were educated to support themselves professionally: one as a singer, the other as a concert violinist and, later, journalist; doubtless their mother reflected not only on the importance of developing female talents, but on the likelihood that her daughters would need jobs.

22. A notable exception is Maud West, who had acted as a male impersonator on the stage and made a specialism of trouser roles in her detective career. See Susannah Stapleton, *The Adventures of Maud West, Lady Detective* (London: Picador, 2019).

23. Elizabeth Burgoyne Corbett (Mrs George Corbett), *When the Sea Gives Up Its Dead: A Thrilling Detective Story* (London: Tower, 1894), 121.

24. Ibid., 41.

25. Ibid., 225.

26. Elizabeth Burgoyne Corbett, *New Amazonia: A Foretaste of the Future* (London: Tower and Newcastle: Lambert, 1889), 75.

27. 'Women as Journalists', *Spectator* 17 June 1893, 800–1; 'Espionnage as a Profession', *Spectator* 18 February 1893, 221–2: 'There has been of late a noticeable tendency to glorify the detective's trade, and invest it with an air of romance . . . It is quite possible that one of the results of this strange taste for detective stories has been the blunting of our former sentiments upon certain nice points of honour, and that we no longer feel the same shrinking dislike of methods which cannot be scrupulously chivalrous.'

28. Catherine Pope, via email correspondence with the author. Catherine Pope, *Florence Marryat* (Brighton: Everett Root, 2020) is an excellent, concise account of Marryat's life and work.

29. Florence Marryat, *In the Name of Liberty* (London: Digby, Long, 1897).

30. Ibid., 128.

31. 'Arrest of an Anarchist in London', *Morning Post* 16 April 1894, 3.

32. 'The Anarchist Polti', *Western Morning News* 17 April 1894, 8.

33. *Weekly Dispatch* 19 November 1865, 13 and other papers reported the capture of James Stephens the Fenian 'head centre', whose wife had been 'tracked from place to place by female detectives' until she unwittingly led them to her husband's place of concealment.

34. Cited in John Forster, *The Life of Charles Dickens* 3 vols (Philadelphia: Lippincott, 1873), vol. 2, 269. The anecdote may be apocryphal, but it carries emotional weight.

35. 'Sad Immorality in High Life', *Monmouthshire Merlin* 15 November 1878, 3.

36. 'Miss Marryat's New Novel', *Pall Mall Gazette* 7 August 1880, 11.

37. Marryat delivered the monologue in New York; in England at venues including the Bury Athenaeum, Chelmsford Mechanics Institute, St James's Hall and the Granville Theatre, London; and in Scotland at the Institution Hall in Dollar.

38. Beinecke Marryat Family Papers Uncat MSS 104.

39. Florence Marryat, 'The Countess Sorrento' in *The Summer Holiday* (London: Greening, 1898), 1.

40. Ibid., 12.

41. Florence Marryat, *Veronique* (London: Bentley, 1869), Preface, vi.

42. George Augustus Sala, 'Private Detectives', *Sala's Journal* 20 August 1892, 385–6.

43. Beth Palmer, 'Florence Marryat, Theatricality and Performativity', *Interdisciplinary Studies in the Long Nineteenth Century* 8 (2009), 7.

44. See Clare Clarke, Adrienne Gavin, Elizabeth Carolyn Miller and Christopher Pittard below. Joseph Kestner's *Sherlock's Sisters* also discusses Pirkis.

45. Adrienne Gavin, 'C. L. Pirkis (not "Miss"): Public Women, Private Lives, and *The Experiences of Loveday Brooke, Private Detective*', in *Writing Women of the Fin de Siècle: Authors of Change* ed. Adrienne E. Gavin and Carolyn W. de la L. Oulton (Basingstoke: Palgrave Macmillan, 2012), 149.

46. 'Death of Capt. F. E. Pirkis', *Surrey Mirror* 14 October 1914, 5.

47. Pirkis wrote to the *Academy* in the 1890s with linguistic questions and observations on subjects such as 'University Slang', *Academy* 1300 (3 April 1897), 386, and 'A Question of Colloquial English', *Academy* 1263 (18 July 1896), 51. For her views on housing see 'Local Improvements', *Surrey Mirror* 21 April 1894, 4.

48. C. L. Pirkis, *The Experiences of Loveday Brooke, Lady Detective* (London: Hutchinson, 1894), 6.

49. 'Literary Notices', *Blyth Weekly News* 27 May 1893, 7.

50. 'What Women Are Doing', *The Queen* 15 September 1894, 449.

51. Pirkis, *Experiences of Loveday Brooke*, 233.

52. C. L. Pirkis, *Judith Wynne* (London: F. V. White, 1884), vol. 1, 121.

53. Elizabeth Carolyn Miller, 'Trouble with She-Dicks: Private Eyes and Public Women in *The Adventures of Loveday Brooke, Lady Detective*', *Victorian Literature and Culture* 33 (2005), 60.

54. This point is well made by Clare Clarke in her chapter on Pirkis in *British Detective Fiction 1891–1901: The Successors to Sherlock* (Basingstoke: Palgrave Macmillan, 2020).

55. Like the eighteenth-century experimental thinker Thomas Day, Walsingham adopts a foundling and educates her to become his wife. In Walsingham's case, however, the experiment is largely accidental.

56. Christopher Pittard, 'Animal Voices: Catherine Louisa Pirkis' *The Experiences of Loveday Brooke, Lady Detective* and the Crimes of Animality', *Humanities* 7:3 (2018), 6.

57. As José V. Saval notes in 'Crime Fiction and Politics' (in *The Routledge Companion to Crime Fiction* ed. Janice M. Allan, Jesper Gulldal, Stewart King and Andrew Pepper [London: Routledge, 2020], 327–34), Raymond Chandler's 1944 distinction between classic 'detective fiction' (which he saw as conservative) and hardboiled 'crime fiction' (which he saw as radical) was deeply influential. Modern critics have shown that some Victorian detective fiction is more liberal than some 1930s crime novels. The genre is complex and capable of ideological ambiguity, in form and content.

58. Although 'Lady Molly' is given that title in Scotland Yard, the first pages tell us 'some say she is the daughter of a Duke, others that she was born in the gutter, and that the handle has been soldered onto her name in order to give her style and influence'.

59. Bodkin, *Dora Myrl*, 2.

60. Ibid., 92.

6 Mrs Warne's Profession: Inventing the Female Detective

1. John Derrig, *Kate Warne: Pinkerton's First Lady* (Fort Myers: Spider, 2014), 43.

2. Accounts of the origin of this fire differ; it was soon ousted in memory by the Great Fire of 1871.

3. Allan Pinkerton, 'Mrs Warn, The Female Detective', *Chicago Republican* repr. *Democratic Enquirer* 19 March 1868, 2.
4. Parker Pillsbury, William Travis Clark and the National Party of New America are also named among the authors and editors of the paper.
5. 'What Women Are Doing and Have Done', *Revolution* 25 June 1868, 395.
6. One of the first 'unknown soldier' monuments of this era is a bronze statue erected in memory of the Danish victory over the Schleswig-Holsteiner at Fredericia on 6 July 1849. The concept of memorialising a single soldier to represent the thousands who died took off in the First World War and led to the well-known monument in Westminster Abbey. One might also compare *L'Inconnue de la Seine*, the famous death-mask of a beautiful young woman – frequently said to be that of a suicide – reproduced in France from the 1880s to the early 1900s. The 'unknown lady' can be enigmatic, both self-less and famous, a subject so impenetrable that the public gaze can safely rest on it as an object.
7. 'What Women Are Doing and Have Done', *Revolution* 25 June 1868, 395.
8. *Lady's Own Paper* 2 May 1868, 284.
9. Ida Husted Harper, *History of Woman Suffrage* 6 vols (Rochester, NY: Anthony, 1886), vol. 3, 398.
10. Frank Morn, *The Eye That Never Sleeps: A History of the Pinkerton Detective Agency* (Bloomington: Indiana University Press, 1982), 54–5.
11. John Stewart, *Pinkertons, Prostitutes and Spies: The Civil War Adventures of Secret Agents Timothy Webster and Hattie Lawton* (Jefferson, NC: McFarland, 2019), esp. 10–16 and 149–50.
12. Allan Pinkerton, *The Expressman and the Detective* (Chicago: Keen, Cooke & Co., 1875), 95.
13. Thomas T. Eckert Papers, Huntingdon Library, California mss EC 1-76, War Department Ciphers Received From 5 August 1862 to 24 March 1863, 370. Discussed in Stewart, *Pinkertons, Prostitutes and Spies*, 137.
14. Ibid., 94.
15. Allan Pinkerton, *The Spy of the Rebellion; Being a True History of the Spy System of the United States Army During the Late Rebellion* (Chicago: Nettleton, 1883), 75.
16. Ibid., 497.
17. Allan Pinkerton, *The Detective and the Somnambulist* (Chicago: Keen, Cooke & Co., 1875), 144.
18. Ward H. Lamon, *The Life of Abraham Lincoln* (Boston: Osgood, 1872), 526–7.
19. 'Claimants for Empty Honors', *Alexandria Gazette* 21 January 1868, 2.
20. S. Paul O'Hara, *Inventing the Pinkertons; or Spies, Sleuths, Mercenaries, and Thugs* (Baltimore: Johns Hopkins University Press, 2016), 9.
21. See, e.g., *The Expressman and the Detective*, 129, where Maroney, the thief in the Adams Express robbery, is reported to have 'brought a woman there and openly lived with her as his wife, who had not only led a life of infamy [prostitution] prior to her meeting with Maroney, but who, even then, was but his mistress.'
22. Pauline Cushman was an actress, of French and Spanish ancestry, who became a spy for the Union side in the early 1860s and was awarded the title of 'Major'. By 1864 she was touring theatres, singing songs and delivering a thrilling

account of her horseback adventures, near-execution and miraculous escape during the war. Her exploits, including stories of the secret messages she carried sewn into her gaiters, were frequently printed in newspapers. A fetching photograph of Cushman in male uniform resembles the swagger of Pauline of the Potomac as she lounges in male uniform on the cover of Alexander's fiction. Her image illustrates the continuity of 'breeches roles' in the Victorian theatre and those roles (real and/or imagined) in the theatre of war. The story of Cushman's recruitment as a spy began in the theatre and her career in espionage ended as a show: she became part of the popular performative narrative of women's contribution to the Civil War, which included women in disguise acting on intelligence missions as decoys and detectives. However, Cushman's story only resembles that of Pauline D'Estraye in the sense that both had French parentage and both were spies. Alexander's narrative, which draws on sensation fiction of the 1860s, is adventure fiction masquerading as history.

23. Wesley Bradshaw (Charles Wesley Alexander), *General Grant's Lady Detective. A Most Singular Narrative Showing How For a Long Time His Every Movement Was Watched and his steps dogged night and day by spies. And how, through the bravery of Miss Maud Melville, The Heroine of Vicksburg, the plot was unravelled and broken up* (Philadelphia: Alexander, 1868), 4.
24. Ibid., 14.
25. Other sensational titles of the 1860s included *Miriam Rivers, the Lady Soldier; or, General Grant's Spy* (1865) and *Kate Sharp; or, The Two Conscripts* (1865), whose heroine enjoyed 'galloping when and where she chose, with enough danger to heighten [sic] the excitement.'
26. Alice Fahs, *The Imagined Civil War: Popular Literature of the North and South 1861–1865* (Chapel Hill: University of North Carolina Press, 2000), 230.
27. William Stephens Hayward, *The Star of the South* (London, Bryce, 1864), 61.
28. William Stephens Hayward, *Revelations of a Lady Detective* (London: British Library, 2012), 88.
29. Ibid., 38.
30. Ibid., 27.
31. An exception is Kimberly Manganelli who, in discussing Mary Elizabeth Braddon's *The Octoroon*, notes that 'American abolitionist fiction gave rise to British sensation fiction.' See Manganelli, 'Women in White: The Tragic Mulatta and the Rise of British Sensation Fiction' in Jennifer Phegley ed. *Transatlantic Sensations* (Farnham: Ashgate, 2012), 138.
32. *Lady Kate, The Dashing Female Detective: First Half* repr. Garyn G. Roberts, Gary Hoppenstand and Ray B. Browne, *Old Sleuth's Freaky Female Detectives (From the Dime Novels)* (Bowling Green, OH: Bowling Green State University Popular Press, 1990), 29.
33. Ibid., 38–9.
34. Roberts, Hoppenstand and Browne, *Old Sleuth's Freaky Female Detectives*, 6.
35. Christine Bold, 'Popular Forms I' in *The Columbia History of the American Novel* ed. Emory Elliott (New York: Columbia University Press, 2005), 285–305. Quoted in Fahs, *The Imagined Civil War*, 230.
36. Rebecca S. Wingo, 'The "Forgotten Era": Race and Gender in Ann Stephen's Dime Novel Frontier', *Frontiers: A Journal of Women Studies* 38:3 (2017), 123.
37. *Lady Kate, The Dashing Female Detective*, 28.

38. In fact, as Rose admits, 'I do not know my real name, I know nothing of the circumstances of my birth.' The absence of parentage that might otherwise be socially stigmatised becomes a strength for the female detective, who is obliged to invent herself and repeatedly succeeds: 'the despised woman detective had done her work successfully and well'. Harlan Page Halsey (Old Sleuth), *Gipsy Rose, the Female Detective* (New York: Ogilvie, 1898), 81, 77.
39. Harlan Page Halsey (Old Sleuth), *Cad Metti: The Female Detective Strategist* (New York: Parlor Car, 1895), 10–11.
40. Pamela Bedore, 'Queer Investigations: Foxy Ladies and Dandy Detectives in American Dime Novels', *Studies in Popular Culture* (Fall 2008), 19–38.
41. *Sunday Journal* 6 November 1887, 1.
42. Jerry Kuntz, *Minnesota's Notorious Nellie King: Wild Woman of the Closed Frontier* (Charleston, SC: The History Press, 2013), 64.
43. Ibid., 110. Nellie had many aliases and her chequered life can only be reconstructed from a mosaic of evidence; there is an element of speculation. Kuntz does an excellent job of fitting together the pieces and construing the most plausible narrative.
44. Essie's story was reprinted in London's *Reynolds's Newspaper* 29 August 1886, 2.
45. 'Miss Flynn Smoked Cigars', *Worcestershire Chronicle* 10 November 1888, 6.
46. *Barber County Index*, Kansas, 6 February 1889, 1.
47. Ibid.
48. 'A Detective's Story', *Derry Journal* 8 September 1880, 6.
49. LeRoy Lad Panek, *The Origins of the American Detective Story* (Jefferson, NC: McFarland, 2006), 149–51 offers some examples of American women working as detectives, while acknowledging that 'The role of women in late 19th century law enforcement and detection is a largely unexplored field.' My own study of US newspapers has furnished a list of names and cases so numerous that they deserve their own book.
50. Hugh C. Weir, *Madelyn Mack, Detective* (Boston: Page, 1914), 4, 260. For a brief account of Holland, see Erika Janik, *Pistols and Petticoats: 175 Years of Lady Detectives in Fact and Fiction* (Boston: Beacon, 2016), 82.
51. *Austin Weekly Statesman* 29 March 1894, 5.
52. *New York Times* 9 December 1884, 3.
53. Not all women-specific crime scenes were in low life; 'Steal from Co-Eds', an article of 6 May 1904, 1 in the *St Paul Globe*, states that the University of Wisconsin are 'negotiating for' a female detective from Chicago to solve a series of major thefts of money and other valuables from an all-women's college, Chadbourne Hall.
54. Pinkerton, *Detective and Somnambulist*, 145.
55. 'Female Ingenuity', *Chicago Daily Tribune* 2 January 1874, 4.
56. 'A New Way to Detect Dishonest Conductors', *Newbern Weekly Progress* 6 December 1859, 2.
57. 'New York's Only Woman Detective', *Sun* 10 March 1913, 5.
58. 'Woman's Scheming Gets "Taxicab Bandits"', *Day Book* 27 February 1912, 29.
59. James H. Collins, *The Great Taxicab Robbery* (New York: Lane, 1912). This account supplies a 'cast' of characters, where the women are at the bottom after forty named men.

60. *Woman's Home Companion* repr. 'A Famous Woman Detective', *Barre Daily Times* 6 September 1912, 1.
61. 'New York's Only Woman Detective', *Greene County Herald* 24 May 1912, 6.
62. Ibid.
63. *Day Book* 28 December 1912, 6.
64. 'Gotham's Only Female Detective Shows Great Nerve When Attacked', *Cairo Bulletin* 14 February 1914, 6.
65. See Judson R. Taylor (Harlan Halsey), *Gipsy Blair: The Western Detective* (New York: Ogilvie, 1883).
66. 'New York's Only Woman Detective', *Sun* 10 March 1913, 5.
67. Ibid.
68. 'Mrs Goodwin, Only Womansleuth, Weds', *Brooklyn Eagle* 29 November 1921, 5. The nosy newspaper noted that Mr Seaholm was Mrs Goodwin's neighbour at the boarding house where she resided and that he had formerly acted as an advertising agent at the *Brooklyn Eagle*, but that Goodwin considered him 'her own secret affair'.
69. *New York Tribune* 28 July 1912, 2.
70. Dorothy Moses Schulz, *From Social Worker to Crimefighter: Women in United States Municipal Policing* (Westport, CT: Praeger, 1995), 15.
71. Ibid., 21.
72. At least she was a matron there by 1893 – from newspaper reports.
73. 'The Female Detective: Police Matron Taylor Plays the Part of Old Sleuth', *Caldwell Tribune* 20 March 1897, 1.
74. 'Held on Another Charge', *Seattle Post-Intelligencer* 24 December 1898, 5.

Conclusion

1. Louise Otto, *Dem Reich der Freiheit werb' ich Bürgerinnen' Die Frauen-Zeitung von Louise Otto* ed. Ute Gerhard, Elisabeth Hannover-Drück and Romina Schmitter (Frankfurt am Main: Syndikat, 1980), 39.
2. 'Kleptomania', *Echo* 27 January 1888, 1.
3. Henry T. Johnson, 'The Scarlet Scar: or the Strange Experiences of a Countess Detective', *Illustrated Chips* 29 February 1896, 2.

SELECT BIBLIOGRAPHY

Alexander, Charles Wesley, *General Grant's Lady Detective* (Philadelphia: Alexander, 1868)
—— *Pauline of the Potomac or General McClellan's Spy: An Authentic and Thrilling Narrative of the beautiful and accomplished Miss Pauline D'Estraye* (Philadelphia: Barclay, 1864)
Allen, Grant, *Hilda Wade: A Woman with Tenacity of Purpose* (London: Richards, 1900)
—— *Miss Cayley's Adventures* (New York: Putnam, 1899)
Bailey, Victor, ed., *Policing and Punishment in Nineteenth-Century Britain* (London: Croom Helm, 1981)
Banks, Elizabeth L., *Campaigns of Curiosity: Journalistic Adventures of an American Girl in London* (London: Cassell, 1894)
Bedell, Jeanne F., 'Amateur and Professional Detectives in the Fiction of Mary Elizabeth Braddon', *Clues: A Journal of Detection* 4:1 (1983), 19–34
Bedore, Pamela, 'Queer Investigations: Foxy Ladies and Dandy Detectives in American Dime Novels', *Studies in Popular Culture* (Fall 2008), 19–38
Beller, Anne-Marie, 'Detecting the Self in the Sensation Fiction of Wilkie Collins and M.E. Braddon', *Clues: A Journal of Detection* 26:1 (2007), 49–61
Bodkin, McD., Q.C., *Dora Myrl: The Lady Detective* (London: Chatto & Windus, 1900)
Braddon, Mary Elizabeth, *Eleanor's Victory* (London: Tinsley, 1863)
Bratton, Jacky, 'Mirroring Men: The Actress in Drag', in Maggie B. Gale and John Stokes ed. *The Cambridge Companion to the Actress* (Cambridge: Cambridge University Press, 2007)
Broadhurst, George H., *The Wrong Mr Wright* (London and New York: French, 1913)
Brown, Jennifer and Frances Heidensohn, eds, *Gender and Policing: Comparative Perspectives* (Basingstoke: Macmillan, 2000)

Burgoyne Corbett, Elizabeth (Mrs George Corbett), 'Behind the Veil, or Revelations of a Lady Detective, Being Further Secrets of a Private Enquiry Office', *Worcestershire Chronicle* 2 July–3 Sept 1892

—— *New Amazonia: A Foretaste of the Future* (London: Tower and Newcastle: Lambert, 1889)

—— 'Recollections of a Lady Detective', *South Wales Echo* 2 April–4 June 1892

—— *Secrets of a Private Enquiry Office* (London: Routledge, 1891)

—— *When the Sea Gives Up Its Dead: A Thrilling Detective Story* (London: Tower, 1894)

Caminada, Jerome, *Twenty-Five Years of Detective Life* (Manchester: Heywood, 1895)

Carnell, Jennifer, *The Literary Lives of Mary Elizabeth Braddon* (Hastings: Sensation, 2000)

Clarke, Clare, *British Detective Fiction 1891–1901: The Successors to Sherlock* (Basingstoke: Palgrave Macmillan, 2020)

Collins, Wilkie, *The Diary of Anne Rodway, Household Words* 19–26 July 1856

—— *The Law and the Lady* (London: Chatto & Windus, 1875)

—— *The Woman in White* (London: Sampson Low, 1860)

Craig, Patricia, *The Lady Investigates: Women Detectives and Spies in Fiction* (New York: St Martin's Press, 1981)

Crowe, Catherine, *Susan Hopley, or, The Adventures of a Maid-servant* (Edinburgh: Tait, 1842)

Cvetkovich, Ann, *Mixed Feelings: Feminism, Mass Culture, and Victorian Sensationalism* (New Brunswick, NJ: Rutgers University Press, 1992)

Daly, Nicholas, *Sensation and Modernity in the 1860s* (Cambridge: Cambridge University Press, 2009)

Darby, Nell, *Sister Sleuths: Female Detectives in Britain* (Barnsley: Pen and Sword, 2021)

Dauncey, Silvanus and George D. Day, *Bilberry of Tilbury: A Musical Farce in Three Acts with Lyrics by George D. Day and Music by Guy Jones* (1898), British Library Add MS 53657 K

Davies, Caitlin, *Private Enquiries: The Secret History of Female Sleuths* (Cheltenham: History Press, 2023)

Davis, Jim, ed., *The Britannia Diaries of Frederick Wilton* (London: Society for Theatre Research, 1992)

Davis, Jim and Victor Emeljanow, *Reflecting the Audience: London Theatregoing, 1840–1880* (Iowa City: University of Iowa Press, 2001)

Donovan, Stephen and Matthew Rubery, eds, *Secret Commissions: An Anthology of Victorian Investigative Journalism* (Ontario: Broadview, 2012)

Douglass, John, *The Lucky Shilling: an original sensational drama in 5 acts*, British Library Add MS 53396 D

Ellis, Edward, *Ruth The Betrayer or The Female Spy* (London: Dick, 1863)

Ellis, George B., *The Female Detective or the Foundling of the Streets*, British Library Add MS 53043 H

Emsley, Clive, *Crime and Society in England, 1750–1900* (Abingdon: Routledge, 2018)

—— *The English Police: A Political and Social History* (Hemel Hempstead: Harvester Wheatsheaf, 1991)

Emsley, Clive and Haia Shpayer-Makov, eds, *Police Detectives in History, 1750–1950* (Aldershot: Ashgate, 2006)

Enns, Chris, *The Pinks* (Lanham, MD: Rowman and Littlefield, 2017)

Fahs, Alice, *The Imagined Civil War: Popular Literature of the North and South 1861–1865* (Chapel Hill: University of North Carolina Press, 2000)

Gavin, Adrienne E. and Carolyn W. de la L. Oulton, eds, *Writing Women of the Fin de Siècle: Authors of Change* (Basingstoke: Palgrave Macmillan, 2012)

Goddard, Henry, *Memoirs of a Bow-Street Runner* (London: Museum Press, 1956)

Goldberg, Max and George Comer, *The Tiger's Grip* (1898), British Library Add MS 53654 L

Hackenberg, Sara, '"The Magician of Civilised Life": The Literary Detective in Mary Elizabeth Braddon's Early Penny Fiction' *Victorian Popular Fictions* 4:2 (2022), 63–78

Halsey, Harlan Page (Old Sleuth), *Cad Metti: The Female Detective Strategist* (New York: Parlor Car, 1895)

—— *Gipsy Rose, the Female Detective* (New York: Ogilvie, 1898)

Hammerton, A. James, *Cruelty and Companionship in Nineteenth-Century Married Life* (London: Routledge, 1992)

Hayward, William Stephens, *The Black Angel: A Tale of the American Civil War* (London: Ward & Lock, 1863)

—— *Revelations of a Lady Detective* (London: Vickers, 1864; repr. London: British Library, 2012)

—— *The Star of the South* (London: Bryce, 1864)

Hazlewood, Colin Henry, *The Female Detective; or, The Mother's Dying Child* (New York: De Witt, 1864)

—— *Happiness at Home* (1871), University of Kent PETT MSS.H.8 SPEC COLL

Heholt, Ruth, *Catherine Crowe: Gender, Genre and Radical Politics* (London: Routledge, 2021)

Hinks, Jim, 'Detective Fictions: The "Baby Farming Detective" in Britain 1867–97', *Journal of Victorian Culture* 27:1 (January 2022), 15–29

Hofer-Robinson, Joanna and Beth Palmer, eds, *Sensation Drama 1860–1880: An Anthology* (Edinburgh: Edinburgh University Press, 2019)

Hollingshead, John, *Ragged London in 1861* (London: Smith Elder, 1861)

Homrighaus, Ruth, 'Baby Farming: The Care of Illegitimate Children in England, 1860–1943', unpublished doctoral thesis (2003), University of North Carolina

Humphreys, Anne, 'Who's Doing It? Fifteen Years of Work on Victorian Detective Fiction', *Dickens Studies Annual* (1996), 259–74

Jackson, Allan Stuart, *The Standard Theatre of Victorian England* (Toronto: Fairleigh Dickinson, 1993)

Jackson, Louise A., *Women Police: Gender, Welfare and Surveillance in the Twentieth Century* (Manchester: Manchester University Press, 2006)

Janik, Erika, *Pistols and Petticoats: 175 Years of Lady Detectives in Fact and Fiction* (Boston: Beacon, 2016)

Jones, David, *Crime, Protest, Community and Police in Nineteenth-Century Britain* (London: Routledge, 1982)

Kestner, Joseph, 'The British Female Detective Written by Women, 1890–1920' in Holly A. Laird ed. *The History of British Women's Writing, 1880–1920* (London: Palgrave Macmillan, 2016)

—— *Sherlock's Sisters: The British Female Detective, 1864–1913* (Aldershot: Ashgate, 2003)

Klein, Kathleen Gregory, *The Woman Detective: Gender and Genre* (Urbana: University of Illinois Press, 1988)

Knight, Stephen, *Crime Fiction, 1800–2000: Detection, Death, Diversity* (Basingstoke: Palgrave Macmillan, 2003)

—— 'Detection and Gender in Early Crime Fiction: Mrs Bucket to Lady Molly', *Crime Fiction Studies* 3:2 (September 2022), 89–105

—— *Towards Sherlock Holmes: A Thematic History of Crime Fiction in the 19th Century World* (Jefferson, NC: McFarland, 2016)

Kungl, Carla T., *Creating the Fictional Female Detective: The Sleuth Heroines of British Women Writers 1890–1940* (Jefferson, NC: McFarland, 2006)

Kuntz, Jerry, *Minnesota's Notorious Nellie King: Wild Woman of the Closed Frontier* (Charleston, SC: The History Press, 2013)

Lamon, Ward H., *The Life of Abraham Lincoln* (Boston: Osgood, 1872)

McDonagh, Josephine, *Child Murder and British Culture* (Cambridge: Cambridge University Press, 2003)

McKenna, Neil, *Fanny and Stella: The Young Men Who Shocked Victorian England* (London: Faber, 2013)

McNaghten, Melville L. [C.B, Chief of the CID], *Days of My Years* (London: Arnold, 1914)

Mandler, Peter, *Liberty and Authority in Victorian Britain* (Oxford: Oxford University Press, 2006)

Mangham, Andrew, ed., *The Cambridge Companion to Sensation Fiction* (Cambridge: Cambridge University Press, 2013)

—— *Violent Women and Sensation Fiction: Crime, Medicine and Victorian Popular Culture* (Basingstoke: Palgrave Macmillan, 2007)

Marryat, Florence, 'The Countess Sorrento' in *The Summer Holiday* (London: Greening, 1898)

—— *In the Name of Liberty* (London: Digby, Long, 1897)

Marshall, Gail, *Actresses on the Victorian Stage: Feminine Performance and the Galatea Myth* (Cambridge: Cambridge University Press, 1998)

Mayes, Ronald, *The Romance of London Theatres* (London: Westby, 1923)

Miller, Elizabeth Carolyn, 'Trouble with She-Dicks: Private Eyes and Public Women in *The Adventures of Loveday Brooke, Lady Detective*', *Victorian Literature and Culture* 33 (2005), 47–65

Mintz, Sidney, *Sweetness and Power: The Place of Sugar in Modern History* (London: Penguin, 1986)

Morn, Frank, *The Eye That Never Sleeps: A History of the Pinkerton Detective Agency* (Bloomington: Indiana University Press, 1982)

Moser, Maurice and Charles F. Rideal, *Stories from Scotland Yard* (London: Routledge, 1890)

Munt, Sally Rowena, *Murder by the Book? Feminism and the Crime Novel* (London: Routledge, 1994)

Newey, Katharine, *Women's Theatre Writing in Victorian Britain* (Basingstoke: Palgrave Macmillan, 2005)

O'Hara, S. Paul, *Inventing the Pinkertons; or Spies, Sleuths, Mercenaries, and Thugs* (Baltimore: Johns Hopkins University Press, 2016)

Orczy, Emmuska, *Lady Molly of Scotland Yard* (London: Cassell, 1910)

Owings, Chloe, *Women Police: A Study of the Development and Status of the Women Police Movement* (Montclair, NJ: Patterson Smith, 1969)

Palmer, Beth, 'Florence Marryat, Theatricality and Performativity', *Interdisciplinary Studies in the Long Nineteenth Century*, 8 (2009)

Panek, LeRoy Lad, *The Essential Elements of the Detective Story* (Jefferson, NC: McFarland, 2016)

—— *The Origins of the American Detective Story* (Jefferson, NC: McFarland, 2006)

Peddie, James, *Secrets of a Private Enquiry Office* (London: Clarke, 1881)

Phegley, Jennifer, ed., *Transatlantic Sensations* (Farnham: Ashgate, 2012)

Pinkerton, Allan, *The Detective and the Somnambulist* (Chicago: Keen, Cooke & Co., 1875)

—— *The Expressman and the Detective* (Chicago: Keen, 1874)

—— *The Spy of the Rebellion; Being a True History of the Spy System of the United States Army During the Late Rebellion* (Chicago: Nettleton, 1883)

Pirkis, C. L., *The Experiences of Loveday Brooke, Lady Detective* (London: Hutchinson, 1894)

—— *Judith Wynne* (London: F. V. White, 1884)

—— *Saint and Sibyl* (London: Hurst & Blackett, 1882)

Pittard, Christopher, 'Animal Voices: Catherine Louisa Pirkis' *The Experiences of Loveday Brooke, Lady Detective* and the Crimes of Animality', *Humanities* 7:3 (2018), 1–16

Pope, Catherine, *Florence Marryat* (Brighton: Everett Root, 2020)

Redding Ware, James, *Before the Bench: Sketches of Police Court Life* (London: Diprose & Bateman, 1880)

—— ('edited by A.F.'), *The Female Detective* (London: Ward & Lock, 1864; repr. London: British Library, 2012)

—— (Andrew Forrester), *Secret Service; or, Recollections of a City Detective* (London: Ward & Lock, 1864)

Reddy, Maureen, 'Women Detectives' in Martin Priestman ed. *The Cambridge Companion to Crime Fiction* (Cambridge: Cambridge University Press, 2003)

Reilly, John W., *Policing Birmingham: An Account of 150 Years of Police in Birmingham* (Birmingham: West Midlands Police, 1994)

Rennison, Nick, *Sherlock's Sisters: Stories from the Golden Age of the Female Detective* (London: No Exit, 2020)

Roberts, Garyn G., Gary Hoppenstand and Ray B. Browne, *Old Sleuth's Freaky Female Detectives (From the Dime Novels)* (Bowling Green, OH: Bowling Green State University Popular Press, 1990)

Rodensky, Lisa, *The Crime in Mind: Criminal Responsibility and the Victorian Novel* (Oxford: Oxford University Press, 2003)

Rubery, Matthew, *The Novelty of Newspapers: Victorian Fiction After the Invention of the News* (Oxford: Oxford University Press, 2009)

Sala, George Augustus, 'Private Detectives', *Sala's Journal* 20 August 1892, 385–6

Saunders, Sam, *The Nineteenth-Century Periodical Press and the Development of Detective Fiction* (London: Routledge, 2021)

Saval, José V., 'Crime Fiction and Politics' in Janice M. Allan, Jesper Gulldal, Stewart King and Andrew Pepper ed. *The Routledge Companion to Crime Fiction* (London: Routledge, 2020)

Schulz, Dorothy Moses, *From Social Worker to Crimefighter: Women in United States Municipal Policing* (Westport, CT: Praeger, 1995)

Shpayer-Makov, Haia, *The Ascent of the Detective: Police Sleuths in Victorian and Edwardian England* (Oxford: Oxford University Press, 2011)

—— *The Making of a Policeman: A Social History of a Labour Force in London, 1829–1914* (Aldershot: Ashgate, 2002)

—— 'Revisiting the Detective Figure in Late Victorian and Edwardian Fiction: A View from the Perspective of Police History', *Law, Crime and History* 2 (2011), 165–93

Sims, George R., *Dorcas Dene, Detective* (London: White, 1897)

Sims, Michael, ed., *The Penguin Book of Victorian Women in Crime* (London: Penguin, 2010)

Slung, Michele *Crime on Her Mind: Fifteen Stories of Female Sleuths from the Victorian Era to the Forties* (New York: Pantheon, 1983)

Smith, Phillip Thurmond, *Policing Victorian London: Political Policing, Public Order, and the London Metropolitan Police* (Westport, CT: Greenwood, 1985)

Stapleton, Susannah, *The Adventures of Maud West, Lady Detective* (London: Picador, 2019)

Stewart, John, *Pinkertons, Prostitutes and Spies: The Civil War Adventures of Secret Agents Timothy Webster and Hattie Lawton* (Jefferson, NC: McFarland, 2019)

Stowell-Kaplan, Isabel, *Staging Detection: From Hawkshaw to Holmes* (London: Routledge, 2022)

Surridge, Lisa, *Bleak Houses: Marital Violence in Victorian Fiction* (Athens, OH: Ohio University Press, 2005)

Sussex, Lucy, *Women Writers and Detectives in Nineteenth-Century Crime Fiction: The Mothers of the Mystery Genre* (Basingstoke: Palgrave Macmillan, 2010)

Tallack, William, *Penological and Preventive Principles* (London: Wertheimer, 1896)

Thomas, Ronald R., *Detective Fiction and the Rise of Forensic Science* (Cambridge: Cambridge University Press, 1999)

Thoms, Peter, *Detection and Its Designs: Narrative and Power in 19th-Century Detective Fiction* (Athens, OH: Ohio University Press, 1998)

Trodd, Anthea, *Domestic Crime in the Victorian Novel* (Basingstoke: Macmillan Press, 1988)

Tromp, Marlene, ed., *Beyond Sensation: Mary Elizabeth Braddon in Context* (Albany, NY: SUNY, 2000)

Watson, Kate, *Women Writing Crime Fiction, 1860–1880* (Jefferson, NC: McFarland, 2012)

Webb, Simon, *Bombers, Rioters and Police Killers: Violent Crime and Disorder in Victorian Britain* (Barnsley: Pen and Sword, 2015)

Weir, Hugh C., *Madelyn Mack, Detective* (Boston: Page, 1914)

Williams, Carolyn, ed., *The Cambridge Companion to English Melodrama* (Cambridge: Cambridge University Press, 2018)

Williams, Gwen, 'Fear's Keen Knife: Suspense and the Female Detective 1890–1920' in Clive Bloom ed. *Twentieth-Century Suspense* (Basingstoke: Palgrave Macmillan, 1990)

Wingo, Rebecca S., 'The "Forgotten Era": Race and Gender in Ann Stephen's Dime Novel Frontier', *Frontiers: A Journal of Women Studies* 38:3 (2017), 121–40

Young, Arlene, '"Petticoated Police": Propriety and the Lady Detective in Victorian Fiction', *Clues: A Journal of Detection* 26:3 (2008), 15–28

Young, Malcolm, *An Inside Job: Policing and Police Culture in Britain* (Oxford: Clarendon, 1991)

Zedner, Lucia, *Women, Crime, and Custody in Victorian England* (Oxford: Clarendon, 1991)

INDEX

INDEX

women police *see* detectives, female;
      police and policing, women's
      role in
work and workers
  actors and actresses *see* theatre,
      actresses
  bus conductors 38
  chimney sweeps 219
  commercial travellers 177
  companions, paid 180–2
  costermongers 25, 101, 131
  delivery drivers 24
  detectives *see* detectives, female;
      detectives, male; private
      enquiry agencies
  domestic servants (maids, cooks,
      gardeners) 16–18, 170–2,
      176, 183
    fictional 107–8, 241–2
    posing as 136, 150, 167–76, **209**,
      250, 284; *see also* detectives,
      female, disguise
  engineers 213

hotel managers 141–2
match-sellers 216
musicians (performers, composers,
    teachers) 220, 223–4,
    333n20, 333n21
seamstresses ('machinists',
    dressmakers, milliners)
    72–4, 136, 156–9; *see also*
    seamstresses, as detectives
sex workers 57–8, 106, 268, 274,
    305
  Back, Emma 307
  brothels 66, 188, 266
  Davies, Margaret 144
  King, Nellie *see* fantasists, King,
    Nellie
  Watts, Clara 157
shopkeepers (grocers, fishmongers,
    drapers) 1–2, 18, 24, 30, 41,
    156
soldiers and sailors 164, 169, 232,
    242, 265
workhouses 182, 215